# party food

# party food

How to plan the perfect party with over
120 recipes for special celebrations

## Bridget Jones

LORENZ BOOKS

This edition is published by Lorenz Books

Lorenz Books is an imprint of Anness Publishing Ltd
Hermes House, 88–89 Blackfriars Road, London SE1 8HA
tel. 020 7401 2077
fax 020 7633 9499
www.lorenzbooks.com
info@anness.com

© Anness Publishing Ltd 2002

This edition distributed in the UK by Aurum Press Ltd
25 Bedford Avenue, London WC1B 3AT
tel. 020 7637 3225; fax 020 7580 2469

This edition distributed in the USA and Canada
by National Book Network
4720 Boston Way, Lanham, MD 20706
tel. 301 459 3366; fax 301 459 1705; www.nbnbooks.com

This edition distributed in Australia by Pan Macmillan Australia
Level 18, St Martins Tower, 31 Market St, Sydney, NSW 2000
tel. 1300 135 113; fax 1300 135 103
email customer.service@macmillan.com.au

This edition distributed in New Zealand by David Bateman Ltd
30 Tarndale Grove, Off Bush Road, Albany, Auckland
tel. (09) 415 7664; fax (09) 415 8892

Publisher: Joanna Lorenz
Managing Editor: Judith Simons
Art Manager: Clare Reynolds
Senior Editor: Doreen Palamartschuk
Editors: Jan Cutler, Jane Bamforth
Recipes: Catherine Atkinson, Alex Barker, Matthew Drennan, Joanne Farrow, Brian Glover,
Nicola Graimes, Lucy Knox, Sara Lewis, Sallie Mansfield, Christine McFadden, Jane Milton,
Keith Richmond, Rena Salaman, Marlena Spieler, Linda Tubby, Oona van den Berg,
Kate Whiteman and Jeni Wright
Designer: Nigel Partridge
Photographers: Karl Adamson, Caroline Arber, Steve Baxter, Martin Brigdale, Nicki Dowey,
Gus Filgate, Michelle Garrett, Amanda Heywood, Janine Hosegood, William Lingwood, Roisin
Neild, Thomas Odulate, Spike Powell, Craig Robertson, Simon Smith, Sam Stowell and
Polly Wreford
Food for photography (chapter openers): Becky Johnson
Production Controller: Wendy Lawson

1 3 5 7 9 10 8 6 4 2

## Notes
Bracketed terms are intended for American readers.
For all recipes, quantities are given in both metric and imperial measures and, where
appropriate, measures are also given in standard cups and spoons. Follow one set, but
not a mixture, because they are not interchangeable.
Standard spoon and cup measures are level. 1 tsp = 5ml, 1 tbsp = 15ml, 1 cup = 250ml/8fl oz
Australian standard tablespoons are 20ml. Australian readers should use 3 tsp in place
of 1 tbsp for measuring small quantities of gelatine, flour, salt, etc.
Medium (US large) eggs are used unless otherwise stated.

# contents

# Introduction

Party-giving should be enjoyable, and timely planning ensures that any event is as relaxed for the organizer as for the guests. The following chapters provide guidelines and reminders to ensure that the organizing is easy and the occasion successful. One of the aims of this book is to provide all the advice necessary to make the planning all part of the party fun and satisfying on both informal and formal occasions.

### Getting started

The process of deciding on dates, times, venues and occasion style often starts the roller-coaster task of putting

*Below To create a sophisticated look, choose one colour for napkins and table linen, and mix different textures such as linen and organdie.*

*Above Pure linen napkins add style and elegance to any dining table.*

together once-in-a-lifetime gatherings. It can often be a stressful time when you are making decisions such as whether traditional ceremonies take precedence over a relaxed celebration or how to assemble different groups of family and friends. Side-stepping a

frantic start helps to avoid dips in enthusiasm later on. Often the initial problems are not as complicated as they appear. Enthusiasm and energy are the first requirements for overcoming any uncertainties, backed up by making useful lists such as key dates, numbers of guests, types of food and drink. It is important to do this before any celebration, large or small, in advance of getting down to the practicalities of invitation writing, room clearing, cooking and greeting.

### Enlisting support

There is no point in playing the party hero and trying to juggle every last item alongside a normal busy life – it is far more sensible and fun to share the load and satisfaction with at least one helper, if not a team of supporters.

Hand pick a reliable and hard-working friend who shares your aims, ethos and humour to join in the process – most people are flattered to be asked for their support, especially on important occasions. Then be thoughtful about who to add to the team. For children's parties, unless the occasion is a surprise, involve the child whose party it is and allow one special friend to be included in the pre-party organization.

Getting together a round-table of enthusiastic organizers is best avoided unless there are specific, separate tasks that are ideal for distributing among several contributors. Finally, there are times when coordinating a committee of people is an essential part of putting together a group event, such as for a club or school, and adopting the same approach to selecting one or two main helpers while ensuring everyone else is usefully involved is an excellent ploy.

## Mix and match

If the occasion is so formal, such as a wedding or christening, or the approach so traditional that there is little room for changing the style and form, it is best to follow the rules of etiquette. For all parties adopt a sensible attitude to all numbers, catering, ambience and entertainment and use tried and tested approaches to ensure success.

**Below** *Add atmosphere to a party with floating candles in a glass bowl.*

When the occasion allows for flexibility, do not take yourself too seriously but aim for enjoyment rather than perfection. Mixing and matching can be an inspiring approach to party planning, especially for informal events. Adopt the "do it with a good will or not at all" approach and loosen up on the rules. Concentrate on the aspects you most enjoy. Those who are not keen on cooking for crowds often do best by selecting just one or two practical one-pot dishes and complementing them with well-chosen bought foods. There is plenty of advice on making the most of bought ingredients in the following chapters.

The same goes for party drinks: while all the experts may dictate offering chilled champagne or certain wines and liqueurs to go with individual courses during a meal, or an eclectic array of drinks, if you – or your budget – dictate otherwise, then do so with conviction and without apology. And if you expect guests to make a contribution by bringing a

**Above** *Classic cocktail glasses will impress your guests at drinks parties.*

bottle, do not be afraid to make the occasion a "bring a bottle party" by spelling it out on the party invitations.

## Enjoy!

Great atmosphere is the most important feature of any party or celebration – and that does not mean ambience alone. Whether you are entertaining in a palace or on a building site, remember to do so with a genuine and warm welcome. Make your guests aware of the type, context and style of the party so that they all come suitably dressed and in the right frame of mind to enjoy themselves. Greet everyone and be sure to encourage them to mingle, making them feel relaxed, at home and with a certain responsibility to participate. At the end of the day, no matter how brilliant the tables, food and decorations, it is the people who make the party.

# party
# planning

Approach successful entertaining with a clear sense of occasion and a

few concise, practical lists. Once you know what you are doing,

involve others in the fun and share the planning with friends or family.

# Grand Design or Simple Style?

A clear picture of the party style and size is the secret of success every time. Before planning venues, invitations, settings, entertainment and food and drink, decide on exactly the right type of party. Energy and enthusiasm are essential for getting things moving but it is best to sort out guidelines within which to plan before ideas snowball and practicalities are forgotten in an initial wave of excitement.

There are established routines and etiquette for many occasions and utilizing these is often sensible. They range from formal dinner parties, society drinks gatherings or balls to weddings, anniversaries and seasonal gatherings. There are also just as many small or substantially large gatherings that are organized for no particular reason other than meeting up and socializing, for example overcoming winter blues, making the most of the summer sun or catching up with a group of friends.

**Below** *An attractive buffet table with plates and napkins piled high.*

### Who's who?
Start with an outline guest plan: is this a gathering for six or sixty, under fives or over fifties, family or friends, bosom pals or business associates? If you are inviting a complete mix of family, friends, colleagues and neighbours a proper plan would be a sensible starting point. Identify the different types and ages; by fitting individuals into groups you will be sure to include something for everyone. This eases the role of host or hostess, which can involve looking after small groups or couples – or worse – individuals drifting about on the fringes of the party.

### Time of day
The party may be to celebrate a marriage, baby naming or Christening, or it may be a social event. It may not be a particularly jolly occasion, for example a post-funeral wake. Double-check arrangements that cannot be changed later, for example timings for ceremonies, photography or performances and estimated travelling time between event and party venue.

**Above** *Summer barbecues can be day or early evening social events.*

Consider the different ages of, or relationship between, guests before fixing times. A two-phase celebration is popular for very different groups; it would typically comprise a formal meal, low-key lunch or early evening drinks party followed by a lively gathering later for younger guests or close friends. This solution works as well for informal occasions – a house warming, open house for a summer barbecue or an annual family gathering – as for weddings. Plan the transition between day and evening, and decide whether those invited to the first part will also stay late.

Formal gatherings for early evening drinks preceding a late supper for a few friends or pre-lunch gatherings must be well orchestrated. Invitations should indicate the time when guests are expected to leave: "Pre-dinner drinks between 6 p.m. and 7.30 p.m." A verbal or informal note to join family or weekend guests for "a drink before lunch" should include the expected time of arrival and departure. Be clear to avoid any confusion.

## Smarten up or dress down?

Once you know whom and when, make a decision on how you want your guests to dress and behave, and follow this through in invitations, food and entertainment. Be clear on invitations if you expect formal dress (white tie and ball gowns; black tie and evening wear; morning wear, or top hats and tails, and hats), lounge suits or smart daywear. For an informal occasion dress will not need to be stipulated. Indicate any special requirements, such as bathing costumes and towels for poolside parties, sun hats and picnic blankets to sit on, and sweaters or shawls for evenings outdoors.

## Before and after

Guests may need accommodation for the night before and/or after the party. After a long journey, house guests will usually want to arrive early enough to freshen up. Include the preparation of guests' rooms in your plans and timings, remembering the little things that make people feel welcome and relaxed – flowers, magazines, drinks, biscuits (cookies) or chocolates as well as towels, soap, shampoo and tissues. Keeping a few disposable, travel-size miniatures, or spare small toothbrushes, toothpaste, small packs of anti-perspirant and sachets of moisturizer in stock is a good idea for party guests who stay unexpectedly.

Pay attention to detail when entertaining youngsters, especially if they may be too shy to ask for forgotten essentials. For a special occasion sleepover you could prepare fun sleepover packs including novelty toothbrushes, fruit-flavoured toothpaste, wacky toiletries, expanding face cloths, reading material such as comics, mini torches, tasty midnight snacks and fruit, and small packs of drinks or bottles of water.

**Above** *Add romantic touches to a table dressed in white for a wedding.*

For large gatherings, check out local hotels and provide guests with details on price, location and availability when sending out invitations. Remember breakfast on the morning after the party and make flexible arrangements.

## Party price

As each name is added to the guest list and every idea mulled and jotted bear in mind the cost. Decide on the type of party to suit the funds available, then work out a realistic budget in more detail before progressing from idea to plan. This is just as important for small, homely events as for once-in-a-lifetime occasions if you want to avoid overspending.

Sorting an outline budget at this stage is essential and easy: make a list of every aspect of the party, adding a realistic (generous rather than mean) cost and contacting suppliers to check special prices. For extravagant occasions involving hotels, venues, caterers, entertainers and so on, make specific enquiries at this first stage. Divide the costs into fixed amounts for the occasion and variable prices that increase with the number of guests – refreshments in particular – remember that the venue size may change if the guest list grows too much. Spreading the cost by paying for some items, such as wine, spirits or beer, completely or partly in advance is one way of easing an overstretched budget, especially when planning a party at home.

**Below** *Simple snacks, drinks and bright decorations are good basics for a party.*

# Have List, Will Organize

dinner parties and drinks parties are good Friday affairs, as are after-theatre or post-exhibition suppers.

Weekends are popular for group events for families and for activity club get-togethers or excursions. While weekend brunches are generally great for those without young children, Saturday brunch can also start family activities on a high note and the afternoon is a good choice for children's parties. If Saturday lunch is difficult for working hosts and guests who have to juggle family commitments, the evening is good

Lists are essential when planning for a special occasion. Suggesting that there should be a system for making them may sound like overkill but even the most super-efficient lists can become so mottled with additions that they become uninterpretable. The answer is to have separate lists with different information. Using a computer or a spiral-bound notepad is brilliant for keeping lists on separate pages but together in one place. Jot the date on each page and include notes of discussions with suppliers, orders placed and ideas as well as the guest list, special requirements, shopping and so on. Using this system it is easy to flip through to check details, and it is a good idea to sticker significant pages you refer to frequently, such as the invitation list where you will tick or

**Above** *Make lists for organizing all aspects of party planning.*

cross off guests' names as replies come in. Start with a list of the usual requirements for different occasions and then personalize it to your style.

### Which day?
Work functions are best from midweek onwards. Friday can be a good day for lunch or an evening party if partners are invited; Wednesday or Thursday are more convenient for "colleague only" events (especially for a comparatively early finish).

Weekday dinner parties can be inconvenient but midweek evenings can be a good choice for drinks gatherings or supper parties designed to end early. Relaxed and informal

**Above** *Champagne is generally served at weddings and formal occasions.*

**Below** *One-pot feasts, such as moussaka, are good for supper parties.*

for large and/or formal dinner parties. Saturday is popular for weddings, allowing time for guests to travel; Friday is ideal when the marriage is witnessed by a small number of relations and followed by a party for friends and associates.

Sunday lunch is extremely versatile: it allows plenty of time for preparation and is suitable for informal or smart arrangements for family, couples, singles or a mixture.

Parties and celebrations for clubs and classes are usually planned for the day and time when the meetings are normally held. Annual dinners tend to be organized for Friday or Saturday evenings, depending on the work commitments of members.

## Scheduling an important celebration

Lists should include all the details, whereas a schedule will set dates and deadlines for the tasks. Draw up a master schedule of key dates, tasks and reminders with references back to the lists for details where necessary. Lists can then be updated as time passes.

A few months may be enough time for organizing simple weddings but one to two years is usually allowed

*Above A stylishly dressed table for a Thanksgiving celebration.*

for extravagant affairs. Timing often depends on the booking requirements of venues and officials; check these carefully. Find out about caterers, entertainment and transport, and check the availability of all related aspects before booking the main event.

Put dates to the lists and check that they are all possible. Then draw up the outline schedule – the master guide to sourcing, booking, confirming and checking every aspect of the celebration. Schedule key dates for everything. Adding minor aspects may seem picky, particularly when coping with a big party, but they can easily be forgotten later. Use a familiar means of layout, if possible, be that a year planner, kitchen calendar, chart on a noticeboard or computer program.

Scrutinize your schedule for bottlenecks and potential problems. If too many tasks coincide make alternative arrangements by moving jobs to different dates or delegate them to helpers. When you are happy that you have not missed anything, make sure the schedule looks neat, tidy and is easy to follow.

## Schedule checks

Below are items to add to the schedule according to the needs of the occasion, placing each against a date when it has to be done.

**Formalities**: legal/paperwork requirements, booking all officials, confirmation
**Venue**: viewing, booking, and confirmation, checking facilities, preparation
**Entertainment**: booking, venue preparation/layout requirements, details of repertoire
**Accommodation**: source details
**Caterers**: references/assessing, booking, menu decisions and/or tasting session, confirmation of numbers, caterer's advance visit
**Special catering**: special diets, finalizing details of presentation
**Food preparation**: ordering, shopping, key dates for advance cooking, days for final preparation
**Bar**: delivery/collection of drinks and glasses, return of items
**Professional help at home**: gardening, cleaning, kitchen help (before or after), butler, waiting staff, bar staff
**Flowers**: booking, venue visit and design liaison
**Guest list**: invitations out, give a date for replies back
**Gifts**: buy, pack

# Choosing a Venue

The occasion, type and size of party, budget, convenience and availability all influence the choice of venue.

## Home options

Entertaining at home can be stylish if there is suitable space. While clearing furniture to the edges of one or two small rooms and allowing everyone to spill into the hall and kitchen may be fine for an informal party, it is not necessarily the answer for a special celebration. Unless there is ample floor and table space plus kitchen facilities sufficient to cater for a sit-down meal, a buffet is most practical. When serving a fork buffet, remember that some guests may prefer to sit down to eat. When finger buffets or snacks are served, guests do not need as much space, especially if the refreshments are handed around.

Make use of outdoor areas and consider hiring an awning or marquee. Tables, chairs and barbecues can be arranged on firm areas; rugs and cushions can be laid on lawns. Be prepared for poor weather and consider erecting large umbrellas.

Above *Put extra tables on patios and courtyards for home entertaining.*

Below *With attention to detail, dressing a table at home can be very stylish.*

## Hotels and restaurants

Select a venue by recommendation, reputation and personal experience if possible. Visit the restaurant for a meal to assess general quality and ambience. When comparing establishments, prepare a standard checklist and do not be embarrassed to make notes while you are there. The following are points to consider:

• How many guests can be catered for and in which room/bar. Check the maximum number of covers usually catered for; point out, if necessary, that you do not want their capabilities to be overstretched. Will a bar adjoining a function room be exclusively for the use of your party or will it also be open to the public? Check bar closing times.

• What types of menus are offered and at what price per head? What is included in the price per head? Are children's portions provided at reduced cost (prudent when a wedding guest list includes many children)?

• Do the regular kitchen staff prepare special functions, or are outside caterers or temporary chefs employed?

• Check wine lists and bar prices. Ask whether you will be able to supply your own wine or champagne and what corkage charge is applied?

• Check arrangements for overseeing the smooth running of the occasion and whether a master of ceremonies is available. Ask about the suitability of spaces for speeches or if amplification equipment is available.

• Accommodation-wise, assess the number and type of rooms, and price per room/person, with or without breakfast. Ask if favourable rates will be offered for a block booking.

• Does the business have existing links with entertainers? At what time in the evening must music end? Are there particular florists who know the hotel/restaurant? Similarly, there may be a useful link with photographers who are familiar with the setting.

• Is the venue easily accessible by car or rail? Is there ample parking?

## Hired hall or rooms

Community, sports, arts, social and religious venues often have rooms for hire. Some may have links with caterers, entertainers and dressers to prepare the venue (and you may be obliged to use bar facilities or caterers);

*Below Always visit hotel or restaurant venues to check the space and facilities before you book.*

accommodation may even be provided in some clubs. Less expensive venues are economical for self-catering. Points to check include:

• Heating (is this included in the cost?).

• Lighting and how it can be adapted to improve the ambience.

• Kitchen facilities for food preparation and storage, heating and clearing up.

• Tables and chairs – check how many there are, the table sizes and ensure they provide enough space for the number of guests.

• Bar facilities and whether alcohol is allowed; entertainment permits.

• Cloakroom facilities.

• Cleaning and preparation of venue – will the space be clear and clean? How far in advance will you have access for setting out tables, decorating the space, laying out food? Clearing up afterwards – will this have to be completed on the evening or next day?

## Marquee hire

This may be a practical solution to gaining all-weather space if you have a large, flat garden. Hire companies provide guidance on size, numbers

**Above** *Brighten up hired tables with table linen and ribbons.*

accommodated and access required for erection. Erected sample marquees or a portfolio of examples should be available. Check the lining is intact, the flooring is solid, and there is provision for power, heating and lighting.

## Picnics

These may be informal and fun, or formal social occasions attached to sporting or entertainment events. Follow custom and etiquette for society occasions, such as the serving of stylish car-boot hampers, or candlelit picnics in a country-house garden. When obtaining tickets for events, check details of times and facilities, parking (and distance from picnic area), dress and conduct code.

## Parties afloat

Boats range from floating restaurants and bars to those with facilities for extensive parties. Smaller vessels can be hired for small groups with or without professional staff, and entertaining up to a dozen friends to a late champagne lunch or early supper is fun. Check that the company rigidly applies safety regulations – if in doubt seek advice from relevant local authorities. Inspect the vessel's facilities thoroughly. Check the duration and route of the trip and access and parking at or transport to the point of departure.

# By Invitation Only

Common sense and consideration are vital for informal invitations while rules of etiquette apply to formal invitations. A note can sometimes follow informal verbal invitations or a telephone call of confirmation a couple of days in advance – typically when organizing dinner parties with friends. The timing for informal invitations depends entirely on how busy and flexible everyone is.

### Invitation information

It may seem like a statement of the obvious but it is surprisingly easy to miss details or to include incorrect (conflicting) dates and days. Invitations need to include the following:
- Guest names, with correct titles.
- Host and/or hostess names.
- Occasion or reason for party.
- Venue.
- Day and date.
- Time: this may be approximate or precise. Before a formal meal, it is usual to indicate a period of about 30 minutes

**Below** *Simple themes work best when making your own invitations.*

### The right time
- Breakfast may be arranged from early until mid morning.
- Coffee mornings are usually scheduled for 11 a.m.
- Brunch can be planned for any time from mid morning to early lunch, between usual breakfast and lunch times.
- Lunch is usually arranged at 12.30 p.m. or 1 p.m. but invitations may be for an early or late lunch.
- Afternoon tea invitations are often scheduled for 3 p.m. or slightly later. Children's tea usually follows the end of afternoon school, usually about 4 p.m.
- Supper is often early or late evening, indicating a light menu rather than dinner.

during which guests are expected (within the first 15 minutes). The time may include the expected duration of the gathering or a time when an evening will end – expressed as "carriages at …" on formal dinner invitations.

- Cocktails and drinks are served from 6 p.m. to 8 p.m.
- Dinner is usually served from 7.30 p.m. until 8.30 p.m., with invitations requesting the arrival of guests about 30 minutes beforehand for pre-dinner drinks.
- "At home" indicates a period of time during which guests may arrive and depart. This is informal and usually includes light nibbles and refreshments rather than a substantial or formal meal.
- "Open house" is the contemporary and particularly informal version of "At home", often extending from lunch (or mid-morning brunch) through to the evening and intended for a mix of families, friends and colleagues of all ages.

- RSVP (*répondez s'il vous plaît*), sometimes with a date, is a polite way of reminding guests that a reply is required.
- Address, telephone and other contact details for replying.
- Dress code and any other information: white tie indicating wing collars, white ties and tails for men, ball gowns for women; black tie and dinner jacket is standard evening wear for men, when women may wear long or short dresses. Notes on a party theme or other special dress requirements should be included.

### Formal invitations

Written requests for the company of guests at a notable occasion are sent at least a month in advance. This is typical of family celebrations, such as weddings, when four to six weeks' notice is practical. (Key guests should be aware of the date well in advance.) Parties organized around public events may be arranged three to six months

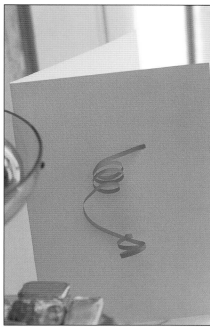

**Above** *Stationery for formal occasions comes in many different styles.*

**Above** *Good quality paper and simple decorations make pretty invitations.*

in advance. Check the closing date for confirming numbers when booking a venue, confirm with suppliers and ensure invitations are sent out in good time in order for replies to be returned by the required date.

### The right title

Addressing guests by an incorrect title may cause offence. Check with the households or offices of those in public or official roles. There are reference books detailing all contemporary and traditionally correct forms of address and greeting, including academic qualifications, religious orders and positions, military ranks, titled persons and those of any office requiring recognition. When in doubt about how acquaintances and relatives prefer to be addressed, check with them, if possible. Otherwise, close family or friends may be able to advise.

Traditionally, a married woman takes the name or initials of her husband when addressed singly or as a couple, for example Mr and Mrs John Smith, Mrs John Smith or Mrs J. Smith. However, some object to this,

preferring to use their first name, and women may retain their own family name after marriage, choosing the title Ms instead of Miss or Mrs. Addressing unmarried couples as "Mr and Mrs" is usually unacceptable to them and both names should be used.

### Inventive invitations

Dress the message up according to the type of party. Concentrate on style and quality for all invitations, from heavy flat cards with fine lettering and discreet decorative edging to bright folded cards that may be fun but fall short of becoming garish.

When using professional designers and printers ask to see samples and prices per quantity and remember that selecting from their usual repertoire may be more convenient and more successful than asking them to create something different and complicated. Craft techniques, art skills or calligraphy can be used to make invitations and party stationery. Involve the children when preparing fun invitations for junior events.

A personal computer can be used to design and print stationery to professional standards. If the printer is not likely to deliver the required quality

in terms of colour and graphics, ready-printed paper, cards and matching envelopes can be used as a base for black-and-white printing.

Finally, creative flair and technology are by no means essential, as ready-printed party stationery is available from quality stationers and general stores. Neat handwriting is all that is required to add individual details.

**Below** *For formal occasions, take care to use the correct titles for guests.*

# Equipment and Materials Lists

Make lists of all equipment needed at the outset to ensure that everything is readily available, budgeted and scheduled. This applies when entertaining at home, particularly for self-catering. When caterers are commissioned they will usually source all equipment related to preparing and serving the food, often including tables and chairs. If you have particular ideas let them be known in advance.

### Buying or hiring?

Hiring is often the only practical option for large celebrations. However, if you regularly entertain medium-size gatherings at home it may be worth buying a basic kit. For example, good quality white china, plain glassware and dishwasher-safe standard cutlery are often available from factory outlets. Plain white flat sheets are an alternative to table linen and perfectly presentable when dressed up for the occasion. For informal, family and children's parties it is worth buying rigid plastic plates and

Above *Table linen, napkins and glassware can all be hired.*

dishes that can be stacked in the dish-washer rather than spending almost as much on disposable ware that will be used just once. Sort out stackable, covered, storage boxes at the same time so that "the kit" can be packed away afterwards for use next time.

### Large items

Tables and chairs are usually included in the hire fee for halls. Check numbers and condition when booking, making sure that they all stand securely when opened. For parties at home, it is usually possible to utilize or borrow spare household or garden tables but chairs can be more of a problem. Hiring folding or stacking plastic chairs may be the answer.

Remember protective floor coverings for pale or precious carpets, especially when planning an indoor–outdoor party with guests of all ages. Specialist non-slip coverings can be useful in hallways or over areas of carpet by the patio or French doors.

When planning a large barbecue party, consider hiring large gas or charcoal barbecues from caterers' suppliers. They will make cooking lots of food easier than coping on the minimum of space on the home barbecue. Outdoor gas heaters can also be hired.

Left *Plain white linen napkins can be decorated with fresh flowers.*

Below *Make sure the barbecue is large enough to cater for all your guests.*

Check availability of entertainment equipment, such as inflatable play centres or bouncy castles, when fixing the party date, to avoid disappointment. Ask if the equipment will be assembled or inflated on delivery or left for you to erect, in which case make sure the necessary tools are also provided.

## Food preparation and serving equipment

Catering hire specialists provide everything from disposable items to starched table linen and napkins, china and cutlery and serving equipment, including folding tables and chairs. When making your lists, sort requirements by category and then check outstanding queries with the hire store. Count and check equipment when taking delivery to make sure that it is all clean, present and undamaged. If there is anything dirty, missing or damaged, let the company know immediately otherwise you may be held responsible and charged for the problem at the end of the hire period. Most of the following items can be easily hired:

**Below** *Check in advance that you have all the cooking equipment you need.*

**Above** *Champagne flutes, ice buckets and cruets can all be hired for parties.*

• Cooking pans, trays and dishes – make sure your oven and burners are large enough to accommodate them.
• Coffee makers and water boilers.
• Serving bowls, trays and dishes – compare the cost of high-quality disposable items with hire charges.
• Table crockery – make a list from the menu, remembering cruets and sauceboats, if necessary, and cups, pots and spoons for coffee. Water jugs (pitchers) and glasses may be included with table crockery.
• Glassware may be hired or borrowed free of charge from wine suppliers or supermarkets – this may include spirit and beer glasses.
• Table linen, napkins and cutlery, plus serving cutlery.

## All the trimmings

List all the decorative trimmings and finishing touches:
• Room decorations and streamers; garden decorations.
• Plants and/or decorations for patio and garden.
• Decorative indoor or outdoor lighting; candles or garden flares.
• Outdoor fireworks.

**Above** *Bright streamers and party hooters jazz up a birthday party table.*

• Table decorations, separated into fresh or silk flowers and others, such as coloured strings, confetti, candles, party poppers, whistles, bubbles, table crackers, indoor sparklers and other mini indoor fireworks.
• Balloons or balloon decorations.
• Guest gifts or children's goodie bags to take away and party-game prizes.
• Small cake boxes.

**Below** *Children love brightly coloured goodie bags to take home.*

# Table Etiquette, Settings and Style

For formal occasions the host and hostess take their places at the ends of the table, with the most important male and female guests on their right (male to host, female to hostess). The remaining guests are seated in order of rank alternating male and female. When there is a master or top table, the most important guests take centre place. This arrangement is adopted for weddings, with the bride and groom in the middle, flanked by their parents and in-laws, with chief bridesmaid and best man at the ends.

Couples are usually seated opposite each other, the idea being that conversation flows around the table, not across it. When the numbers of men and women are equal, they are seated alternately around the table.

Above *Use traditional etiquette to avoid confusion: cutlery is placed on either side of the plates in order of courses.*

Above *Make sure there is ample elbow-room between each table setting.*

Below *Coloured modern cutlery mixed with elegant antique silver pieces.*

Seat people who are likely to have something in common next to each other. It is considerate to avoid pairing individuals whose opinions clash dramatically. When placing guests among several tables, try to achieve a compatible but interesting mix on each table. When there are children at formal occasions, it is sensible to put them on tables near the entrance, for easy cloakroom access. Guests with babies or small children may need space for prams or high chairs.

Make sure the writing on place cards is large enough to be legible by guests as they walk around the table. Display a seating plan on a board near the entrance to dining areas at large formal gatherings.

## Formal table settings

The simple rule for formal settings is to lay cutlery for opening courses on the outside, starting from the right, and work in towards the plate.

• Use a large dinner plate to check the space for each setting and leave plenty of elbow-room between settings.

• Working from the right, lay the bread knife, soup spoon, fish knife or small side knife for the first course, large knife for the main course and dessert-spoon. Working in from the left, lay the fish fork or small fork for first course, fork for main course and dessert fork.

• For slightly less formal arrangements, the dessertspoon and fork may be laid across the top of the setting, spoon at the top (on the outside), with its handle to the right and fork below (on the inside), with its handle to the left.

• Cheese knives and utensils, such as a lobster pick or escargot tongs, may be brought in with the appropriate course. The cheese knife may be laid across the top, below the dessertspoon and fork.

• Arrange glasses at the top right above the setting in the order in which they are used. Include a water goblet or tumbler, white and red wine glasses.

• Distribute serving cutlery, cruets and butter dishes evenly around the table.

**Above** *Chevrons are just one way of folding linen napkins.*

**Below** *Cutlery can be bound together to add interest to an empty bowl.*

## Contemporary style

Flaunt convention to make a design statement. The civilized rule when exploring new table-laying territory is to be practical and avoid confusing diners or causing embarrassment. If the cutlery is not laid in conventional positions it should be clear for which course it is intended. Bread knives can be laid on side plates, cutlery for the first course can be laid on a base platter with a napkin or brought in with the food, leaving the main course cutlery on the table. For stark effect leave the table bare, laying perfectly starched linen napkins at each place and bring out cutlery as courses are served. Go for graphic lines and clean textures on table decorations, including any flowers and candles.

Base platters that remain in position under plates for first course and main course look attractive. They should be significantly larger than, and comfortably hold, the main-course plate so that it does not rattle. Glass, metal, wood or china in bold colours look especially dramatic under white or black plates. Match napkins to the base platter, arranging them on top as part of the setting.

## Fun and lively

Strew the table with streamers and fun decorations in carefully coordinated colours. Bold flower petals and succulent leaves make a change from the usual floral decorations. Crystals, beads and glass baubles can be used to good effect in centrepieces or corner decorations. Use low or very tall candles to create pools of light. Make sure they do not block the view. Add crackers and indoor table fireworks for lively intervals between courses.

**Below** *Outdoor entertaining can be formal and stylish.*

**Above** *A wide selection of novelty items are available for children's parties.*

## Mix and match

Ultimately, the best parties and meals are those where good food and entertaining company are shared in a relaxed atmosphere.

Mixing and matching food, table style and room setting can result in a wonderfully eclectic party. There is no reason why all the china, glassware, cutlery and linen should match; picking out one colour to use for decorations will transform a complete muddle of equipment into a lively style.

# Presentation and Buffets

Reflect the style in atmosphere and presentation, from the first impression on entering the house to the lingering memories of an enjoyable party.

### Formal sit-down meals

Give guests something to dress up for, balancing a sense of occasion and ceremony with a formal but relaxed atmosphere.

• The home or hired venue should be sparkling clean, sweet smelling and attractive with flowers or appropriate decorations. Aim for understated sophistication. Every area that guests will notice must be pristine.

• The table is the centrepiece, so devote time to planning it. Coordinate colour, shape and texture in decorations and presentation. Lay the table well in advance rather than as an afterthought. Lighting should be flattering, rather than bright, but never gloomy. Candlelight is perfect, so use candles around the room and set fairly low on the table or well above eye level of seated diners.

• The dining area should be pleasantly warm rather than uncomfortably hot. Be ready to reduce heating discreetly or provide ventilation as everyone warms

up over a meal, then to warm the room again later, if necessary.

• If possible, allow a beautiful table to be appreciated before everyone sits down. Leave the door to the prepared dining room open so that guests catch a tantalizing glimpse as they arrive. Allow time for seating guests at the table rather than rushing them.

### Buffet basics

You can decorate the edge of a buffet table with flowers, garlands, bows or other trimmings. Table coverings and

**Above** *Highly decorative floral displays look good on buffets.*

edges can be flowing but they must not be so long that they become a hazard as people pass close by.

A fork buffet should include food that is easily eaten with just a fork. Plates should be arranged at one end of the table so that guests move along and help themselves. Displaying forks, napkins and any accompaniments on a small table slightly away from the end of the buffet will encourage guests to move away from the food. Buffet tables are often placed against a wall but moving the table into the room is better, encouraging guests to walk around and serve themselves without having to stretch over dishes.

If the buffet is self-service, all the food should be easy to serve with a spoon, tongs or slice using one hand. Try to arrange food in dishes of different heights, and display one or more large dishes as centrepieces.

Arrange food in a logical order rather than randomly on the table. Moving guests from main dishes on to

**Left** *A silver and white theme creates a classy dining table.*

accompaniments is logical if the menu takes that form. Replenish or replace dishes as necessary.

When the food takes the form of a main course, rather than a collection of complementary dishes, the savouries are usually cleared away before sweet dishes are brought out. This can be awkward in large gatherings if some guests are ready for dessert before others have finished the main course, so setting out cheese and desserts on a separate table is better.

## Fabulously simple

Instead of setting out one large buffet table, you can distribute dishes individually among several occasional tables, adding a stack of small plates, forks and paper or linen napkins in each case. This is a brilliant way of presenting an eclectic collection of dishes, each to be sampled and savoured alone. Reflect the stylish approach by serving beautifully displayed food on plain white plates and keep decorative room trimmings uncluttered, just one step on from minimalism.

For this approach, the trick is to keep "waves" of prepared foods in reserve in the kitchen. Instead of laying them all out at once, replace empty platters as the food is consumed. Moving from one style of food to another is easy – rather like serving different courses of a meal – and it is a good idea to allow a palate-clearing pause between one variety and the next. For example, a range of marinated seafood may be followed

**Above** *Decorate a table for an autumnal lunch with fruits of the season.*

by a selection of roasted miniature vegetables and accompanying dips, and finally by the finest home-made chocolate truffles. Remember the rule: less is more.

## Informal and fun

It is easy to lose a sense of style when casually decorating a home and displaying an informal buffet. Focus on a limited choice of fun decorations and controlled use of colour to avoid overdoing it with garish clutter.

Presenting just a small number of seriously delicious dishes or one or two types of the finest-quality ingredients is much more sophisticated than laying out an ill-matched mix of home-made and bought bits and pieces. For example, perfect seafood paella, a tureen of superlative soup and glorious platters of charcuterie and cheese will each make a fabulous meal when served with lots of fresh home-made bread and a herb-filled leafy salad.

**Left** *Bright table linen and plates complemented by colourful utensils add up to informal Mediterranean style.*

# organizing your party food

Food with flair is the result of calm forethought rather than frantic kitchen activity. Take time out to consider all options to avoid being overwhelmed by choice when leafing through recipes or shopping for ingredients.

# Planning Points

The easiest way to ensure a successful party is by tailoring your requirements to a suitable list of key points. Consider the following planning points:

• The occasion and type of meal are good starting points. Is the celebration formal or informal? Is it for adults or children, or both? Are you serving nibbles and finger food, a fork supper or a sit-down meal? A mixture of dishes can come together successfully as refreshment without fitting into accepted menu courses and this is true for seated eating as well as stand-up situations.

• Numbers and special requirements are important. Thinking up a menu that is over-ambitious to cook for a large number of guests can lead to disaster. An extravagant spread of many courses that is suitable for a dozen guests to sample in small quantities may be difficult to prepare and leave some guests embarrassed not to have done

**Above** *Lobster Themidore and fillets of turbot with oysters are stylish dishes for special occasions.*

justice to the food. You should plan to accommodate special diets right from the beginning, for example, include vegetarian, vegan, or low-fat dishes on the menu. If guests have specific needs – such as gluten-free food – it is easier to plan suitable dishes as part of the main menu rather than preparing a set of alternatives at the last minute.

• Facilities should come high on the list of considerations. When finishing or serving food away from home, at a hired venue, or a picnic for example, make sure that every dish can be transported, reheated or cooked at the venue as appropriate. Check out facilities available at the venue, if necessary. At home, the danger is overstretching facilities, so avoid planning too many dishes requiring

last-minute cooking or heating to fit in the oven or for the top of the stove. Some recipes cooked at different temperatures cannot be adapted for cooking in the same oven. Also make sure you have enough crockery and cutlery for the menu.

• Food options are endless, so cost and capabilities are vital. When buying ready-made or commissioning caterers be aware of prices before dreaming up a menu to blow the budget. When planning to cook, work within your capabilities; being adventurous is fun within reasonable limitations but beyond this it can become a problem. Enlist the help of others or combine bought and home-made to be practical when there is a lot to be done.

Money can evaporate when using expensive ingredients and it is easy to isolate a pricey shopping list and get carried away, forgetting that it all adds up with drinks and other party costs.

**Match courses or dishes**

For formal menus, plan courses that complement each other and balance substantial and light dishes. The same criteria apply to finger or fork buffets, but there is more flexibility when guests don't have to eat dishes in order.

**Below** *Tarts and quiches are popular choices for a buffet or brunch.*

### Selecting recipes

Confident cooks who entertain often and enjoy providing culinary theatre for guests may opt for lots of last-minute cooking, especially when they have kitchen space to accommodate spectators. Otherwise it is sensible to plan the menu around cook-ahead dishes, with last-minute cooking limited according to ability and the occasion. Being with your guests at a dinner party is important, while doing whirling dervish impressions between stove and buffet table can be stressful for both partygoers and you. Consider the following points:

• Balance hot and cold dishes to minimize last-minute work. One or two hot dishes are usually sufficient for a formal, main-meal buffet.

**Above** *Cut the first slice of cakes so guests can then easily help themselves.*

• Go for recipes based on familiar techniques.
• Select dishes that are practical to serve as well as prepare.
• For stand-up buffets, avoid dishes that are difficult to eat with only a fork.
• When arranging a finger buffet, select foods that are bitesize or easy to handle and bite without being messy.
• Leafy salads fill plates and can be difficult to eat when standing up, so guests tend to take less from buffets. Serve dressings separately from salads

that are likely to wilt so that they can be added to taste when served; this prevents the salad from become soggy.
• Creamy salads and dishes that can be piled neatly on plates or in which ingredients cling together are popular.

### Increasing quantities

Recipes that can be increased in quantity successfully include soups, casseroles, sauces for pasta and recipes for individual portions (such as a specific number of chicken portions).
• When increasing the volume of stews and casseroles by more than three times, re-assess the volume of liquid as the proportion can be reduced slightly.
• Pies with pre-cooked fillings and a lid can be made in larger portions and cooked in larger dishes without vastly increasing the cooking time.
• Baked pasta dishes (such as lasagne or cannelloni) are excellent candidates for cooking in quantity.
• It is easier to boil large quantities of pasta in separate batches than to try to overfill a pan. Undercook it very slightly, drain and rinse, then toss with a little olive oil and reheat briefly in a suitable covered dish in the microwave.
• When increasing quantities by more than double, do not multiply up the herbs, spices and garlic several times as they may become overpowering.

**Above** *Baked dishes, such as lasagne, are good choices for supper parties.*

• Accompanying sauces for hot dishes and dressings for salads do not have to be increased by as much as the main ingredients when increasing the recipe by more than two or three times.

### Menu cards

Displaying a menu card is an excellent way of letting everyone know what they will be eating or identifying dishes on a buffet. Arrange several menus on a large buffet table and remember to identify those dishes that are suitable for vegetarians or special diets.

**Below** *Use bought or home-made menu cards to identify buffet dishes.*

# Cooking Plans, Shopping and Storage

With the menu organized it is time to get down to practicalities and, yet again, making the right lists eases everything along.

## Cooking plan

Make a list of all the cooking. It is a good idea to copy the recipes and keep them together in a plastic folder in the kitchen when preparing them.

Divide the list into those recipes to cook well in advance and freeze, adding notes on when to remove them from the freezer, with likely thawing time and any finishing touches or reheating time. Note down any seasonings or enriching ingredients that have to be added at the last minute and include this on the checklist of things to do.

List the dishes that have to be cooked just before the party, that is the day before or on the same day. Note any advance preparation next to each dish. For example, salad dressings can be made a day or two ahead and chilled; some salad ingredients can be trimmed or peeled and washed the day before, then chilled ready for use – spring onions (scallions), celery sticks and tomatoes are good examples.

When all the dishes are listed, with the days on which they have to be made, it is then easier to draw up a cooking plan. Order the recipes according to the day on which they have to be made, then go through this list to make sure it is all possible. If you have far too much work for any one day, check whether any can be made in advance. If you have chosen too many last-minute dishes, adjust the menu before embarking on a shopping spree.

On your cooking plan, list different items to be prepared separately – this way you are less likely to underestimate the work involved. As well as volume of work, make sure that you have enough containers, work surfaces and note the cooking appliance needed for each dish.

## Shopping lists

Working from numbers and menu, check the recipes and increase the quantities if necessary. Then work out

**Above** *Use good quality meat cuts and poultry from the butcher's.*

**Below** *Keep fresh fish and shellfish chilled until ready to cook.*

the shopping list, checking store-cupboard ingredients. Rather than having one mammoth list, divide it according to type of food, items that can be bought in advance and perishable last-minute purchases. Include any notes, reminders or alternatives on the lists to make shopping as efficient as possible.

## Orders and deliveries

Scrutinize the list for items that should or can be ordered: meat cuts from a local butcher; fish to be prepared by the fishmonger; bread to be reserved at the supermarket or ordered from the baker and so on. Take advantage of delivery services offered by super-

**Left** *Local greengrocers may deliver fresh fruit and vegetables to your door.*

**Above** *Use temporary containers as colourful ice buckets.*

**Below** *Defrost frozen items slowly and then keep them cool.*

markets and organic produce that can be bought over the Internet. Do not be shy about asking for a delivery from local suppliers if you are placing an exceptionally large order.

Seek out mail-order suppliers for specialist or fine quality ingredients. Virtually all foods are available by this method and it is a particularly good option for specialist items, such as excellent raw or baked hams or high quality fish and shellfish.

### Keeping cool and safe
Check refrigerator and freezer space well in advance. If you are cooking and freezing dishes ahead, make sure you have plenty of storage space. Sort and clean the refrigerator. Assess the amount of storage space you need and sort out practical options – a helpful neighbour

may have refrigerator space or, in cold weather, an unheated utility room or a suitable clean, dry outside area can be useful for less perishable items.

• Chill bottles of wine, beers and soft drinks in a large, clean plastic bin or several buckets part-filled with water and ice.

• Use chiller boxes and ice packs when the refrigerator is full – borrow or buy these in advance.

• Make temporary chiller boxes by lining rigid plastic stacking boxes with double-thick, heavy bubble wrap and covering the bottom with ice packs or ice in sealed plastic bags. Place on the floor in a clean, safe and cool area to hold ingredients or less-delicate dishes. Cover the top with more ice packs to keep the cold in.

• Prioritize your refrigerator space for highly perishable food such as fish, meat, poultry and dairy products. Fish should be kept in the coldest section of the refrigerator.

• Cool cooked dishes as quickly as possible. Cover them securely and chill them promptly.

• Leave items to be served cold in the refrigerator until the last minute.

• Thaw frozen items properly, keeping them cool.

**Above** *Some kinds of vegetables can be prepared and chopped in advance.*

### Coping with leftovers
There are inevitably leftovers after a large party. Being prepared for coping with them makes clearing up far easier. Buy plenty of large plastic bags and clear film (plastic wrap). Some foods, such as cheese, should be wrapped and chilled promptly. Transfer leftovers to suitably small containers, cover and chill. Leftover cooked vegetables or green salads can be transformed into delicious soup with a minimum of fuss.

**Below** *Wrap leftovers promptly after a meal and transfer to a refrigerator.*

# Cook Ahead, Stay Calm

### Meat and poultry sauces and casseroles

Hearty meat and game casseroles freeze well, for 3–6 months. Poultry casseroles using portions do not have as good a texture as when they are freshly cooked, but diced poultry casseroles and sauces freeze well. Mushrooms and crisp vegetables are not as good after thawing as when freshly cooked. Add some finely diced vegetables for flavouring the casserole during the cooking, then add more sautéed vegetables when reheating for a good texture. Fine-textured or minced (ground) meat sauces – bolognese, chilli con carne – are successful when frozen and thawed.

**Left** *Stocks, sauces and casserole dishes can often be cooked ahead.*

It may be possible to cook the majority of a meal or buffet in advance, spreading the work load over a period of time. You will then have it all ready in the freezer, leaving accompaniments and side dishes for last-minute preparation. Select the right type of dishes for success. Try some of the following ideas remembering that the freezer life depends on the ingredients used in the dishes more than the type of dish.

### Soups

Smooth soups freeze well for up to three months. Do not add cream, yogurt, fromage frais or egg yolks before freezing. Reheat gently, then add the dairy ingredients before serving.

### Pâtés

Smooth, rich pâtés freeze well for up to one month. They are best served sliced or scooped, as they can look slightly tired when served from the dishes in which they were frozen. Home-made pâtés and spreads (fish, poultry or meat) are excellent for topping canapés.

**Above** *Most soups and some types of sauces can be cooked in advance.*

**Above** *Make stocks and freeze in ice cube trays until ready to use.*

**Above** *Cook minced (ground) sauces in advance and freeze until needed.*

**Above** *Make curry pastes and sauces ahead of schedule.*

## Stuffings

Breadcrumb, meat or fruit stuffings can all be frozen up to one month ahead. Rice is not so good as the grains soften and become slightly granular.

## Sauces, gravies and dips

Reduced cooking juices and flour-thickened sauces and gravies freeze well for up to 3 months. However, those based on eggs and oils are not suitable, as they curdle. Finely chopped or puréed vegetable salsas are excellent freezer candidates. Home-made dips also freeze well – try avocado dips (guacamole), chickpeas and pulses (hummus), or roasted vegetables puréed with cream cheese. Light, mayonnaise-based dips do not freeze well as they tend to curdle.

## Vegetable dishes

Although the majority should be freshly cooked, there are some useful dishes to freeze ahead. Creamy mashed potatoes and vegetable purées freeze well for up to 6 months – great for decorative gratin edges, pie toppings or reheated in the microwave and stirred before serving. (You will be amazed at how quickly fabulous mash disappears from a buffet – with butter, chopped fresh herbs and a little grated lemon rind mash is a delicious accompaniment and easy to eat.) Grated potato pancakes are also excellent: lay them out on a baking tray ready for rapid reheating and crisping in a hot oven. Firm vegetable terrines also freeze well for up to 1 month.

## Pastries

Filled pastries should be frozen raw, then cooked at the last minute. Puff or filo pastries that are time-consuming to prepare but quick to cook are ideal. Buy chilled rather than frozen pastry. Brush shaped filo pastry with a little butter or olive oil (or a mixture) before

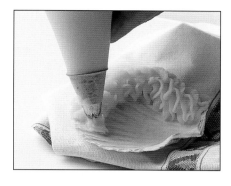

**Above** *Pipe mashed potato into scallop shells for Coquille St. Jacques.*

**Above** *Make samosas or small pastries in advance and freeze.*

freezing to prevent it from cracking. Cook small pastries from frozen. Large pastry items – pies, tarts, and pastry-wrapped fish – should be frozen raw and thawed before cooking. They will keep well for 1–3 months, depending on the ingredients in the filling.

Cooked choux pastries, such as profiteroles, freeze well unfilled. Crisp the pastries very briefly in a hot oven when thawed, then cool and fill. If serving savoury buns hot, fill then reheat them; depending on the filling, they may be filled before freezing and, if small, reheated from frozen.

## Batters and baked goods

Pancakes are versatile; interleave them with clear freezer film (plastic wrap), then pack in a freezer bag. They keep well for a few months and are excellent filled with savoury or sweet mixtures, and baked. Baked sponge cakes, meringues, muffins and breads freeze

**Above** *Fish cakes can be made in advance and frozen individually.*

**Above** *Brush small savouries with a little melted butter before freezing.*

well also. Protect delicate items by packing them in rigid containers. Fill gâteaux and desserts when they are part-thawed.

## Ices

You can prepare iced desserts up to a week or two in advance, but any longer and they can become "icy" with ice crystals. Richer mixtures keep better than lighter recipes: cream-rich parfaits frozen in moulds are a good choice.

## Safe thawing

Thaw cooked dishes overnight in the refrigerator or a cool place and reheat to their original temperature. This is important for meat and poultry sauces.
• Defrost frozen items to be served chilled (pâtés, sponge cakes, gâteaux) in the refrigerator for up to 24 hours. Transfer delicate items to serving platters while frozen, cover and thaw in the refrigerator.

# Simple Presentation

Anticipation of good food is an enjoyable part of the dining process, so creating a visual feast is as important as making food taste terrific. Getting the look just right for a smart dinner party is less daunting than creating a buffet that does not look messy or ridiculously over-elaborate. Achieving food that is easy to serve as well as appealing and delicious is the ultimate aim, and it is not difficult.

### Appetizing presentation

Here are a few simple rules for food presentation – they apply to individual or large portions, fork suppers, dinner parties or buffets:

• Drips and drizzles should be wiped off dishes, especially cooking dishes.
• One or more folded clean dishtowels can be wrapped around hot dishes.

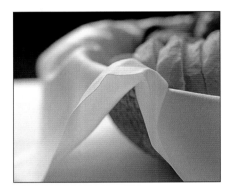

**Above** *Line bread baskets with crisp linen napkins.*

**Below** *Present hot serving dishes wrapped in clean napkins.*

• The serving dish should suit the food: neither too small nor too large, it should be deep enough to hold liquids without slopping, and large enough for items to be cut, scooped or spooned out without overflowing.
• Select dishes to complement the colour, shape and pattern of the food. Plain foods can be served on patterned crockery but fussy, bitty ingredients look best on plain designs or simple white crockery.

### Appropriate garnishes

Any garnish should complement the food in style, flavour, texture, colour and shape. These finishing touches should enhance not mask the dish and they must not clash with the main ingredients.

Herb, vegetable and salad garnishes should complement the flavours of the dish or cooking style. For example, salad garnishes go well with pan-fried main courses and fairly dry bakes or pastries, but they are ghastly floating in a delicious hot sauce or gravy, where

**Above** *Serve appropriate sauces and accompaniments with each dish.*

they do nothing other than become limp and wreck the temperature, flavour and texture of the food.

Crisp croûtons, puff pastry shapes (*fleuron*) and shreds or shapes of pancake or omelette are all excellent for introducing contrasting shapes and textures. Nuts, roasted seeds and crisp-fried noodles or pasta shapes contribute texture. Diced or coarsely shredded potatoes, carrots and beetroot (beet) can be deep-fried to make delicious garnishes.

### Divine decorations

Some good-looking sweet dishes are best left to make their own perfect statements with perhaps little more than a dusting of icing (confectioners') sugar – fabulous fruit salads, creamy roulades, whirly meringues, sparkling jellies and feather-light baked soufflés, for example. Others will benefit from a little decoration.

Sweet decorations should complement the main dish in colour, texture, flavour, style and form. The decoration should not overpower or clash with the dessert in any way. Be aware that it is easy to overdo the decoration on sweets, so avoid a cheap-looking concoction.

Many desserts are inherently decorative – set or baked in moulds, using decorative ingredients, topped with swirled cream, or served with colourful fruit sauces. A minimalist hint at decoration is often all that is needed – a single strawberry leaf with a part-sliced fruit; a cluster of perfect red currants; the smallest mound of chocolate curls; a simple dusting of dark cocoa powder (unsweetened); or a tiny scattering of golden-toasted flaked (sliced) almonds.

Elaborate piped decorations may not make a contemporary fashion statement but they can be lusciously alluring when applied with style. The fatal mistake is adding one swirl too many. Instead of using a decorative nozzle, try a plain one or use a medium-size spoon to apply cream and a fork to swirl it lightly.

### Buffet sense

When adding finishing touches to buffet food, keep individual dishes simple, remembering that they will make a mosaic of colour and form when they are together on the buffet. Make the food look approachable and easy to serve when you expect guests to help themselves, otherwise elaborate or awkward-looking creations will be avoided by all but the most confident.

• So that food is easy to reach, stagger the arrangement of dishes and do not overfill the table. Instead, top up plates or dishes or remove and replace empty dishes occasionally.

• Do not overfill dishes or platters.

• When possible, present individual portions of food that are easier to serve and make them smaller than you would for a sit-down meal as diners usually prefer to sample a range of foods from a buffet than to take a full-size portion of one dish.

• Cut large items into small portions and remove the first piece, resting it on a serving spatula or laying it on the first guest's plate. This applies to items such as quiches, pies, pizzas and gâteaux.

• When serving whole hams, roasted poultry or large pieces of meat, the best solution is to present the whole item, then make a display of carving the first batch as part of the invitation to guests to eat. Encourage everyone to cut as much as they require, check occasionally and enlist the help of a friend to check that enough is carved.

### Food centrepieces

Buffet tables will benefit from some form of centrepiece, which is usually a large main dish or an elaborate dessert. Alternatively, a fabulous display of fruit

**Above** *Stunning cakes and tortes make good buffet centrepieces.*

or a superb cheese board arranged on a raised stand, with splendid breads and crackers in a huge basket all look good towards the back of a buffet table. These form a focal point and backdrop, and are ready to bring forward when the main course has been consumed; they also help to keep the buffet looking neat, whole and appealing.

**Below** *Raised dishes or platters save space on a buffet table.*

# Garnishing and Decorating

The possibilities are endless, and much creative use can be made of the main ingredients in the dish, presenting them with a slightly different twist. These classic, simple ideas are versatile and effective.

### Herbs

Sturdy sprigs sit well alongside main food, while fine, feathery sprigs can be placed on top. Tiny sprigs are best for small or delicate items.

• Chopped herbs bring fresh colour to soups, casseroles, sauces, rice, pasta and vegetables. As they also add flavour, they should be used with discretion. Neat lines of finely chopped herbs, applied from a large chef's knife, add dimension to large areas of pale and creamy mixtures.

• Fried parsley is delicious with fish and seafood, and it brings crunchy texture to creamy sauced dishes. Wash and thoroughly dry small tender sprigs of curly parsley, then drop into hot deep oil and deep-fry for a few seconds until bright green and crisp. Drain well on kitchen paper.

### Vegetables

Finely sliced vegetables, such as cucumber, (bell) peppers, carrots or tomatoes, can be overlapped in threes or arranged in groups.

• Julienne, or fine matchstick strips,

**Above** *Cut four lengths of chives and use another chive to tie them together.*

look good in neat little heaps or criss-cross rows. Root vegetables – carrots, beetroot (beet), potatoes or swede (rutabaga) – are good raw or cooked as appropriate. Other suitable vegetables include celery, courgettes (zucchini), fennel, peppers or cucumber.

• Fine dice of raw or cooked vegetables look good in rows or heaps. Adjacent rows of contrasting coloured vegetables look very smart.

• Ribbons pared using a potato peeler can be used raw or cooked, depending on the vegetables. Carrots and courgettes are ideal.

• Grated or shredded raw carrots, white radish or cooked beetroot, look good heaped in tiny mounds or other neat arrangements.

• Decorative shapes can be cut from lightly cooked sliced root vegetables,

**Above** *Chopped fresh parsley sprinkled on savoury dishes is an effective garnish.*

sliced courgettes, blanched (bell) peppers, pared cucumber peel or the outer flesh and skin of quartered tomatoes. Use tiny aspic cutters or a small, sharp knife.

### Citrus shapes

Slices and wedges are easy and effective. Wedges are easier to squeeze if the juice is required to sharpen the food. Slices – whole, halved or cut into sections – are useful for sweet dishes.

• Twists are fine slices with a single cut from centre to edge and the cut edges separated in opposite directions.

• Shreds of citrus rind can be cut using a cannelle knife (zester). Simmer them in boiling water until tender, and then drain. For sweet dishes, quickly roll the shreds in caster (superfine) sugar and leave set them aside on a board to dry.

**Below** *Bundles of herbs tied together can be used to garnish savoury dishes.*

**Below** *Chillies can be arranged as garnishes for hot and spicy dishes.*

**Below** *Cut vegetables into julienne strips to add a splash of colour.*

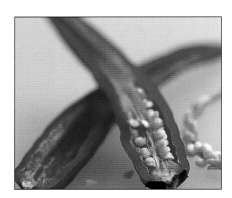

**Above** *Cut small chillies with scissors or a sharp knife to make chilli flowers.*

**Below** *Make cucumber flowers by folding alternate cut slices inwards.*

## Salad ingredients

A chiffonade of bright salad leaves makes an extremely fresh garnish. Roll one or two leaves together fairly tightly and use a sharp knife to cut the finest slices, then shake these out into shreds.

• Curls are highly decorative and slightly oriental. Shred spring onions (scallions), leaving the shreds attached at the root end. Pare short, thin, curly strips off carrots using a vegetable peeler. Cut fine julienne of celery. Place the prepared vegetables in a bowl of iced water and leave for at least 30 minutes, or until they curl.

• Tomatoes and red radishes can be decoratively cut to resemble flowers. Use a small, sharp, pointed knife and, starting at the base, make small "V"-shaped cuts with the points at the top. Make sure the flesh is still attached at

the wide base. Make another row of cuts around the base, and then continue making successive neat rows of cuts up to the top of the vegetable. Always curve the knife around the shape of the vegetable to keep the section of cut flesh evenly thin. Place in a bowl of iced water until the cuts open out to create a flower shape.

Vandyke is the name given to a zigzag cut used to divide radishes and tomatoes decoratively in half. Use a small, fine, pointed knife to make zigzag cuts around the middle, cutting in as far as the centre. Carefully pull the two halves apart. This technique is also useful for citrus fruit and apples; eating apples can be sprinkled with lemon juice and sugar and placed under a preheated grill (broiler) until the sugar turns golden and caramelizes.

**Above** *Individual twists of sliced lemon look good grouped together.*

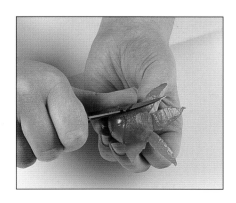

**Above** *Tomato flowers are made by peeling back the skin of cut tomatoes.*

## Breads

Croûtons, croûtes and croustades are all crisp and browned bread garnishes. Croûtons may be small, neat dice or hearty chunks; croûtes are thin or thick but fairly small slices served on the side or used as a base for serving main ingredients; croustades are small containers that can be filled with a variety of savoury mixtures.

Croûtons and croûtes are fried in a mixture of oil and butter. However, if the slices of bread are brushed with a little oil before being cut up they can be spread out on an ovenproof dish and baked until crisp and golden.

• To make croustades, cut thick slices of bread, then cut them into cubes or rounds and hollow these out neatly. Brush sparingly all over with a little oil and bake until crisp and golden.

**Above** *Brush croûtons with a little oil before baking.*

**Above** *Use a sharp knife to make ridges in avocados and then slice thinly.*

### Pastries

Puff pastry shapes can be savoury or sweet: glaze savoury shapes with beaten egg before baking or brush sweet ones with a little egg white and sprinkle with sugar. Use aspic cutters or large biscuit (cookie) cutters to stamp out shapes.

• Filo pastry shreds are decorative, crisp and delicious with savoury or sweet dishes that have a soft texture. Roll up the pastry, then cut it into 1cm/½in wide slices. Shake these out on to a greased baking sheet and brush with a little oil before baking until golden. Dust with caster (superfine) sugar for sweet decorations.

The shreds can be sliced more finely and arranged in neat nests to be filled with savoury or sweet ingredients.

### Pancakes

Thin crêpes or pancakes make excellent garnishes for clear soups and leafy green salads. To cut shreds, tightly roll up one or two pancakes and with a sharp knife slice them into very fine or thin slices, then shake them out. Alternatively, use aspic or biscuit cutters to stamp out shapes.

**Below** *Toasted coconut is a delicious decoration for many desserts.*

For sweet decorations, melt some unsalted (sweet) butter in a frying pan and cook the shreds or shapes, turning once or twice, for a few minutes, until crisp. Transfer to a board or plate and sprinkle with sugar.

### Nuts, seeds and grains

Dry-fry nuts, seeds or grains in a heavy frying pan until they are lightly browned. Stir them constantly so that they brown evenly. Remove from the pan immediately. Use the nuts, seeds or grains to garnish soups, salads (savoury or sweet) or creamy desserts.

• Lightly toast nuts on a piece of foil under a medium-hot grill (broiler), turning them frequently so that they brown evenly. Use to garnish soups, salads, vegetables or sauced dishes. They are also good on desserts, gâteaux and ices. For sugary nuts, lightly toast halved blanched almonds, then immediately toss them with sugar and transfer to a plate to cool.

• Praline is made by tossing lightly roasted nuts, usually almonds, in caramel. Toast blanched almonds or hazelnuts under a grill or in a heavy, dry pan. Make a caramel sauce and stir in the nuts, then pour the mixture on to an oiled baking sheet. Leave to cool completely and set. Crush the praline with a rolling pin and use to decorate creamy desserts, gâteaux or ices.

### Jelly garnishes and decorations

Aspic is the savoury jelly used to glaze chilled cold dishes or make attractive garnishes. Available in packet form, for either fish or poultry, or made by adding dissolved gelatine to clarified fish or chicken stock, set the jelly in a thin layer in an oblong container. Use aspic cutters to stamp out tiny shapes or turn the jelly out on to a board and chop it neatly. Aspic can also be set on sliced black or stuffed green olives,

**Above** *Fresh seasonal fruits look stunning on this Genoese sponge cake.*

herb sprigs or tiny colourful vegetable shapes in ice cube trays.

• Fruit jelly, home-made or from a packet, can be set and cut into shapes or chopped as for aspic. It can also be set over pieces of fruit in ice cube trays.

### Creamy finishes

Whipped cream can be swirled or piped over desserts using a decorative or plain nozzle. Small swirls make decorative edging while large and luscious whirls are good toppings for individual desserts. For a looser feel, drop spoonfuls of cream on to the dessert and sprinkle with chopped toasted nuts.

**Below** *Boston Banoffee pie decorated with piped whipped cream.*

**Above** *Iced Christmas torte with sugared leaves.*

Use double (heavy) or whipping cream. When whipping cream, make sure it is well chilled and use cold utensils, then whip it until it stands up in soft peaks – slightly softer than you need as it firms when piped or spooned. Swirled cream provides contrast and interest in savoury or sweet dishes, such as smooth soups and fruit or chocolate sauces. Trickle a little single (light) cream into the dish, then drag it slightly with a cocktail stick (toothpick).

Feathered cream is attractive in sauces. Drop small dots of cream into the sauce, then drag them with a cocktail stick into feather shapes.

### Sugared decorations

These are effective as decorations on all sorts of sweet dishes. Select tiny bunches of currants, small whole fruit or edible flowers, such as rose petals, and small leaves from mint, scented geraniums or blackcurrants. Make sure the fruit or flowers are clean and dry.

Lightly whisk a little egg white and brush over the fruit or flowers, then dust generously with caster (superfine) sugar. Transfer to a wire rack and leave until crisp and dry.

### Chocolate shapes

Melted plain (semisweet), milk or white chocolate can be used to make a variety of shapes. Melt the chocolate in a bowl over a pan of hot, not boiling, water. Pour the chocolate on to a board covered with baking parchment, then spread it out evenly and thinly using a metal spatula. Leave until just set but not brittle.

Use cutters to stamp out shapes, and use a ruler and sharp knife to cut geometric shapes. Use a large, sharp cook's knife to make chocolate caraque or long curls: hold the knife at an acute angle and scrape off the surface of the chocolate in large curls. Transfer each curl to a separate board and leave until they are firm. To make chocolate leaves, instead of pouring the chocolate on to a board, brush it over the back of washed and dried perfect rose leaves. Apply two or three coats, then set the leaves aside to dry. Ease the leaves away from the chocolate once it has set.

### Ice bowls

An ice bowl makes an impressive serving dish for ice creams and sorbets (sherbets). Make the bowl well in advance and store it in the freezer. Fill it with scoops of ice cream a few hours before dinner, return to the freezer and dessert is ready to serve at once!

**Below** *Serve ice cream or sorbets in a spectacular ice bowl.*

### Making an ice bowl

**1** Select two bowls, one about 5cm/2in smaller than the other. Stand a few ice cubes in the bottom of the larger bowl and place the smaller bowl on top so that the rims of both bowls are level. Tape the bowls at intervals at the edge. Slide slices of fruit or flowers between the bowls and pour in cold water to fill the gap.

**2** Freeze the bowls. Use a skewer to push the fruit or flowers down between the bowls if they float during freezing. To release the ice bowl, remove the tape and pour a little hot water into the small bowl and stand the bottom bowl in hot water. As soon as the ice bowl is released place it in the freezer.

# party themes

Make the most of every party opportunity by focusing on a particular approach. Whether the occasion demands etiquette and sophistication or relaxation of the rules, there are plenty of options to consider. Once the style is set, follow it through with enthusiasm.

# **Shaken** and **Stirred:** the **Drinks Party**

Today's drinks party is a celebration of relaxed sophistication. From easy evenings with friends to an opportunity for semi-formal pre- or post-wedding congratulations, sharing drinks and nibbles is sociable. Plan carefully to ensure the occasion flows smoothly.

## **Setting the scene**
Try the following checklist for straightforward drinks party planning. Make lists of all your ideas while you write shopping lists and notes on aspects to organize.
- Define the occasion precisely.
- Focus on the ambience.
- Decide on the type of drinks.
- Select the style of finger food.

## **Occasion**
Drinks party invitations range from "stylishly casual" to "lounge suit and tie" – a balance of relaxed formality in varying proportions. Within this context, define your occasion before making precise plans. For example, a wedding may provide the opportunity for a gathering of friends not invited to the ceremony and main meal, or a celebration with colleagues and

*Below* Colourful drinks add to the thrill of the cocktail hour.

business clients, neighbours or other associates outside your immediate circle of personal friends.

Whatever the occasion, the number of guests and whether you intend inviting one or more groups of people are important. There is no reason why a drinks party should be connected to any particular event – this is precisely the sort of opportunity to catch up with friends or meet and greet acquaintances. The party may be short – lunchtime or pre-dinner – or an open-ended evening. So there is plenty of scope for setting subtle differences in ambience once you have clear aims.

## **Drinks**
Decide on the type of drinks: cocktails, champagne, wine or an open bar. Cocktails are classic pre-dinner drinks. Champagne is always acceptable and perfect when there is a special toast to raise. Red and white wines are a popular choice. Providing an open bar (that is, offering a selection of shorts and mixers, wine or beer) is the most difficult and expensive, but this can be successful for a limited number of guests, especially if you know them well. Always provide mineral water and a good choice of soft drinks as alternatives to alcohol.

## **Food style**
The food should fit the occasion, ambience and drinks. A plentiful supply of chunky and satisfying finger food is ideal for the sort of relaxed drinks party that drifts into late evening. Dainty canapés and cocktail nibbles are sufficient for a short pre-dinner party. Generous quantities of extra-special, stylish finger food go down well on special occasions. Among the myriad of food options, remember bread and cheese; hot fondues and dips; or international savouries, such as Japanese sushi or Spanish tapas.

**Above** *Arrange nibbles on platters so that guests can easily help themselves.*

## **Serving snacks**
Distribute plates or bowls of snacks around side tables and surfaces (protect surfaces to avoid damage from spills). Offer nibbles as you mingle, or move them near groups of guests and encourage everyone to dip in. Take platters of hot canapés around or enlist the help of a friend or co-host.

**Below** *Hire a range of different cocktail glasses for an authentic touch.*

**Above** *Avocado-filled eggs make excellent little canapés.*

**Right** *A selection of canapés and light bites suitable for a drinks party.*

## Planning finger food

For stylish refreshments, present a modest range of excellent items. Select a number of complementary types of food, including variety in colour, texture and flavour. The following examples show how to match crisp and smooth textures and different ingredients and dishes. Broaden the variety by including a range of sandwich, tart or pastry fillings or toppings. In addition to the main snacks, distribute bowls of good quality bought (or home-made) nibbles, such as roasted nuts, breadsticks and Chinese rice crackers.

- Mini open sandwiches, crisp short pastry tartlets, fruit and cheese savouries on sticks, and crudités with dips.
- Filo-wrapped savouries, bread-based canapés, filled salad vegetables, and smoked salmon and/or ham rolls.
- Bitesize pizza pieces, Spanish tortilla squares, miniature fish cakes, cheese or meat croquettes, and crudités.
- Miniature kebabs, fish goujons, dried fruit wrapped in prosciutto, walnuts sandwiched with cream cheese.
- Smoked salmon sandwiches, marinated mini-mozzarella cheese skewered with cherry tomatoes.
- Excellent chocolate truffles.

## Making canapés

The trick to making impressive canapés without an army of experts is by adopting a conveyor-belt method.

Buy large square sandwich loaves of white, wholemeal (whole-wheat) or rye bread and leave them unwrapped at room temperature for a day. Trim off the crusts, and then cut each loaf lengthways into large, fairly thin slices. Spread with the chosen topping, such as a savoury butter, flavoured soft cheese, pâté or spread. For speed, use a topping that can be piped, rather than spread, such as soft cheese or creamy mixtures. The bases can be prepared to this stage a day ahead; cover with clear film (plastic wrap) and pack in a plastic bag. Cut into squares or fingers.

Arrange the canapés on serving platters and then add the garnishes. For efficiency, prepare a tray that can be added to the topped canapés quickly and easily.

Fuss-free options include: lumpfish row, peeled cooked tiger prawns (shrimp), stuffed green olives, pecan nut halves, halved cherry tomatoes, halved canned artichoke hearts or peeled and halved cucumber slices.

## Portions

The amount guests will eat depends on the time of day and length of the party. The following is a rough guide to the number of bitesize canapés or snacks to prepare for comparatively formal occasions. It is as well to be aware that the more relaxed and lively the gathering, the more people are likely to eat.

- Allow 5 items per person as an appetizer with drinks before a meal.
- Allow 10–12 items per person for an early evening drinks party (assuming that guests will be going on to dinner elsewhere).
- Allow 12–14 items per person for evening refreshments following a late lunch party, wedding breakfast or reception. (Remember to increase this when inviting additional guests in the evening that have not shared the main meal.)
- Allow 14–16 small items per person for light lunchtime or supper refreshments.

at a time, keeping the rest of the pastry covered with clear film (plastic wrap) to prevent it from drying and cracking. Brush with a little melted butter or olive oil, or a mixture of both. Cut the sheet widthways into 7.5cm/3in wide strips.

For fingers, place a little full-flavoured filling across one end of a pastry strip. Fold the end and sides of the strip over, and then roll it up. To make triangles, place a little mound of filling in the middle of the strip about 4cm/1½in from the end. Fold the corner of the pastry and filling over into a triangle across one end, then continue folding the triangle of filling over along the length of the strip.

### Perfect pastries

These can be prepared in advance; they are easy to eat, satisfying and versatile. Try the following tips for streamlined preparation:

**Puff pastries**: prepare three different full-flavoured, well-seasoned cooked fillings. For speedy preparation make squares, triangles and oblong shapes.

Brush the rolled-out pastry lightly with beaten egg before cutting it into 6cm/2½in squares. These can be paired to make square pastries or folded in half into triangles or oblongs. Use one filling for each shape and place a small mound in the appropriate place on

*Above Little pastries, such as piroshki, are always popular party foods.*

each square – centre slightly generous amounts for squares (leave an equal number blank for topping); in one corner for triangles; and to one side for oblongs. Top the squares and fold the others in half. Press the edges together and place on baking sheets. Brush with beaten egg and bake at 220°C/425°F/ Gas 7 for 7–10 minutes, until well puffed and golden. Cool on wire racks.

**Flaky filo savouries**: filo pastry triangles or fingers are extremely easy and quick to make. Work on one sheet

### Kebabs and cocktail-stick snacks

For party finger food, make kebabs and snacks on sticks that are super tasty and neat:

• Thread no more than three miniature items on mini-kebabs.

• Cook trays of marinated ingredients, such as chicken or beef, then cool and thread them on to mini-wooden skewers. Reheat on ovenproof serving platters. Try cubes of chicken or gammon, mini-meatballs, mini-sausages, slices of spicy sausage, squares of (bell) pepper, small pickling onions, halved baby aubergines (eggplant) or cherry tomatoes.

**Below** *Flaky filo fingers are easy to make for large numbers.*

**Below** *Leek, saffron and mussel tartlets are tasty finger food.*

**Below** *Little cheese pies with raisins and pine nuts make great nibbles.*

## Filling ideas for pastries

• Mash a 50g/2oz can of sardines in olive oil with the oil from the can, 1 crushed garlic clove, 2 finely chopped spring onions (scallions), the grated rind of 1 lemon, a squeeze of lemon juice, salt and a pinch of chilli powder.

• Mix finely chopped or minced (ground) cooked ham with a little freshly grated Pecorino cheese, a generous dollop of wholegrain mustard and plenty of chopped fresh chives.

• Mix plenty of finely chopped sun-dried tomatoes, pine nuts, a few chopped raisins and a generous pinch of dried oregano into cream cheese.

• Mash feta cheese to fine bread-crumbs and mix with chopped spring onion, a little oregano and enough ricotta cheese to bind the mixture into a paste.

• Mix chopped, well-drained cooked spinach with chopped spring onion, 1 chopped garlic clove (optional), a little freshly grated Parmesan cheese and enough ricotta to make a firm paste. Season with salt, pepper and a little nutmeg.

• Make sure cocktail-stick (toothpick) bites are bitesize rather than too large to pop into the mouth in one go. (Biting savouries off sticks can mean that the piece left on the stick falls off.)

• Strips of tender foods that roll well are good spread with soft cheese or used as wrappers for firm ingredients. Roll smoked halibut or salmon, cured or cooked ham, salami, peeled roasted (bell) peppers or canned pimientos.

• Olives, melon balls, halved cooked baby new potatoes, cubes of

**Above** *Many supermarkets now sell good-quality prepared sushi.*

cucumber, pieces of dried fruit (prunes, apricots or dates) and radishes are tasty wrapped in cooked or cured meat.

## Simply stylish sushi

Sushi is delicious and practical as it can be prepared ahead, arranged on platters, covered and chilled. Ideally, make the sushi a few hours in advance; however, it can be prepared the day before. Keep it well wrapped to prevent the rice from hardening. Remove from the refrigerator about 30 minutes before serving.

• Rolled sushi: buy mini-sheets of toasted and seasoned nori seaweed to make cocktail-sized rolled sushi rice. Top with dressed cooked sushi rice and add two or three strips of ingredients such as cucumber, spring onion (scallion), cooked carrot or cooked dried shiitake mushrooms marinated in soy sauce and a little sherry. Roll up firmly and neatly. Wrap each roll in clear fim (plastic wrap), twisting the ends firmly. Cut into small pieces before serving.

• Mini-moulded sushi: shape mini-sushi squares by pressing the dressed, cooked rice into ice cube trays. Place a small square of smoked salmon, smoked halibut, thin omelette or thinly sliced smoked or marinated tofu in the bottom of each ice cube compartment before pressing in the rice and topping each one with another square of the same or a piece of nori. Unmould on to a board and top with a suitable garnish, such as lumpfish roe, quartered cucumber slices and/or pieces of pickled ginger. Serve with small bowls of wasabi or light soy dipping sauce.

**Below** *Butterfly prawn (shrimp) spiedini with chilli and raspberry dip.*

# Fabulous Fork Food

Formal or casual, this type of food is fun to prepare, simple to serve and effortless to eat. Make light of the planning by adopting a completely practical approach to this style of buffet instead of stretching it beyond its limits.

## Menu options

The fork buffet menu may be for a two- or three-course meal, laid out in stages, or a series of complementary refreshments presented together. Display a menu to let guests know what to expect and to encourage self-service. Although food must be complementary and marry well to form a meal if that is the intention, a party buffet is an occasional treat, so well-balanced nutritional value is not necessarily a priority.

*Below Cut large tarts into slices so that they are easy to eat with just a fork.*

When offering a first course, serve it from a separate side table before placing main dishes on the buffet to avoid any confusion over what should be eaten first. When serving a comparatively small number (10–20 guests) it may be easier to present the first course served on small plates, with accompanying cutlery. These can be arranged on a side table or handed around from trays.

For a stylish main course, focus on one or two main dishes and add easy-to-eat main accompaniments, such as creamy mashed potatoes, rice, pasta or couscous. To avoid overflowing plates, limit the number of vegetable or salad accompaniments to one or two that really make the most of the main dish.

When serving a range of savoury refreshments rather than a traditionally well-balanced main course, select dishes that are contrasting rather than complementary. However, avoid

**Above** *Tomato and courgette timbale is a light dish and ideal fork food.*

clashing flavours as guests often sample a little of each dish instead of eating just one or two.

Desserts are not likely to be confused with the main course, so they can be arranged towards the back of the buffet table to be moved forward when the main dishes have been cleared away.

Cheese can be seen as an alternative to main dishes, so if you want it strictly as a separate course, set the cheese board and accompaniments on a side table away from the main buffet.

## Practical fork food

There is nothing worse than doing battle with food that is difficult to eat while balancing a glass and trying to make conversation.

• Serve ingredients in small pieces or that can be broken easily with the side of a fork.

• Select foods and dishes that cling together well and are easily scooped up on a fork.

• While moist dishes are successful, excess thin sauce can be difficult to eat and will drip easily.

• Match dishes or ingredients with complementary sauces or dressings

**Above** *Stuffed vine leaves can be home-made or bought from the deli.*

rather than serving a main dish and accompaniments in different sauces that clash or are too runny.

## Favourite foods

The following dishes are always popular and are easy to serve:
• Pasta bakes, such as lasagne and cannelloni. Try fillings with seafood, poultry, vegetable or ricotta cheese as alternatives to meat.
• Dishes full of bitesize chunks in lightly thickened sauces – lamb or chicken curries, boeuf à la bourguignonne, beef casseroles, coq au vin made with boneless chunks of chicken, ratatouille.
• Comforting mince (ground beef) dishes – chilli con carne, moussaka and bitesize meatballs in tomato sauce.
• Moreish rice dishes, such as creamy risotto, slightly spicy kedgeree and rice

salad with a fine yet light, slightly creamy dressing.
• Creamy potato salad, fine-cut coleslaw, tomato and mozzarella salad made with halved cherry tomatoes.

**Below** *Savoury rice dishes are easily eaten with just a fork.*

## Stylish options

Add one or two stylish variations to a fork supper. Try one of the following:
• Savoury moulds and creamy mousses, such as seafood or vegetable terrines, fish or seafood mousses, tender foods or eggs in aspic.
• Dressed salmon, Coquille St. Jacques or other seafood gratins.
• International specialities such as a saffron risotto with shredded Parma ham and basil, seafood paella or spicy Moroccan-style tagine.

## Desserts

These are often overlooked for informal fork buffets: this is unfortunate because their are plenty of options. Individual pots or dishes are easy to eat but they do take up space. Large items and big bowls that cut easily or can be spooned out are most practical.
• Fruit salads, mousses and fools.
• Filo pastries with soft cheese, nut, fruit or chocolate fillings.
• Superlative trifle, light-as-air meringues, luscious chocolate desserts.
• Miniature portions of desserts, such as cheesecake, individual gâteaux, bitesize shortcake or tiny fruit tarts.

**Below** *Fresh feta cheese, good quality olives and bread are excellent party fare.*

# **Dinner** from the **Buffet**

Balance dinner-party formality with self-service simplicity by offering a traditional menu buffet style. This is an excellent way of sharing a special meal with a larger number of guests than you would normally want to invite to dinner. The ambience can be stylish, with attractively garnished food, elegant table settings and all the trimmings that make memorable celebrations, but without the need for close attention from host or hostess during the meal. A buffet is a good way to entertain whether in a hired room or in a marquee erected at home.

### **Table tips**

Lay out a buffet table to one side of the dining room or in a separate area – this may be another adjacent room, hallway or dining area within the kitchen. Prepare a separate side table for dessert, if necessary, and have the cheese course set out ready for self-service or to be taken to the table when appropriate. Allow room for guests to walk past the buffet without disrupting others seated at the table. Plan the "flow" of guests, arranging food to encourage logical movement in one direction. Prepare a discreet table, trolley or area on which to deposit used plates from the first and main courses, remembering to include a suitable container to take cutlery.

Set the dining table or several different dining tables – a conservatory, hallway or patio can be used instead of, or as well as, the usual dining area. When preparing several tables, take care to arrange them so that they are linked without any one being isolated.

Select a cold first course that can be plated and placed on the tables before guests sit down. Have table heaters, if necessary, for hot main-course dishes, so that they can be arranged on the buffet before guests sit down to the appetizer.

### **Simple dishes ensure success**

The food does not have to be fork friendly – everyone will be sitting down to eat – but it should be approachable for self-service.

• A main course made up of individual portions looks neat and attractive, and

*Below* Make sure there are plenty of napkins on or near the buffet table.

*Above* Choose a selection of dishes that are suitable for self-service.

guests will not be intimidated by having to cut or carve. Individual pastries, fish steaks or rolled fillets, or chicken breast portions are typical.

• Casseroles made up of evenly cut ingredients are a good choice.

• Select dishes that can be kept hot successfully without spoiling. Sauced portions or wrapped ingredients that will not dry out easily are the best choices. Pan-fried or freshly grilled items that have to be served freshly cooked are best avoided.

• Instead of plain cooked vegetable accompaniments, select a gratin, purée, casserole or bake that will stay hot without spoiling.

• Bowls of refreshing complementary side salad can be placed on the dining table after the first course.

• Cold salsas, sauces or condiments for main dishes can be placed on the dining table.

• Platters of individual desserts look elegant and are easy to serve – try making individual versions of large recipes, such as little fruit tarts, mini-gâteaux, meringue pairs, little choux pastries and individual mousses or moulded sweets.

## Menu reminders

Remember the usual rules for creating good menus: go for complementary flavours, contrasting textures and appealing colours. In addition, when serving the food buffet-style consider the following ideas:

• Easy appetizers: arrange stylish portions of salads that will not wilt on individual plates at the table. Try marinated roasted vegetables and mini or cubed cheese; cured meats with olives, Parmesan flakes and crusty bread; little cheese or vegetable mousses with crisp savoury biscuits (crackers); home-made fish or meat pâté with tiny dinner rolls; smoked salmon marinated with chopped fresh dill and mustard in olive oil; or pickled herring with shredded cooked beetroot (beet) and horseradish.

• Simple-to-serve main dishes: cubed boneless chicken or turkey breast; venison, beef, lamb or pork all make delicious casseroles enriched with wine and spirits; or cook breast fillets of chicken, turkey, pheasant or duck in wine sauces reduced to a thin glaze for coating. Cook boneless portions of fish, poultry or meat in filo or puff pastry, adding herb butter before wrapping. Game, poultry or vegetarian pies are suitable for formal and informal buffet meals, and whole cooked salmon is always popular.

• No-fuss accompaniments: simple leafy salads with dressings served on the side; creamy mashed potatoes flavoured with herbs, garlic, spring onions (scallions) and olives; roasted mixed vegetables dressed with citrus

**Above** *Whole meat joints can be carved and served at the buffet.*

rind and herbs after cooking; vegetable gratins; or casseroles of Mediterranean vegetables, such as ratatouille.

• So to dessert: for an elegant statement, make a simple salad of two or three fruits with an intriguing hint of additional flavour – try mango and raspberry dressed with orange juice and a little honey; strawberry and papaya with a hint of lime rind and

**Above** *Home-made truffles make a wonderful finishing touch to any party.*

juice; chilled pears poached in cider with melon and chopped preserved stem ginger; or pineapple marinated with cardamom and sprinkled with coconut. Classic individual dishes, such as crème caramel or crème brûlée and meringue nests, are all good for a buffet.

**Below** *Contrasting colours and textures provide an appetizing display.*

# Dinner Party Planner

Many dinner parties may be sheer fun, others sedate and some involve a sense of duty but all should be sociable and stylish. Achieving the latter ultimate goal does mean putting in a little forethought and planning – but do not be daunted, entertaining is the most rewarding part of greeting and meeting. Ultimately, dinner parties should be enjoyable.

## Style guide

Hitting the high point means making a few well-calculated plans:

• Scour the guest list for flaws to be sure of surrounding the table with people who will amuse each other (even if they don't entirely agree).
• Adopt a definite approach to ambience: relaxed businesslike, society smart, well-acquainted casual, lively and up-beat, socially sexy, friendly calm, or intimate.

**Below** *Herb-crusted rack of lamb with Puy lentils.*

**Above** *Home-made rolls add a special touch to a dinner party.*

• Plan the menu, table décor, room trimmings and lighting, background music, pre- and post- dinner nibbles and petits fours to fit in with the required ambience.
• Check out linen, crockery, cutlery and serving dishes in advance.
• Ensure cloakroom and other areas open to guests fit in with the ambience.

**Above** *Cappuccino soup of Puy lentils, lobster and tarragon.*

• Be sure to allow time for spring cleaning – or organize cleaners to do so for you – a few days beforehand and last-minute tidying up.

## Menu impressions

Effortless catering is always the most impressive. As a guest, there is nothing worse than acting as spectator to the host's or hostess's insecurities and kitchen inadequacies. Keep it simple and do not attempt anything out of your league.

• Check guests' diets beforehand if you do not know them well – just ring and ask if there is anything they do not eat.
• Plan a practical menu, with the majority of dishes ready in advance and requiring little last-minute attention.
• Buy the best ingredients you can afford and use simple methods.
• Use familiar recipes or try out new ones beforehand.

## Planning and timing

From the menu, make a shopping list and then a list of "things to do" in the order in which they have to be done. Make sure you double check that you have included everything:

• Pre-dinner drinks and nibbles.
• Appetizer and bread.

- Fish or soup course.
- Sorbet (sherbet) to cleanse the palate.
- Main course.
- Vegetables and side salads.
- Dessert and biscuits (cookies).
- Cheese board and crackers.
- Coffee and chocolates or petits fours.
- Wine for each course, water and after-dinner drinks.

You may not want to include everything from this definitive list, but make a note of what has to be done and by when. If there is too much to do on the day or at the last minute, change some of the dishes to cook-ahead items or reduce the number of courses. Pre-plan shopping, cooking, serving and clearing up as you go along. Remember to allow time for relaxation and getting yourself in the mood well before guests arrive.

## Quantity guide

The following is a rough guide when serving 4–8 people. The quantities vary according to the number of courses and type of dishes, but the amounts give some idea of the portions that "look" generous without being daunting. As numbers increase over about ten, the amounts per person

**Below** *Prosciutto with potato rémoulade uses fresh seasonal ingredients.*

tend to go down (except for individual items). You may well be preparing a multi-course menu with small portions for each course or you may know that guests have modest appetites.

When inviting people you do not know well, the solution is to opt for pre-portioned foods that you can count out per person and to prepare generous amounts of vegetables and salads rather than risk running out.

### Appetizers, per portion:
- 250ml/8fl oz/1 cup soup.
- 75g/3oz shellfish or 115g/4oz prepared fish.
- 25g/1oz salad leaves (such as watercress or lettuce).

### Main course:
- 175g/6oz prepared fish, 1 fish steak or 1 small whole fish per portion.
- 175–225g/6–8oz portion of poultry or meat or 1 modest poultry or game breast fillet per portion.
- 225g/8oz poultry, game or meat for casseroles per portion.
- 1 roast duck serves two to three.
- 1 roast pheasant serves two.
- 1 small game bird per portion.

**Above** *Medallions of venison with herby horseradish dumplings.*

### Accompaniments, per portion:
- 75g/3oz vegetables such as beans, peas, broccoli and carrots, or salad.
- 1 baked potato.
- 3–5 boiled new potatoes.
- 2–3 roast potatoes.
- 50g/2oz uncooked rice.
- 75–115 g/3–4oz uncooked pasta.
- 2–3 thick slices of crusty white or wholemeal (whole-wheat) bread.

**Below** *Frozen Grand Marnier soufflés are wonderfully easy for a special dinner.*

# Fondue Flair

Although the fondue drifts in and out of fashion, it is always enjoyable and definitely a hassle-free option for light-hearted social gatherings. Serving fondue involves the minimum of time-consuming cooking, provides entertaining dining and allows guests to participate in the cooking process and select and sample as much or as little as they wish.

## Fondue style

The following styles of fondue are open to interpretation and variation to create a variety of different menus:
• Classic Swiss-style cheese fondue is fabulously creamy with crusty bread and crisp vegetables or fruit.
• Fondue Bourguignonne consists of cubes of lean tender steak cooked in a pot of hot oil, and then eaten with accompanying sauces. Poultry and other meats are also cooked this way.

## Fondue etiquette

Long-handled forks with different coloured ends (for identification) are used to dip ingredients into the fondue pot. Forgetting the colour of your fork is greatly frowned upon, as is leaving ingredients to cook in the pot for too long. When someone drops a piece of food off the fork into the pot, they are traditionally expected to kiss the other diners of the opposite sex!

**Above** *Garlic croûtes make a change from the cubes of bread that are traditionally dipped into a Swiss cheese fondue.*

• Fondue Chinois is an interpretation of the Mongolian firepot method of cooking a mixture of raw ingredients in simmering broth. Seafood, marinated chicken, little Chinese-style dumplings (dim sum) and vegetables are lowered into the broth, and then scooped out in miniature baskets. The wonderful broth is the final treat of the meal, usually with added vegetables, noodles or other ingredients simmered briefly before it is served.
• Dessert fondues are sweet dips served with pieces of fruit, finger biscuits (cookies) or cake for dipping. Chocolate fondues can be dark (bitter-sweet) or luscious with white chocolate and cream. Warm, thick fruit fondues laced with liqueur are perfect with mini-sponge cakes or cubes of brioche.

## Dip and dine

Cheese fondue is simple to make and effortless to eat. Depending on the ingredients and accompaniments, it fits well into the simplest or most sophisticated dinner party setting.

Buy good quality crusty baguette early on the day or a day ahead, so that it is slightly stale, and cut it into bitesize chunks for dipping. Chunks of celery, fennel and apple also go well with cheese fondue. Firm, ripe cherry tomatoes and large juicy seedless grapes are easy to dip and delicious with a robust fondue.

**Below** *Croûtons make bitesize dippers, but slices of fresh bread are good too.*

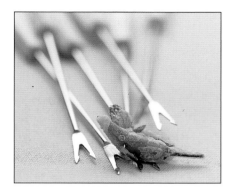

**Above** *Always use long-handled forks to cook your food.*

Any other accompaniments should be simple – a crisp, refreshing side salad of leaves and herb sprigs clears the palate perfectly. Little new potatoes drizzled with a hint of good olive or walnut oil and sprinkled with chives balance the rich cheese, as does a simple salad of tomato strewn with finely chopped red onion.

### Fondue sets

Sets are available that incorporate a pot, stand, forks and a burner. Cheaper sets with just a rack and burner can also be bought, as can individual pots and pans, forks and skewers.

### Cutlery

Dinner forks can be used for dipping food into a fondue. However, when cooking food in the fondue, forks with wooden handles are needed, as the metal of a fork or skewer will get hot when left in the fondue. Small wire baskets can be used to fish out food that has been deep-fried or cooked in stock. Chopsticks or wooden tongs are the authentic equipment for cooking sukiyaki and tempura. For dipping, food can also be speared onto skewers.

### Simple cheese fondue

For the simplest cheese fondue, the basic proportions to serve four as a main course (with accompaniments) are 500g/1¼lb cheese to 250ml/ 8fl oz/1 cup wine. The finished fondue should have a creamy consistency.

For a fabulous fondue, gently heat 1 halved garlic clove, 1 thin slice of onion, 1 blade of mace and 1 large bay leaf in 150ml/¼ pint/⅔ cup dry or medium-dry white wine until just simmering. Cover and set aside for several hours or overnight. Finely grate 225g/8oz each of Gruyère and Emmenthal cheese and 25g/1oz fresh Parmesan. Place the cheeses in a large bowl and thoroughly but lightly mix in 30ml/2 tbsp plain (all-purpose) flour with a little freshly ground black pepper until the cheese is evenly coated. (Take care not to compact the grated cheese into clumps or it will not melt as easily.)

Strain the wine into a heavy fondue pan and heat until boiling. Reduce the heat to low, so that the wine is kept hot but off the boil, and immediately begin to stir in handfuls of floured cheese. After adding a couple of handfuls, allow the cheese to melt before adding more. Continue adding the cheese, melting it gently and stirring constantly. Finally, add 45ml/ 3 tbsp Kirsch and bring to the boil, stirring, until the fondue is smooth and slightly thickened. Add salt and ground black pepper, if required, and a little freshly grated nutmeg. Transfer the pan to a spirit burner at the table and regulate the flame to keep the fondue hot but not boiling.

### Alternative cheeses

Dolcelatte makes a creamy blue cheese fondue when used half and half with Gruyère. For blue cheese fondue that bites back, use Gorgonzola, Bleu d'Auvergne or Roquefort. Pep up blue cheese fondues with brandy instead of Kirsch.

• Other suitable cheeses include Beaufort, mozzarella, Edam, Fontina and Cheddar; try them for their subtle differences of taste and texture.

• For an economical choice, opt for mature (sharp) Cheddar and fruit cider. Add a generous dollop of wholegrain mustard and omit the Kirsch.

**Below** *Classic Swiss cheese fondue with baby vegetables*

## Fondue Bourguignonne

This dish demands the finest beef and perfect condiments. Complementary side salads and warm crusty bread are the traditional accompaniments. Bring the beef to life with an imaginative mixed green salad, such as lightly dressed fine green beans on a bed of peppery rocket (arugula) and sprinkled with shredded basil, or try finely shredded fennel, celery and (bell) peppers on a generous base of rocket, watercress or salad leaves. Baked potatoes topped with sour cream, or crisp new potatoes roasted in their skins also taste terrific with the beef.

The choice of condiments and sauces can set the style for fondue Bourguignonne: they can be simple to prepare, such as a sophisticated béarnaise sauce or mayonnaise flavoured with garlic, chopped herbs, mustard or tomato. Chutneys, relishes, gherkins, pickled dill cucumbers and finely chopped onion are often served, and barbecue sauce is sometimes

*Below* Spicy Moroccan meatballs with harissa dip.

offered. Slightly spicy fresh tomato salsa or herby green salsa contribute a lighter feel.

Allow 175–225g/6–8oz good quality fillet or rump steak per portion. Trim off all the fat and cut it into 2cm/¾in cubes. Arrange the steak on small individual plates. Individual bowls of condiments and sauces are a good idea or large bowls can be passed around the table. Whatever the choice, the accompaniments can be prepared and chilled in advance.

Heat oil in the fondue pan on the stove, and then place it on the spirit burner at the table to keep it hot for cooking the meat. Remind guests that their forks are hot and the cooked meat should be scraped off for eating.

## Fondue Chinois

This is quite different and light. The quality of stock is vital, so make it with 450g/1lb lean pork, 1 chicken leg and thigh quarter, 1 quartered large onion, 4 spring onions (scallions), 2 slices of fresh root ginger, 2 garlic cloves, a few sprigs of fresh coriander (cilantro) leaves and 1 lemon grass stalk or a strip

**Above** *Crunchy vegetables perfectly complement a savoury fondue.*

of pared lemon rind. Place in a large pan, cover with cold water and bring to the boil. Skim the stock, then reduce the heat and cover the pan. Leave the stock to simmer very gently for 1½ hours. Strain and season lightly.

To serve the broth: when all the ingredients have been cooked, taste the broth, which will be concentrated by this stage. Dilute the broth to taste with boiling water or adjust the seasoning and add some shredded spring onions and greens. Simmer the soup for a few minutes before ladling it into bowls.

### Safety notes

• If oil is overheated it could burst into flames. If it catches light, carefully place a lid or a large plate over the top of the pan to cut off the air supply. Never pour water on to burning oil.

• Make sure that the food for dipping is dry, as wet food will cause the oil to spit.

• Protect your hands when moving a hot pan.

• Check that the fondue pot is secure on its stand on the table and that it cannot be knocked over accidentally.

• Never leave a lighted burner or candle unattended.

**Above** *Biscotti, small fruits and cakes are wonderful with sweet fondues.*

**Right** *Crab cakes cooked in oil with a chunky, spicy cucumber relish.*

## Ingredients to cook

Prepare a selection of ingredients to cook in oil or stock – remember that dumplings for simmering can be bought from specialist stores. Try peeled raw tiger prawns (shrimp), scallops, cubes of chicken breast fillet or pork, pork meatballs flavoured with sesame, ginger and garlic, dim sum, tofu and

**Below** *Crème Anglaise with raspberry meringue and summer fruits.*

vegetables such as mustard greens or Chinese leaves. The ingredients can be marinated separately with aromatics or seasonings, such as soy sauce, five-spice powder, shredded ginger, spring onions (scallions) or chopped garlic.

## Dipping sauces and accompaniments

Whether plain or marinated, the cooked ingredients are dipped in a little sauce before they are eaten. Provide individual dishes of dipping sauce for each diner. A mixture of soy sauce and dry sherry, with a drop of sesame oil, a little finely shredded spring onion and finely chopped garlic is powerful and delicious. Plain soy sauce, hoisin sauce or plum sauce also make good dips.

Shredded vegetables, such as cucumber, spring onions (scallions) and Chinese leaves, are refreshing accompaniments, and plain boiled or steamed rice completes the meal.

## Sweet fondues

• Some fruits, such as grapes and apples, are suitable for dipping into savoury as well as sweet fondues. Take advantage of fruits in season for sweet fondues: strawberries, cherries, plums, peaches, apricots and nectarines are all suitable, as well as exotic fruits such as figs, pineapple, papaya, mangoes, star fruit and lychees. Fruits available all year, such as bananas and the citrus fruits, also dip well. Underripe fruit can be lightly poached in sugar syrup, fruit juice or a fruity wine.

• Cakes, biscuits and cookies: slices of dense-textured cake and sweet biscuits or cookies make excellent dippers for sweet fondues. Try Madeira cake, meringues, biscotti or Danish pastries.

# Brunches and Lunches

Parties between mid-morning and mid-afternoon range from laid-back indulgence time to lively and invigorating gatherings, from sophisticated low-key relaxation to fun with friends.

## Dining and sharing

Brunch or lunch is often closely linked to shared activities, such as family excursions, sport or shopping; they may be part of a weekend house party; or a follow-on with overnight dinner or party guests. Food should be inconspicuously successful rather than dominating on these occasions, which calls for well-planned and completely practical menus. Prepare ahead or serve the easiest cook-and-share dishes; creative deli shopping is the clever choice.

Cook-ahead options include large or individual quiches, such as classic quiche Lorraine; set omelettes, such as Italian-style frittata or Spanish tortilla that can be served hot or cold; and chunky soups. Sweet breads, muffins and fruit compotes or salads are all good cook-ahead items. Refresh baked goods briefly in the oven before serving. Cook-and-share dishes are ideal for kitchen gatherings, when

**Below** *Keep family and informal entertaining relaxed by using simple napery, crockery and cutlery.*

guests congregate to help cook and serve and then eat in an informal atmosphere. Pancakes or waffles are ideal for eating over a long, relaxed joint cooking session. Egg dishes, such as fluffy omelettes or scrambled eggs, are also good options for sociable cook-together brunches.

Self-assembly open sandwiches are ideal for kitchen lunches – just lay out all the prepared ingredients and breads for guests to help themselves. For relaxed success, have all breads, ingredients and accompaniments prepared and laid out in platters, bowls and baskets.

Creative deli shopping makes a superbly simple meal. For menu sense and stylish presentation, focus on one type of food or, for larger gatherings, keep different types of ingredients separate. Display a selection of different salami and cured raw meats, such as prosciutto and bresaola, on a large platter. Arrange cooked or smoked poultry and meat on another tray, and seafood and smoked fish together. Present cheeses on a board. Garnish each platter lightly with herbs and wedges of citrus fruit. Provide olive oil for drizzling over.

Include dried and fresh fruit, pickles and breads to complement the savoury platters. Croissants, bagels and mixed breads can be served with savoury as well as sweet foods; brioches, sweet breads and fruit buns go with fruit conserves, marmalade, honey or maple syrup. Sour cream, fromage frais or cream cheese go well with savoury or sweet ingredients, including smoked salmon or croissants with fruit conserve.

## Summertime chill-out

Light foods are ideal for relaxed brunches or lunches in the sun. Offer warm crusty bread, light rye bread, mini-rolls, croissants or thinly sliced bread and butter as accompaniments.

**Above** *Fish chowders are excellent for winter lunches and brunches.*

**Below** *American pancakes with crisp bacon make a tasty brunch dish.*

**Below** *Chive scrambled eggs in brioches are the ultimate brunch treat.*

**Above** *Iced melon soup with mint sorbet is a refreshing summer dish.*

Include one, two or more courses, or just set out an array of foods in a cool kitchen for everyone to wander and sample as they please, such as:
• Chilled fruit soups, lively citrus sorbets (sherbets) or fresh fruit salads are stylish and refreshing. Alternatively, serve prepared exotic fruit, melons and berries on a bed of ice.
• Muesli ingredients are satisfying with fruit – oat, barley and rye flakes, nuts, seeds and dried fruit can be mixed or served in separate bowls. Offer honey, maple syrup, yogurt and milk for moistening the fruit and grains.
• Offer simple grilled (broiled) seafood – lobster, large prawns (shrimp), scallops or oysters – dressed with butter and served with lemon.
• Summer dishes, such as dressed salmon, chicken salads or baked ham, are good cook-ahead main dishes.
• Asparagus or globe artichokes are a treat with melted butter and lemon.

### Winter indulgence
Cold weather is the time for lingering over several courses of favourite foods and dishes.
• Serve warm compotes of dried fruit lightly spiced with cinnamon and cloves.
• Simmer porridge slowly, then serve it with brown sugar and extra cream.
• Opt for an indulgent cooked breakfast, with gloriously aromatic grilled bacon, sausages, kidneys, tomatoes and crisp fried bread. Fried potatoes or potato pancakes and poached or fried eggs are essential.
• Poached kippers or smoked haddock are delicious with poached eggs, and buttered, lightly cooked spinach.
• Serve pats of butter creamed with chopped parsley and grated lemon rind to dress plain cooked eggs – baked, poached or boiled. Creamy scrambled eggs are special when served with smoked salmon.
• Remember to round off winter breakfasts with warm fresh American muffins or toasted English muffins with butter and marmalade.

### House-guest breakfasts and brunches
A take-it-or-leave-it kitchen buffet of fresh fruits, yogurt, cereals and warm breakfast breads provides an informal and successful start to the day. This can be extended to include sophisticated cold platters or cooked dishes.
• Wake-up trays of tea or coffee and biscuits or cookies in the bedroom provide welcome refreshment.
• Prepare cook-ahead dishes to avoid early morning work before guests rise.
• Set the breakfast table or prepare everything last thing the night before, after guests have retired, if possible, so that you can relax in the morning.

### Lingering over a roast lunch
The great British tradition of Sunday roast lunch with all the trimmings is still comforting in cool weather. Start by serving a tray of little canapés or nibbles with pre-lunch drinks – offer small quantities of tiny smoked salmon sandwiches, salted nuts and pretzels. Serve a small portion of smooth, light soup as a first course. Then cleanse the palate with a melon or citrus fruit cocktail or a small portion of sorbet. For the main course, try the following traditional combinations:
• Rib of beef with Yorkshire pudding, roast and boiled potatoes, roast parsnips, buttered carrots, crisp, lightly cooked cabbage, rich port-reduced cooking jus, horseradish sauce and wholegrain mustard.
• Leg of lamb with new potatoes, baby carrots in tarragon butter, fine green beans, red-wine cooking jus, mint sauce and redcurrant jelly.
• Shoulder of pork with crisp crackling, roast potatoes, sage and onion stuffing, stir-fried red cabbage with raisins, creamy mashed swede (rutabaga), apple sauce and gravy.
• Chicken with parsley and thyme stuffing, salad or new potatoes roasted in their skins, roasted carrot wedges, crunchy broccoli, lightly cooked spinach and bread sauce.
• Desserts can be traditional favourites, such as fruit pies or crumbles and custard, or baked rice pudding with a poached fruit compote, or lighter alternatives, including crème caramel, fruit salad or a light mousse, chilled soufflé or creamy cheesecake.

**Below** *Succulent roast rib of beef cooked to perfection, served with horseradish, is a Sunday lunch treat.*

# Children's Parties

Setting the scene for children's parties is enormous fun. Selecting a favourite character and using bought stationery and decorations is comparatively quick but it can be expensive. Picking an individual theme is more flexible and it can be based on anything from a popular figure to a favourite subject.

**Below** *Young guests will feel special with individual place name cards.*

## Fun themes

The following are a few ideas to use as the basis for designing – or buying – invitations, goodie bags, decorations and games. They can be used as a theme for fancy dress or making masks, as well as on stationery and decorations. Draw simple images in bold black pen (or use a computer) and copy or print to make cut-out decorations to hang on the wall or stick on the corners of the table. Paint splashes of colour on the copies and add glitter. The birthday cake and novelty foods, such as cut-out cookies and sandwiches, should also match.

• Clowns – you could also hire a juggler to teach the young clowns.
• Pirates – a good theme for a treasure hunt; make sure everyone has a loot bag to take home.
• Witches and wizards – enlist a magician to add a little magic.

**Above** *A children's party is an ideal opportunity to create a bright table.*

• Dragons and monsters – friendly or fierce, hire a musician for musical participation and entertainment on the theme or set up a monster karaoke session.

**Below** *Sugar mice in bright colours will go down a treat with youngsters.*

**Above** *Decorate home-made letter cookies with pretty ribbon.*

• Wild animals – a great theme for hiring a face-painting entertainer or enlisting the help of a few willing adults to paint young faces.

• Balloons – use the balloon theme for decoration and fancy dress, and hire a balloon modeller to keep the youngsters entertained.

• Puppet party – have a hand puppet-making party and hire a puppet show.

• Girls' makeover – for little girls or teenagers, put together fun make-up kits and demonstrate a few beauty tips or persuade a gifted friend to help.

For a simpler party, all of these themes would work equally well combined with traditional party games, such as musical statues,

**Below** *Make simple place cards from coloured card cut-outs.*

musical bumps, pass the parcel, pin the tail on the donkey, simple Simon, sardines and hunt the thimble.

## Table magic

Use disposable or wipe-clean table covers and disposable or shatterproof plates and tumblers with colourful drinking straws. Make a centrepiece of candies and sweets or floating balloons. Decorate plain paper tablecloths with colourful cut-outs on the party theme, sticking them firmly in place. Keep decorations towards the middle of the table so that they do not get in the way and cause more spills than necessary. Secure the table cover in place with sticky tape or ties so that it cannot be pulled to one side as little people jump off chairs.

It is better to have lots of small plates of food within easy reach than a few large platters. Have tuck boxes with bitesize foods ready at every place. Follow with little dishes of ice cream. Try a neat pyramid of fun little cakes instead of a big cake.

## Small sweets

Children love sweet desserts, so opt for small portions of simple sweet dishes. Buy small colourful dessert containers for visual appeal.

**Above** *Bright plastic cups and crockery are practical for children's parties.*

• Fruit set in jelly is still a winner, especially with ice cream. Canned mandarin oranges, peaches or pineapple are all easy to eat. Halved or quartered fresh strawberries or whole fresh raspberries work well.

• Start ice cream sundaes in advance. Pile scoops of chocolate, strawberry and vanilla ice cream in dishes and keep them in the freezer. Add spoonfuls of prepared fruit and drizzle with chocolate or strawberry flavour sauce just before serving. Top with a whirl of whipped cream and a little iced cookie or jellied sweet (candy).

**Below** *Individual cup cakes can replace a large birthday or celebration cake.*

# Barbecue Entertaining

**Above** *Serve small snacks that guests can nibble while the food is cooking.*

**Below** *Chargrilled pineapple with pineapple and chilli granita.*

**Above** *Long, hot days herald the start of the barbecue season.*

Achieving a relaxed atmosphere is the most important key to success for outdoor entertaining. The ultimate compliment guests can pay is being so at ease that they spontaneously become involved in cooking and serving at a barbecue. This *al fresco* impression of super-easy, impromptu entertaining is, in fact, usually the result of careful planning.

## Barbecue food basics

The whole barbecue ambience is geared towards savouring the cooking process as well as the eating, so the menu should provide a relaxed first course that allows everyone to nibble while the main-course food items sizzle to perfection. For some occasions the idea of a main course of grilled food plus side dishes can be abandoned to a glorified sampling session. However, for the majority of occasions the following is a safe approach.

• An appetizer of dips, Italian-style antipasti or Greek-style meze works well. This may be finger food to nibble while standing around with drinks or trays of salads or marinated savouries to eat with bread at the table.

• The main course can be grilled selected ingredients with planned accompaniments or a wider choice of "main" items and a range of side dishes. The latter can turn the whole barbecue into a relaxed and lengthy multi-course tasting session.

• It is a good idea to include fruit that can be grilled on the remains of the barbecue for dessert – bananas are terrific grilled in their skins and served with maple syrup and ice cream or cream; halved and stoned (pitted) peaches sprinkled with brown sugar and wrapped in foil can be cooked on the rack above dying embers; sliced fresh pineapple can be grilled on the barbecue or cooked in foil with rum and brown sugar; or marshmallows can be toasted on long forks.

## Moreish morsels

Serve little dishes of the following to keep everyone happy while the barbecue heats and cooks the main course. Offer crusty bread and breadsticks with the savouries.

**Below** *Sweet romano peppers stuffed with mozzarella cheese and olives.*

**Above** *Grilled bananas and ice cream are a classic barbecue dessert.*

• Mix thinly sliced garlic and chopped black olives with chopped fresh oregano and olive oil as a marinade for cubes of feta or mozzarella cheese.
• Halve baby plum tomatoes and toss with a little sugar, chopped red onion and plenty of chopped fresh mint. Drizzle with walnut oil.
• Buy plain canned rice-stuffed vine leaves and cut each one in half. Heat a crushed garlic clove with some dry white wine, plenty of olive oil, 2–4 bay leaves, a handful of pine nuts and a few fresh sage leaves. Bring to the boil, then remove from the heat and leave to cool before pouring over the halved stuffed vine leaves. Cover and chill for several hours or overnight. Sprinkle with lots of chopped fresh parsley and grated lemon rind before serving.
• Roast a mixture of baby carrots, pickling onions, turnips, radishes and chunks of red (bell) pepper together in olive oil in the oven until tender. Transfer to a serving dish, sprinkle with a dressing made from lemon juice, sugar, seasoning, a little mustard, capers and olive oil. Leave to cool and serve sprinkled with shredded fresh basil.
• Heat a few bay leaves and a handful of fennel seeds in olive oil in a large pan. Add cleaned button (white) or closed-cap mushrooms and season

lightly. Cover and cook, stirring often, until the mushrooms have given up their liquid and are greatly reduced in size. Uncover and continue cooking until the liquor has evaporated, stirring occasionally. The mushrooms should be virtually dry and just beginning to sizzle in the remains of the olive oil. Transfer to a serving dish and drizzle with more olive oil. Leave to cool, then sprinkle with chopped parsley, a little chopped garlic and grated lemon rind. Serve with lemon wedges.

## Bastes and glazes

Marinating is not essential but food should be brushed with oil, butter or another basting mixture to prevent it from drying out during grilling. The following can be brushed on foods during and after cooking.
• Olive oil flavoured with herbs, garlic, citrus rind or chillies.
• Dijon or wholegrain mustard diluted to a thin paste with sunflower or olive oil and sweetened with a little sugar.
• Equal quantities of tomato ketchup and wholegrain mustard mixed and thinned with a little sunflower oil.
• Sunflower oil flavoured and sweetened with clear honey and lemon or orange juice for a sharp contrast.
• A little tahini (sesame seed paste) stirred into natural (plain) yogurt, and

**Above** *Serve a selection of side dishes to accompany the cooked food.*

with a crushed garlic clove and finely chopped spring onion (scallion).
• Tomato purée (paste), a good pinch of sugar and a crushed garlic clove stirred into olive oil.
• The grated rind and juice of 1 lime mixed with natural yogurt with a pinch of dried red chillies, chopped fresh root ginger and chopped spring onion.

**Below** *Tongs are invaluable for turning and moving food over the hot coals.*

## Marinating food

The point of marinating is to infuse flavour and moisten the food before grilling. Marinating also helps to tenderize meat. As a guide, a good marinade includes ingredients to keep the food moist during cooking – typically oil mixed with other liquid – aromatics and seasoning. Salt encourages moisture to seep from the food during marinating, so it is best to salt the food after marinating and just before grilling or partway through the cooking time.

• Always cool a hot marinade before pouring it over the food.

## Grilling times

Cooking times are influenced by many factors, including the type of barbecue, heat of the coals, closeness of the cooking rack to the coals and thickness of food. All poultry, pork, sausages and burgers should be thoroughly cooked through. The following is a guide:

**Total cooking time** (turn items halfway through):
**Fish steaks:** 6–10 minutes
**Small whole fish (sardines or small mackerel):** 5–7 minutes
**Large prawns (shrimp) in shells:** 6–8 minutes
**Chicken quarters:** 30–35 minutes
**Chicken drumsticks:** 25–30 minutes
**Boneless chicken breast fillet or turkey breast fillet:** 10–15 minutes
**Beef steaks (about 2.5cm/1in thick):** 5–12 minutes (depending on required extent of cooking)
**Burgers:** 6–8 minutes
**Lamb chops:** 10–15 minutes
**Pork chops:** 15–18 minutes
**Sausages:** 8–10 minutes
**Halved and seeded (bell) peppers:** 5–8 minutes

• Keep food covered and cool during marinating – in the refrigerator if it is left for any more than an hour.

• Drain the food well before cooking and heat the marinade to boiling point in a small pan. Use this for basting food during cooking, then bring any leftover marinade to the boil and use it to glaze the food before serving. (Do not serve any remaining marinade from fish, meat or poultry without first boiling it as it will contain bacteria from the uncooked ingredients.)

## Simple marinades

**Lemon, thyme and caper marinade:** for fish, seafood, poultry, gammon or game. Gently heat several sprigs of thyme in a little olive oil until they are just beginning to sizzle, then remove from the heat and add the grated rind and juice of 1 lemon. Whisk in freshly ground black pepper and some more oil, so that there is about twice the quantity of oil to lemon juice. Add 15ml/1 tbsp chopped capers and whisk well.

**Orange, garlic and red wine marinade:** this is good for all meats, game and red or green (bell) peppers. Peel a whole head of garlic and place the cloves in a small pan. Add 2 bay

*Above Fish brochettes with lime, lemon, garlic and olive oil marinade.*

leaves and 60ml/4 tbsp olive oil and cook gently for 5 minutes, stirring occasionally. Add the grated rind and juice of 1 orange, 5ml/1 tsp sugar, freshly ground black pepper and 300ml/½ pint/1¼ cups robust red wine. Bring to the boil and cook for about a minute, then remove from the heat and leave to cool before pouring over the ingredients to be marinated.

**Mustard and rosemary marinade:** a versatile marinade for oily fish, especially mackerel, and for poultry,

*Below Brush fish or meat frequently with a marinade during cooking to keep it moist.*

**Above** *Home-made beef or lamb burgers are popular dishes.*

meat, peppers, onions or mushrooms. Whisk 30ml/2 tbsp wholegrain mustard with 60ml/4 tbsp olive oil, 5ml/1 tsp sugar and pepper. Gently heat 250ml/ 8fl oz/1 cup dry white wine or dry (hard) cider with 3–4 fresh rosemary sprigs until boiling. Whisk into the mustard mixture and leave to cool before using.

### Shortcuts for success

• Chicken joints, such as quarters and drumsticks, require lengthy cooking. For safety and speed when entertaining a crowd, pre-cook the portions in a covered roasting pan in the oven until just cooked but not well browned. Pour over a marinade or add seasoning. Cool and chill. Brown and thoroughly reheat the chicken on the barbecue.
• Potatoes take up lots of space, so pre-bake them in the oven until tender, then brush with oil and finish on the barbecue for crisp, well-flavoured skins.
• Boil small new potatoes in their skins until just tender, then toss with olive oil, a pinch of sugar, seasoning and a little mustard. Thread on metal skewers and grill until crisp and well browned.
• Grated potato pancakes are terrific on the barbecue. Make them in advance, cooking them until they are set but only very lightly browned. Cool, cover and chill. Grill on the barbecue until crisp and well browned.

### Vegetarian barbecues

When cooking a mixed barbecue, organize a separate cooking area for vegetarian foods.
• Vegetables for marinating and grilling include halved and seeded peppers; slices or wedges of aubergine (eggplant); whole mushrooms; halved small beetroot (beet); par-boiled carrots; slices of butternut squash; halved courgettes (zucchini); blanched asparagus; and blanched fennel.
• For easy vegetable burgers, mix cooked and mashed carrots and potatoes, finely shredded white cabbage, chopped spring onions (scallions), finely chopped celery and chopped red pepper. Season, flavour with crushed garlic and shredded basil, then add enough fresh wholemeal (whole-wheat) breadcrumbs to bind the mixture firmly. Shape into burgers and brush with oil before grilling.
• Grill halved peppers cut sides down, remove them and fill with chopped fresh tomato, garlic and finely chopped fresh oregano, then grill skin sides down until well browned and tender. Serve topped with shavings of Parmesan cheese.

### Food safety

• Keep food chilled until just before cooking.
• When serving food outside or keeping it ready for cooking, shade the table from the sun and cover food to keep insects off.
• Keep separate utensils for removing cooked fish, meat or poultry from the grill so as not to contaminate them with juices from raw or part-cooked items.
• Grill poultry and meat, and their products, high above the coals, or over medium heat, so that they cook through before becoming too brown outside.

• Marinate firm tofu with garlic and herbs in oil, then wrap in vine leaves and brush with oil for grilling.
• Marinate slices of firm halloumi cheese in olive oil with garlic and herbs, then grill until crisp and golden on both sides. Serve immediately.

**Below** *Lobsters are excellent barbecue food. Serve with good mayonnaise.*

# Packing up a Picnic

Plan all the practical aspects of packing, transporting and consuming a picnic on separate lists compiled from menu requirements alongside the choice of food.

Picnic baskets are attractive and, while they are not the most practical choice for transporting food and equipment on large or informal family picnics, they are stylish for carrying china, cutlery and glassware for grand picnic meals. Lightweight crates that fit neatly into the storage area of a car are ideal for holding equipment. Wrap dishtowels and table linen around and between fragile items. Rigid plastic or disposable dishes, plastic cutlery and drinking containers can be stacked without fear of damage. Open baskets are light to carry and useful for bread.

Insulated bags keep food cool and in good condition. Soft bags are easy to carry and insulated backpacks are particularly practical when packing modest picnics. Although more awkward to carry, rigid chiller boxes protect delicate foods and bottles from damage as well as keeping food cool. Sort out or buy storage containers that stack neatly in chiller boxes to avoid tedious searching and shuffling when assembling the prepared picnic. Hi-tech

**Above** *A day beside the sea is an ideal opportunity for a summer picnic.*

storage boxes (designed for camping expeditions) can be plugged into the electrical supply of a car to act as a mini-refrigerator or as a modest oven for reheating food.

### Relaxing in comfort
Folding chairs and tables may be *de rigueur* for flamboyant evening picnics but they are also comfortable for relaxed and informal meals. Decent chairs are far better than tiny, uncomfortable stools.

Rugs and cushions are a good choice. Damp-proof groundsheets or rugs with plastic backing are ideal. Pack umbrellas, sunshades and spare sun hats. Remember insect-repellent and storm candles.

### Individual hampers
Children and adults alike love personal food packs and they are easy to prepare, distribute and eat. Colourful boxes that stack in a chiller bag can be filled with a selection of fun food packs. Drink packs can be packed separately and snack bags can contain fruit for a sweet course.

Individual adult hampers can be just as exciting and inventive as children's versions, especially when stylishly packed in extra-large linen napkins and tied into neat bundles. Try out a sample bundle, checking the amount and type of food it will hold and the number that can be stored in an insulated bag. Bundle contents can include portions of tasty cheese and charcuterie; small seeded rolls or baguettes, a small bowl of salad or marinated baby vegetables; and a little pot of condiment, salsa or dip. Individual bottles of champagne or wine can be included for a special touch.

**Above** *Filled baguettes, fruit and snacks form the basics of a tasty picnic.*

**Below** *Individual picnic packs are especially popular with children.*

**Above** *A wicker basket is practical when transporting bottles of wine.*

## Safe carrying

Wicker baskets are good for carrying cutlery, crockery, loaves of bread, crackers, biscuits and cakes. Perishable foods that deteriorate in quality should be carried on chiller packs in insulated bags. Lightweight insulated bags and insulated lunch boxes are practical for out-and-about snacks. Stacking rings that are used to separate plates of food for microwave heating are useful for stacking plated items in a chiller box. Sturdy foods in plastic containers are easier to transport and more successful than delicate items with the potential for ending up as disasters.

## Supermarket dash

Simple or special, it is easy to buy a complete picnic menu from a good supermarket or deli without having to compromise on quality. There is more to discover than the usual baguettes, cheese and fruit, so try adding some of the following to the shopping list:
• Breads: select interesting breads, wraps or flour tortillas for scooping up or holding salads, cooked meats or cheese. Try bagels, Italian-style crusty breads or ciabatta, rye breads, naan, mini pitta breads, chapatis, pancakes or crêpes.

Buy a full-flavoured extra virgin olive oil, walnut, macadamia or pumpkin seed oil to go with breads or rolls. Pour a little oil on to saucers and serve chunks of bread to mop it up.
• Salads and vegetables: select washed, ready-to-eat produce that does not have to be cut up but can simply be emptied into bowls and eaten by the sprig without cutlery or as crudités with sour cream, fromage frais, garlic and herb soft cheese, soft goat's cheese or garlic mayonnaise. Among the leaves try watercress, rocket and lamb's lettuce; and select from cherry tomatoes or baby plum tomatoes, trimmed sugar snap peas or mangetouts (snow peas), cauliflower and broccoli florets, baby carrots, baby corn or radishes. Washed parsley, coriander (cilantro) leaves, fennel and basil are also brilliant.

Plain cooked beetroot (beet), vacuum packed without vinegar, is excellent drizzled with walnut oil and sprinkled with ground black pepper; it is also irresistible with soft goat's cheese or mascarpone and a trickle of raspberry vinegar. Canned artichoke hearts are good drained.
• From the deli: smoked salmon or mackerel, pickled herring (packed in oil if possible) and peeled, cooked prawns (shrimp) are versatile with sour cream and lemon wedges. Cured and cooked meats, fish or meat pâtés and terrines are all ideal for picnics. Choose good quality olives and marinated (bell) peppers instead of the mixed salads.

**Below** *A stylish hamper for carrying china, cutlery and glassware for grand picnic meals.*

## Simply different

These are just a few ideas for dishes that are easy to carry and simple to eat.

• Cut a large loaf into horizontal slices and sandwich them back together with complementary fillings. Wrap tightly in clear film (plastic wrap). Cut into vertical slices to make attractive-looking ribbon sandwiches.

• Slit a large baguette lengthways, scoop out the crumb and fill with layers of mozzarella cheese and roasted spring onions (scallions) and (bell) peppers. Drizzle the layers lightly with good olive oil and sprinkle with shredded basil. Replace the top of the

**Below** *Select alcoholic and non-alcoholic drinks to suit your guests.*

baguette, press firmly together and wrap tightly in clear film. Leave overnight in the refrigerator. Cut into wide chunks to serve.

• Sandwich soft wheat tortillas together into a neat stack with a filling of ricotta cheese, salami, cooked chicken and spring onions. Shred the salami and cooked chicken, and chop the spring onions. Spread each tortilla with ricotta and sprinkle with salami, chicken and spring onions before adding the next. Press the stack firmly together and wrap in clear film. Make a spicy tomato salsa to serve with wedges of the tortilla stack.

• Cut short fine strips of spring onion, carrot, cucumber and cooked ham. Thin smooth peanut butter with a little

**Above** *Filled baguettes in colourful napkins are practical and fun.*

tahini (sesame paste) and olive oil, then add a crushed garlic clove and a few drops of sesame oil. Add a dash of chilli sauce, if you like. Spread this paste thinly over Chinese pancakes and place a little of the shredded vegetables and ham on each. Roll each pancake up tightly and wrap in clear film.

## Stepping out

The grand picnic party, so popular with gentility of previous generations, is still a fabulous way of celebrating at a special event. Summer season events such as a day at the races, sailing regattas or country-house operas typify picnic grandeur. The picnic may be served with ceremony and silver at a table (with chauffeur-cum-butler) or for stylish lounging on rugs and large cushions but always with linen napkins, proper cutlery, china and glassware.

• First courses: arrange smoked salmon sandwiches on a serving platter or plates and offer a separate bowl of lemon wedges.

Prepare individual pots of pâté, spread or mousse, sealed with clarified butter and garnished with herb sprigs.

Serve curly Melba toast, rye crisp breads or small shaped dinner rolls as an accompaniment.

Pack chilled soup, such as classic vichyssoise, gazpacho or a fruit soup, in a vacuum flask and take separate containers of cream or chilled garnishing ingredients to add to individual portions.

• The main dish: poached salmon steaks can be dressed at the last minute with a slightly thinned herb or lemon mayonnaise.

An impressive pie or pastry dish, such as game pie or pork pie in large or mini versions, travels well.

Cold roast whole or stuffed boned chicken, turkey, duck or pheasant can be served with a mayonnaise-based sauce or lighter salsa; alternatively, individual boned breast fillets can be coated with mayonnaise and aspic.

Baked glazed ham can be accompanied by pickled peaches poached in spiced syrup made with cider vinegar instead of water.

• Desserts: for exciting fruit salads combine a limited number of complementary fruits, such as

**Above** *Coleslaw, gherkins and creamy potato salad are all picnic favourites.*

strawberries with papaya and lime, pineapple with mango and toasted shreds of fresh coconut, or physalis with cherries. Whole tropical fruits such as passion fruits, rambutans and mangoes are delicious just on their own.

Fruit tarts and flans filled with confectioner's custard, vanilla custard or a sweetened cream and topped with summer berries are practical when the pastry case is baked in a serving dish.

Set custards baked in individual pots are easy to carry ready for turning out on to serving plates at the last minute.

• And finally, serve two or three perfect cheeses with finger oatcakes, classic Bath Oliver biscuits or plain crackers.

Pack home-made chocolate truffles or high quality after dinner mints in a cool box to serve with coffee. (Take a vacuum flask full of boiling water and instant coffee granules separately rather than keeping the coffee hot for several hours.)

## Simple picnic feasts

Try these food combinations for escaping into simple indulgence or to excite the palate as part of an impressive menu:

• Creamy ripe goat's cheese with sweet fresh figs, and take a small pepper mill full of black peppercorns for freshly ground pepper.

• Fine slices of prosciutto, Parma or Serrano ham with little bunches of sweet seedless grapes and lime or lemon wedges.

• Ruffles of finely sliced smoked venison with halved strawberries and cucumber slices.

• Smoked loin of pork and succulent ready-to-eat dried apricots trickled with walnut oil, and lemon wedges.

• Mozzarella cheese slices layered with finely shredded fresh basil and chopped fresh coriander (cilantro) leaves, trickled with good olive oil and served with lemon wedges.

**Above** *A quick trip to the local deli can provide you with all the picnic basics.*

## Outdoor escapes

Summer excursions and picnics may be the main focus for outdoor feasts but there are other occasions when food goes down well in the fresh air:

• On Hallowe'en or bonfire nights cook turkey burgers on the barbecue; wrap potatoes in foil to cook them on the barbecue or pre-bake them in the oven and then finish them on the barbecue. Finish with your favourite muffins, served warm with lots of whipped cream and chocolate sauce.

• The seaside can be exhilarating for winter walks, especially when seafood – large tiger prawns (shrimp) in their shells, prepared squid and skewered swordfish or tuna – is served straight from a portable barbecue and accompanied by pats of garlic and parsley butter with lots of crusty bread. A vacuum flask of light, clear vegetable or seafood broth with chopped herbs and finely diced vegetables goes well with grilled seafood.

• When the snow provides the opportunity for outdoor sport, assemble an impromptu afternoon party with toasted chestnuts, crumpets and English muffins on a barbecue. Mulled wine is a warming drinks option.

# party basics

You do not have to be a five-star chef to throw a good party bash but having a few snazzy food and drink ideas to hand is a real help. From exciting deli-selections to confidence with basic recipes, inspiration and essential information are the ingredients for planning the perfect menu.

# Just Nibbles

Tune in the party by serving the right type and quantity of snacks with drinks when guests first arrive. Too few or poor quality nibbles look mean and awkward; too many or filling snacks overfill guests before the meal. Flavours should preview the courses to follow; for example, it is not good form to serve powerful, spicy snacks before a delicate meal.

### Off-the-shelf selection

The array makes it difficult to resist trying some of the amazing commercial creations, but it is best to do this in your non-entertaining time. Select plain snacks and classic products rather than bizarre concoctions. Many bought savouries are wildly over-seasoned and they completely dull the palate for a delicate meal. Plain salted nuts, Chinese-style rice crackers, simple breadsticks, lightly flavoured croûtons, and good quality crisps (US potato chips) and cocktail crackers complement home-made snacks.

### Roasted nuts

Place blanched almonds and plain, shelled pistachio and macadamia nuts in a large, shallow ovenproof dish. Sprinkle with a little salt and cook at 200°C/400°F/Gas 6 for about 6–10 minutes, or until pale golden. Shake the dish well to coat the nuts with the salt and leave to cool. For a deliciously elusive hint of spice, sprinkle the nuts with two or three pinches each of grated nutmeg and ground mace.

**Below** *Feta cheese with roast pepper dip with chillies on toast.*

**Below** *Pistachio nuts, almonds and macadamia nuts are good party snacks.*

**Above** *Good-quality bread, cheese, olives and wine are essential party basics.*

### Marinated olives

Lightly crumple 4 bay leaves and place in a small pan with 15ml/1 tbsp fennel seeds, the grated rind of 1 lemon and 2 peeled and sliced garlic cloves. Pour in a little olive oil and cook gently for 15 minutes so that the ingredients barely sizzle. Remove from the heat and whisk in the juice of 1 lemon, 5ml/1 tsp caster (superfine) sugar and a little salt and pepper. Stir in 250ml/8fl oz/1 cup olive oil. Drain a 250g/9oz can pitted black olives in brine, then add them to the oil and mix well. Transfer to a covered container and leave to marinate in the refrigerator for 2–7 days. Drain the olives before serving. (The oil is fabulous for dressing cured meats, vegetables and salads.)

## Marinated cheese

Prepare the marinade used for olives to flavour bitesize cubes of feta cheese or mini-mozzarella cheeses. The fennel seeds are good with the cheese but they can be omitted and replaced by several sprigs of fresh oregano instead. Alternatively, instead of fennel and oregano, sprinkle the drained cheese with finely shredded basil when serving. Gouda or Jarlsberg cheese is excellent soaked in the same marinade with fennel, cumin or caraway seeds.

## Vegetable crisps

Home-made potato crisps are special when combined with other vegetables, such as beetroot (beet), sweet potatoes, celeriac and carrots.

Peel and thinly slice the potatoes and/or vegetables using a hand peeler, food processor or mandolin. Rinse well in cold water, drain and dry thoroughly on clean dishtowels. Make sure all the slices are separate before deep frying a handful at a time in hot oil until they

*Below Lemon and herb marinated olives are tasty party nibbles.*

are crisp and golden. Drain thoroughly on paper towels and season lightly with salt.

## Roasted cardamom cauliflower crudités

Split 8 green cardamom pods and heat gently in a large pan with 60ml/4 tbsp sunflower oil until the pods are just sizzling, then cook for 2 minutes. Break a trimmed cauliflower into bitesize florets. Add the florets to the pan and toss to coat thoroughly in the oil, then turn them out into a shallow ovenproof dish, scraping all the oil over them. Roast at 220°C/425°F/Gas 7 for 10

*Above Spiced plantain chips with hot chilli sauce.*

minutes, turning once, until lightly browned. Season lightly and cool. Discard the cardamoms when transferring the cauliflower florets to serving bowls.

## Baguette croûtons

Cut a good baguette with good, soft centre crumb into quarters lengthways. Cut the quarters across into large bitesize chunks. Spread these out in a large roasting pan and bake at 160°C/325°F/Gas 3 for about 40 minutes, turning occasionally, until crisp, dry and lightly browned. Finely chop 1 garlic clove and cook lightly in 30ml/2 tbsp olive oil for 1 minute. Add 5ml/1 tsp each of dried oregano and thyme, then pour in a further 60ml/4 tbsp olive oil. Heat gently for a few minutes, then trickle evenly and thinly over the croûtons. Season lightly with salt and toss well, then return to the oven for a further 5 minutes. Toss with plenty of finely chopped fresh parsley and finely grated lemon rind, if you like, just before serving.

For lightly flavoured croûtons, heat 2 bay leaves, a blade of mace and the pared rind of 1 lemon with the oil instead of the garlic, oregano and thyme. Leave to stand for several hours before pouring over the croûtons.

# Salsas, Dips and Dippers

A few good salsas and dips go a long way, and a repertoire of basic recipes can be varied to create exciting snacks. Try them as fillings for hollowed vegetables or halved hard-boiled eggs; spread them on soft tortillas, wraps or pancakes and roll up into tasty picnic snacks or slice them into stylish canapés.

## Matching dippers to dips

Vegetable crudités, breadsticks, croûtes and crackers taste good with most dips. For a juicy dip, select dippers to scoop up and hold juice or absorb a little – thick, curly crisps (US potato chips) and tortilla chips work well.

**Below** *Crunchy tacos are perfect with tomato salsa and guacamole.*

## Do's and don'ts for dips and dippers

Do …
• Make smooth, fairly soft, but not sloppy, dips for easy eating.
• Select sturdy and fairly short nibbles to dunk – chunky lengths of celery, carrot, (bell) pepper and fennel; mini breadsticks; pitta bread fingers and crackers.
• Use cocktail sticks (toothpicks) for small, firm bits to dunk.
• Match dippers to dips.
• Serve dips in small bowls on platters, surrounded by enough dippers for the entire bowlful of dip.

Don't …
• Make the dip too thick to scoop easily.
• Prepare dips that separate or become watery on standing.
• Serve fragile dippers that break or bend; avoid fine crisps (US potato chips), fine puff pastries and flopping wedges of pitta.
• Offer nibbles that are too small to dunk without putting your fingers into the dip.
• Serve a huge bowl of dip that does the rounds for 30 minutes only to become messy.
• Offer dressed or sauced dunks that discolour and flavour the dip.

• For crisp potato wedges cut medium to large potatoes into quarters lengthways and place in a plastic bag. Add a little sunflower oil and salt, and then mix well. (Add a generous pinch of dried oregano or rosemary if appropriate for the dip.) Turn out into a roasting pan and cook at 240°C/ 475°F/Gas 9 for about 40 minutes, turning two or three times, until crisp and browned. Serve freshly cooked.

These can be three-quarters cooked in advance, then finished in the oven at the last minute. Sweet potatoes and new potatoes also work well.
• For crisp skins, halve baked potatoes and scoop out the middle, leaving a fairly thick shell. Brush all over with oil, place in a greased roasting pan and season lightly with salt. Roast at 200°C/400°F/Gas 6 for about 30 minutes, or until crisp and browned.

## Red salsa

Play with this basic mixture to impress your personality on it and excite your palate – add a little extra sugar or chilli, perhaps, and increase the paprika for a deeper, warmer flavour. To lighten the salsa and add a lively zing, omit the tomato purée (paste) and stir in a little lemon juice. The salsa complements fish, poultry, meat or cheese; it makes a terrific dip with fingers of pitta bread or cheese cubes on sticks; and it is delicious on bitesize croûtes, topped with halved, boiled quails' eggs.

Mix 60ml/4 tbsp tomato purée, 1 finely chopped red onion, 1 seeded and finely chopped red (bell) pepper, 1 seeded and finely chopped mild red chilli, 1 crushed garlic clove, 10ml/2 tsp caster (superfine) sugar, 2.5ml/½ tsp paprika and 30ml/2 tbsp balsamic vinegar until thoroughly combined. Peel and chop 450g/1lb ripe tomatoes, then stir them into the mixture. Add salt and pepper to taste. Cover and chill for 1–3 days in the refrigerator.

### Cucumber and avocado salsa

This fresh, lively salsa complements fish and seafood, salami and cured meats, and grilled (broiled) and barbecued meats and burgers. It enlivens creamy cheeses. As a dip, it is wicked with potato wedges or skins, and chunky cheese straws.

Peel and finely chop 1 cucumber, then place it in a sieve. Sprinkle with

*Below* Tomato-based salsas are very versatile: add chillies, coriander or garlic.

salt and leave over a bowl to drain for 30 minutes. Meanwhile, finely chop 1 large seeded green (bell) pepper, 1 seeded mild green chilli, 1 bunch of spring onions (scallions) and mix with 15ml/1 tbsp caster (superfine) sugar, 45ml/3 tbsp good olive oil and the grated rind and juice of 1 lime. Squeeze the cucumber and then dry it on kitchen paper before adding it to the salsa. Halve, stone and finely chop 2 avocados, then mix them into the salsa. Chop a big bunch of coriander (cilantro) leaves and stir them into the salsa. Cover and chill for several hours or up to 1 day. Before serving, finely shred a handful of tender basil sprigs and stir them in.

*Below* Pitta bread makes excellent dippers for creamy dips.

*Above* Spicy pumpkin dip served with cucumber crudités.

### Onion and chive dip

This is delicious as a filling for baked potatoes or with crispy barbecued new potatoes; it is a good accompaniment for baked gammon or a filling for scooped-out cherry tomatoes.

Peel and quarter 6 onions. Mix 15ml/1 tbsp sugar, 15ml/1 tbsp wholegrain mustard, 30ml/2 tbsp sunflower oil and 30ml/2 tbsp cider vinegar in a shallow ovenproof dish just large enough to hold the onions. Turn the onions in this mixture, then roast at 200°C/400°F/Gas 6 for about 45 minutes, turning once or twice, until tender. Cover and cool.

Purée the onions with their juices. Gradually stir the onion purée into 450g/1lb curd cheese. Finely snip a handful of chives into the dip, add a little freshly grated nutmeg and mix well. Taste for seasoning, then chill.

### Gorgonzola and parsley dip

Mash 225g/8oz Gorgonzola cheese and mix in 225g/8oz/1 cup ricotta cheese. Finely chop 50g/2oz flat leaf parsley and mix it into the dip with freshly ground black pepper. Stir in 250ml/8fl oz/1 cup crème fraîche and seasoning to taste. Chill before serving.

# Salad Talk

In a flurry of curly leaves or a frisée of fine shreds, every salad should make a stunning statement. Move on from making irrelevant "side salads" to presenting classy creations by marrying vegetables with taste bud-tingling dressings and well-textured toppings.

### Salad reminders

Harmonize all aspects of a salad; the base, main ingredients, dressing and topping or garnish should contrast and blend to perfection.

• Include a limited selection of complementary flavours and textures rather than a mishmash of ingredients – this is especially relevant with rice or pasta salads.

• Dress leafy salads at the last minute, otherwise they become limp. For buffets, serve the dressing separately.

• Sprinkle crisp or crunchy toppings over when serving, or offer them separately for buffets.

• Have a generous taste of the dressing to check the seasoning and balance of

*Below Classic Caesar salad is a popular party dish.*

sweet to sour. The dressing must complement not mask the salad.

• There should be enough dressing to coat but not drown the ingredients.

• Light-textured and thin dressings complement soft and crisp ingredients; crunchy and firm ingredients support creamy coatings.

• Unless they should be served chilled, remove salads from the refrigerator about 30 minutes before serving.

### Full-of-flavour leaves

The palate-cleansing properties of fresh leaves are welcome with firm, substantial main dishes, such as grilled poultry or meat and hearty raised pies or pastries. They are also an excellent base for sautéed or grilled fish and seafood, finely sliced cured meats or crumbly or creamy cheeses.

For exciting leafy ensembles mix green flavours with subtly different textures. Crisp iceberg, cos or romaine lettuces contrast with lamb's lettuce, lollo rosso or Little Gem (Bibb) leaves.

Baby spinach brings a firm, rather than crisp, texture and a subtle, slightly musty flavour. Peppery watercress and savoury rocket (arugula) bring positive textures as well as lively flavour.

**Above** *Olive oil and ripe black olives add plenty of flavour.*

Herb sprigs are excellent in leafy salads, either singly or in a burst of mixed flavours. Chopping the herbs changes the result completely, distributing their flavour rather than providing the occasional interesting mouthful; so include small sprig ends with their tender edible stems.

### Salad portions

Estimating salad portions for large gatherings is not easy; simply multiplying portion sizes for a meal for four or six by a larger number for a buffet does not work. Portion sizes are smaller for buffet salads. As a rough guide for gatherings of over 20, 1 large lettuce (lollo rosso, iceberg, cos or romaine) will provide eight portions, 500g/1¼lb tomatoes will be enough for six, 1 small white cabbage will serve 12 when finely shredded, 500g/1¼lb new potatoes will serve four and 500g/1¼lb shredded carrots will serve six to eight.

### The crunch factor

The greater resistance of crunch is different from crisp and it is a texture that supports substantial ingredients and flavours or creamy dressings very well. Fennel, celery, radishes, cucumber, carrots, celeriac, red or white cabbage, courgettes (zucchini), (bell) peppers, beansprouts and onions are packed with crunch. For super-crunchy salads, add drained and thinly sliced canned water chestnuts.

### Tender not soft

Cooked root vegetables, tomatoes, mushrooms, canned bamboo shoots and olives are examples of tender ingredients that can be marinated in dressings to impart or absorb flavours. A suitable marinade should not spoil their textures but it will enrich the salad and give it depth.

### Tip-top finishes

The decorative garnishes or toppings for salad add vital flavour and introduce interesting textures.
• Chopped, slivered or whole nuts can complement main ingredients or be a focal point. Walnuts, pecans, pistachios, macadamia nuts and hazelnuts are all excellent on salads.
• Lightly roasted seeds bring strength of flavour and texture. Linseeds, pumpkin, sesame, sunflower, mustard and poppy seeds are all delicious individually or together. Pine nuts are delicious, tender and nutty and go especially well with spinach.
• Lightly roasted grains bring texture and flavour, and they go well with seeds and/or bacon. Barley, rye and/or oat flakes can all be roasted in a dry, heavy pan until lightly browned and crisp.
• Croûtons bring crunch and they can be tasty with herbs and/or garlic.
• Crisp sautéed diced bacon or gammon, salami or chorizo are full of flavour and texture.

Above *White beans with green peppers in a spicy dressing.*

### Asides to centrepieces

Salads make appealing first courses or light main courses and many are just a twist away from becoming impressive centrepieces for picnics or buffets. The trick is to marry punchy main ingredients with a salad base full of character, then link them with a sympathetic dressing. Experiment with the following examples:
• A substantial full-flavoured leaf and herb base is brilliant for pan-fried fish, poultry, cheese or tofu. Sliced scallops, peeled raw tiger prawns (shrimp), chunks of salmon, strips of chicken or turkey breast fillet, cubes of halloumi cheese or firm tofu can all be

marinated with a little olive oil, garlic and lemon rind, then pan-fried and tossed into the salad while hot. Deglaze the pan with lemon juice or balsamic vinegar, a sprinkling of sugar, seasoning and a final drizzle of olive oil to make a delicious dressing. To serve the salad cold, transfer the pan-fried ingredients to a container, pour over the deglazed dressing and cool, then mix with the leaves before serving.
• Use shredded crunchy salad in a light oil-based dressing as a base for ruffles of thinly sliced cured meats; julienne of cooked meats; quartered hard-boiled eggs and diced smoked salmon or ham; or diced firm cheese. Add a creamy dressing and crunchy topping.
• A mixture of soft and crisp, lightly flavoured leaves (for example lollo biondo, lamb's lettuce and shredded iceberg) is a good base for fresh fruit, rich dried fruit and creamy cheese. Crisp and juicy green grapes, sliced dried apricots and sliced ripe Brie combine well. Add a topping of coarsely chopped walnuts and dress with a drizzle of walnut oil. Add lemon wedges as a little zest to taste.

Below *Refreshing tabbouleh with masses of chopped fresh herbs.*

# Sauces, Dressings and Relishes

A good home-made sauce elevates plain cooked foods to a stylish dish. Here are a few classic recipes:

## Tomato sauce

This good basic sauce freezes well. Thaw it for several hours at room temperature or in the microwave. Apart from the myriad of uses in compound dishes, the sauce goes well with plain cooked fish, poultry or meat.

For the simplest informal supper party, serve fresh pasta with tomato sauce, topped with lots of finely shredded fresh basil and coriander (cilantro), and shavings of Parmesan cheese. Add a punchy, crunchy salad of shredded fennel and white cabbage with chopped spring onion (scallion) and toasted pine nuts.

Chop 1 onion, 1 celery stick, 1 carrot and 1 garlic clove, then cook in 30ml/2 tbsp olive oil with 2 bay leaves and 1 large sprig each of fresh thyme and oregano for 15 minutes. Cover the pan to keep the moisture in and prevent the vegetables from browning. Add 1kg/2lb chopped ripe tomatoes, 30ml/2 tbsp tomato purée

*Below Pickles add full flavour to accompaniments and condiments.*

(paste), 15ml/1 tbsp sugar, 2.5ml/½ tsp paprika and a little seasoning. Heat, stirring, until the tomatoes give up some of their juice, and simmer then cover the pan and cook gently for 40–45 minutes, until the vegetables are tender and the tomatoes reduced. Discard the bay leaves and herb sprigs, then purée the sauce. Use the sauce as it is (slightly coarse) or press it through a fine sieve for a smooth texture.

## Mayonnaise

Home-made mayonnaise is superb, and the flavour can be fine-tuned to your personal taste by adjusting the balance of sunflower and olive oils (or using different types of oil) and the quantity of lemon juice.

Home-made mayonnaise contains raw egg; pregnant women, the very young and the elderly are generally advised not to eat raw eggs.

Commercial mayonnaise, however, is pasteurized to destroy any micro-organisms in the egg and it can be a safer option for buffet dishes that are likely to be left sitting for several hours in a warm room.

*Below Home-made garlic mayonnaise with crudités.*

**Above** *Home-made mayonnaise is quick to make and so delicious.*

Use an electric beater to whisk 1 large (US extra large) egg with a little salt and pepper, 2.5ml/½ tsp Dijon mustard and the juice of ½ small lemon, until thoroughly combined. Mix 150ml/¼ pint/⅔ cup each of sunflower and olive oil. Whisking constantly, gradually add the oils to the egg in a very thin trickle, broken at first, then more constantly as the mixture thickens and becomes creamy. The finished mayonnaise should be thick, pale and glossy. Add salt, pepper and lemon juice to taste if required.

• The mayonnaise can be made in a food processor by processing the egg mixture first, then gradually dropping and trickling in the oil with the motor running. Scrape the mixture down frequently. A large food processor bowl may be too large for a single quantity.

• For a rich mayonnaise, use egg yolks rather than whole egg and allow 2 egg yolks to 250 ml/8 fl oz/1 cup oil.

## Flavouring mayonnaise

A well-flavoured mayonnaise can be served as a filling for baked potatoes or a dip with potato wedges.

• Add 1 crushed garlic clove to the egg. For a mellow flavour, first cook 1 garlic clove in a little olive oil until lightly browned.

• Stir in 60ml/4 tbsp chopped fresh chives, parsley, tarragon, dill or fennel, or a handful of shredded basil leaves.

• Stir in the grated rind of 1 lemon, lime or orange. Use the juice of 1 lime instead of the lemon juice. (Orange juice is not sharp enough to balance the oil and egg mixture.)

• To make a spicy rouille, add 1 crushed garlic clove, 5ml/1 tsp paprika and a good pinch of cayenne pepper to the egg. Taste the prepared mayonnaise for seasoning and add a little extra cayenne if you like. Rouille is a traditional accompaniment for fish soups, served with slices of warm baguette, but it also goes with a wide variety of other foods or it makes a delicious dip for plain breadsticks.

### Excellent salad dressing

This is a good basic oil and vinegar salad dressing, which can be varied to suit all sorts of salads. Different types of oil (sunflower, grapeseed, walnut, hazelnut or pumpkin seed) or vinegar (remember all the flavoured vinegars) can be used, and there are many types of mustard that will vary the flavour. Strong nut oils should be used in modest amounts with light grapeseed or sunflower oil.

Below *Herbs, garlic or lemon rind can enliven a plain salad dressing.*

Above *Quail's eggs served with mayonnaise dip and olive oil.*

Whisk 5ml/1 tsp sugar, salt and freshly ground black pepper, and 7.5ml/1½ tsp mustard (wholegrain or Dijon, mild or strong to taste) with 30ml/2 tbsp balsamic or cider vinegar until the sugar and salt have dissolved. Whisking hard and constantly, slowly pour in 150ml/¼ pint/⅔ cup olive oil. The dressing will emulsify and thicken slightly. Store in an airtight jar in the refrigerator and shake before serving.

### Flavouring dressings

Try some of the following additions.
• Add 1 chopped garlic clove.
• Add 30ml/2 tbsp chopped parsley, mint, tarragon or chives.
• Add the grated rind of ½–1 lemon.
• To make a spicy peanut dressing, omit the mustard and use 30ml/2 tbsp crunchy peanut butter. Add the juice of 1 lime and a pinch of dried red chillies.

### Beetroot relish

This sweet and sour preserve is terrific with cooked meats or cheese. Serve it with a Christmas buffet or in summer to complement barbecued foods.

Peel and coarsely grate 450g/1lb raw beetroot (beet). Peel, core and coarsely grate 450g/1lb cooking apples.

Finely chop 450g/1lb onions. Peel and chop 25g/1oz fresh root ginger. Mix all the ingredients in a pan and add 2 crushed garlic cloves, 5ml/1 tsp each of ground cinnamon and nutmeg, 225g/8oz/1 cup soft brown sugar and 450ml/¾ pint/scant 2 cups cider vinegar. Bring to the boil, stirring occasionally, then reduce the heat and cover the pan. Simmer the relish for about 1½ hours. Pot the relish in warmed sterilized jars immediately the pan is removed from the heat. Cover with airtight lids and store for at least 2 weeks before eating. It makes about 1.3kg/3lb.

Below *Beetroot relish.*

go well with dips or pates, and are good filled or topped with salads, roasted vegetables, grilled or cured meat.

• Herb butter: cream 60ml/4 tbsp chopped fresh herbs into 115g/4oz/½ cup butter.

or thick and crusty slices. Croutes complement soft foods or make a good base to absorb juices.

Making the Best of Bread

# Stunning Cheese Boards

Whether the cheese board is an international extravaganza or a celebration of one or two good cheeses depends on the occasion and the role of the cheese in the menu.

### Dinner-party cheese course

When the cheese board is served as a dinner-party course among many there may be just one or two cheeses or a small selection of different types. Offering one fine example is quite acceptable, typically Brie or a similar universally popular type of cheese. It is fun to focus on something special you know your guests will appreciate, such as a good blue or tangy goat's cheese.

The more usual approach to the basic dinner-party cheese board is to include an example each of hard, blue and semi-soft cheese. One or two other cheeses are often added according to what is good at the deli. Availability and quality are important and it is better to limit the cheeses to a few good quality examples than to offer many second-rate selections.

**Above** *Keep to a few fresh, good-quality cheeses for the cheese board.*

• Vary the sizes, shapes and textures of pieces of cheese.
• Ensure that there is enough of each cheese for every guest to have a modest sample; buy more than one of a small cheese if necessary.
• Cheese may be served after the main course and before dessert, in the French style, or after the dessert and before coffee. If it is practical, the cheese can be brought to the table and offered at the same time as the dessert, allowing individuals to decide which they would prefer to eat first.

### Cheese on the buffet

The selection of cheeses may be one of many courses of food or it may be the main focus for a buffet. The modern cheese and wine party is way beyond squares of hard cheese on cocktail sticks: it is a celebration of cheese.
• When serving a wide variety, keep the different types of cheese separate. Large pieces can be given their own

platters or stands. If there is more than one type of hard white, semi-soft or blue cheese, group them by type on separate boards or platters.
• Contrasting colours and shapes are important, so include cheeses with different rinds, and display logs, pyramids, squares, domes or rounds as well as wedges and wheels.
• One or more whole cheeses in perfect condition are a real delight. Order from a good supplier well in advance, requesting that the cheese be in peak condition for the party. A whole Brie and a half or whole Stilton are a good classic combination.

### Presentation tips

Wooden or marble boards are traditional but china platters and glass or china cake stands work extremely well. Baskets lined with heavy linen napkins, topped with fresh vine leaves are an attractive backdrop for cheese.
• Remove cheese from the refrigerator several hours beforehand and leave it in a cool room. Unwrap any pre-packed cheeses and cover them loosely.
• Always have separate knives for hard, soft, blue and goat's cheeses.
• Allow enough space on the board or base for cutting.
• Do not clutter a board with grapes if it already contains several cheeses; it is better to serve the fruit separately.

**Below** *Remove cheese from the refrigerator shortly before serving.*

## Accompaniments

Crackers should be plain. Oatcakes, water biscuits, Bath Oliver biscuits and Melba toast are excellent. Flavoured and salted biscuits ruin good cheese.

• Crusty bread with plenty of substantial, soft crumb should be offered as well as biscuits. When offering cheese as the main food for a meal or buffet, choose a good selection of breads that are light in flavour but substantial in texture.

• Serve bowls of watercress or rocket (arugula) sprigs with the cheese. A light green salad can clear the palate.

• Celery sticks and pieces of fennel.

• Fresh figs, apples, pears, grapes, physalis, fresh dates and apricots go well with all cheeses. Dried fruits to serve with cheese include apricots, dates, peaches, pears and figs.

• Nuts in the shell or shelled.

• When serving cheese as a main course, black or green olives, or sweet ripe tomatoes may be offered.

• Chutneys, pickles, relishes and salsas are delicious with a main-course cheese board. Sweet-sour flavours are particularly successful.

**Below** *Chopped egg and onions with white cheese and olives.*

**Above** *Serve oatcakes and crackers with cheese.*

• Offer an excellent oil with the cheese – walnut, hazelnut, macadamia or olive oils may be trickled on a plate as a condiment for cheese.

## Lower-fat options

Watching everyone else indulge in a lavish cheese course is dismal for guests who have to limit their intake of saturated fat. It is possible to offer lower-fat options without compromising on quality.

• Ricotta cheese is comparatively low in fat and delicious with fresh or dried fruit. Slit and stone fresh dates, then separate the halves leaving them joined underneath. Fill with a little ricotta and top with a fine shaving of Parmesan.

• Creamy medium-fat soft goat's cheese is delicious with fresh figs. Slit each fig almost down into quarters, leaving them joined at the base. Fill with a little soft goat's cheese and serve with freshly ground black pepper.

• Sandwich walnut halves together with low-fat soft cheese.

• Slit ready-to-eat dried apricots and fill them with a little low-fat soft cheese, then add a young mint leaf to each.

• Ready-to-eat dried apricots are delicious with feta cheese. Place small cubes of feta in slit apricots.

• Make delicious potted cheese with nuts by mixing very finely chopped walnuts with low-fat soft cheese. Add a little walnut oil to intensify the flavour, if you like. Pistachio nuts and pistachio nut oil can also be used – do not chop the nuts as finely as the walnuts and use the pistachio nut oil sparingly as it is very strong. Serve with celery and fennel.

## Cheese savouries

Hot savouries can be served instead of a cheese board. The important point is to keep everything small to add a final burst of flavour at the end of the meal or before the dessert rather than to introduce another filling course.

A small pot of cheese fondue, neat fingers of cheese on toast or Welsh rarebit are all suitable. Little croûtes topped with goat's cheese and grilled (broiled) can be served with peppery watercress or rocket. Miniature tartlets made with cheese pastry can be filled with warm Stilton topped with a grape.

**Below** *A small pot of cheese fondue can be served as the final course.*

# Wine for All Occasions

The variety of drinks available, as well as attitudes to entertaining and drinking have changed significantly in the last couple of decades such that providing liquid refreshment involves more than buying a few anonymous bottles of red and white wine. There is better information in supermarkets, and wine merchants who provide reliable, practical advice are no longer limited to élite outlets. Parties offering an "open bar" are not common but it is usual to offer a mixed selection of pre-dinner drinks. Cocktail parties are fun occasions and can be combined with dressing up in 1920s style.

Whatever the occasion or refreshment, non-alcoholic drinks are important, as most people prefer to avoid alcohol completely when they are driving and many also prefer to drink small amounts. Generous quantities of table water are essential at every meal to complement wine, and a selection of sophisticated alcohol-free aperitifs should be offered on every occasion.

*Below Choose a selection of red and white wines to suit different tastes.*

*Above There is a choice of several wine glasses from your wine merchant.*

### Party wines

For the majority of parties it is still usual to provide white or red wine. Offering a choice of dry to medium-dry white is a good idea, especially when the menu is finger food rather than a main meal. Medium-bodied and soft reds are more flexible than their robust counterparts. Take advantage of wine-tasting opportunities at supermarkets, wine merchants or warehouses, particularly the latter where there is always a selection of wines for tasting.

Sparkling white wine is fun for parties, but always offer still wine as an alternative. Champagne is the choice for special celebrations. If you are planning a large gathering and want to serve expensive wines, it is worth taking expert and practical advice from a reputable wine merchant. You may well find expensive wines and sparkling wines offered there on a sale-or-return basis for whole cases.

## Wine with food

The tradition of serving white wine with fish or poultry, and red with meat or cheese is still a good rule of thumb, but the vastly increased choice and changing cooking styles have widened the goalposts dramatically. Personal wine preference is just as important as bowing to expert opinion, so if you want to share your favourite wines with friends, do not feel inhibited even if they do not feature in wine guides or fashionable columns.

As a general rule, match light foods with light wines; crisp textures with crisp wines; and robust foods with characterful or full-bodied wines. Never

*Below Sparkling wine or champagne is popular for a special occasion.*

Above *Crisp, dry white wines complement fish, seafood and poultry.*

make the mistake of using cheap and nasty wine in special cooking but use a good wine and complement it by serving the same or similar at the table. For example, when cooking fish, poultry or meat in wine or serving a wine sauce buy enough wine for cooking and serving with the meal.

## First courses

When champagne or sparkling wine is offered as an aperitif it is often served for the first course. Light and crisp white wines complement salad-style appetizers and fine soups, while slightly more complex or fuller whites support fish or vegetables, pâté and egg dishes.

## Fish, poultry and meat

• Fish and seafood take crisp, dry white wines, including Sauvignon Blanc, Chablis, Muscadet sur lie or Chardonnay from Alto Adige. Firm-fleshed fish, shellfish and richer fish dishes or pâtés take the more robust whites, such as white Rioja, Australian Sémillon, oaked Chardonnays, and Californian Fumé Blanc.
• Chicken takes a soft red, such as mature burgundy, Crianza, Reserva Rioja or Californian Merlot. Light cooking methods, such as poaching in white wine, call for lighter wine but

Above *Choose full-bodied reds to accompany beef or pork.*

this could well be a rich white to match a creamy sauce.
• Turkey is slightly more powerful than chicken. An impressive red is essential for Thanksgiving or Christmas. St-Emilion, Pomerol claret, Châteauneuf-du-Pape, Australian Cabernet-Merlot or Cabernet Shiraz blends are all suitable.
• Duck benefits from a young red with some acidity, such as Crozes-Hermitage, Chianti Classico or Californian or New Zealand Pinot.
• Game birds take a fully aged Pinot Noir from the Côte d'Or, Carneros or Oregon while powerful venison is matched by concentrated red Bordeaux or northern Rhône wines, or Cabernet Shiraz and Zinfandel.
• Beef takes medium- to full-bodied reds. Serve reds from lighter Bordeaux wines or a medium Châteauneuf-du-Pape to the most powerful Zinfandels, Barolo, Barbaresco or Coonawarra Shiraz. Syrah or Grenache match mustard and horseradish condiments.
• Cabernet Sauvignon complements lamb, especially ripe examples from any of the producing countries.
• Pork takes full-bodied, slightly spicy reds, such as southern Rhône blends, Australian Shiraz, California Syrah or Tuscan Vino Nobile or Brunello.

## Pasta

Match the wine to the sauce or type of pasta dish, for example the dominant flavours may be fish, poultry or meat. Light to medium reds go well with tomato-based sauces. Good Soave complements creamy pasta dishes, especially those containing seafood.

## Desserts

Sauternes, Barsac and Monbazillac are classic wines for creamy desserts and custards. Rich Sauternes and high-alcohol dessert wines complement chocolate desserts. German or Austrian Rieslings or late-harvest Muscat from North America are great with baked fruit desserts and tarts. Slightly sweeter sparkling wines, such as Asti or Moscato d'Asti, are light and wash down Christmas pudding, gâteaux and meringues. Rich desserts, fruit cakes and nut-based specialities, such as pecan pie, will take a liqueur Muscat, sweet oloroso sherry or Madeira.

## Cheese

Traditionally, cheese was always served with red wine, and although the combination of full rich and powerful

*Below High-alcohol dessert wines go especially well with chocolate desserts.*

*Above Whatever type you select, always go for a good quality corkscrew.*

cheese with a full red is an enjoyable one, the very heavy, tannic wines tend to mask the subtle nuttiness and lingering slight sweetness that comes with good ripe cheese.

Happily, the picrture is now a little more varied. Any red wine or substantial white served with the main course can be finished off with cheese. Selecting wine to complement cheese is different and the idea of matching flavours and full-ness is a good one to consider. Fresh, crisp and slightly acidic and dry cheeses are best matched by crisp, fruity wines. Mellow, richer and creamy cheese takes a more rounded white, such as a full Chardonnay, or a light red. Blue cheeses are well matched by sweet wines.

• As a general rule, offer a choice of a substantial white and a soft red.
• Light whites, such as Sauvignon or Chenin Blanc, go well with light cheeses, such as the crumbly mild whites and fresh light goat's cheese.
• Chianti, Merlot or Rioja support the more substantial, ripe and well-flavoured semi-soft cheeses.
• New Zealand Cabernet Sauvignon or Côte du Rhône marry well with the medium-strong hard cheeses.
• Save Australian Shiraz and Californian Cabernet Sauvignon for well-matured hard cheese.
• Fruity wines, such as Vouvray, Chenin Blanc or rosé, match mild and creamy blue cheese while the stronger blues with a piquant flavour take the more robust reds.
• Sweet wines, such as Monbazillac, complement the stronger blue cheeses. Classic combinations include port with Stilton and Sauternes with Roquefort.

## Serving wine

Much of the ceremony and paraphernalia of wine opening is conspicuous rather than practical.

## Temperature

White wines should be chilled and reds served at room temperature. Over-chilling whites dulls their flavour – light whites should be served at 10°C/50°F, or just below, while the fuller Chardonnays, dry Sémillons and Alsace wines can be slightly less cool. The chilling time depends on the starting temperature of the bottle, but as a general rule allow a couple of hours in the refrigerator.

Leave red wines in a warm room for a couple of hours before serving. Heating them on a radiator is a bad idea as this clouds the flavours and aromas. Some light reds, such as young Beaujolais, can be served lightly chilled.

## Allowing wine to breathe

Opening red wine in advance and allowing it to breathe before drinking is intended to take the tannic or acidic edge off the flavour of young reds. However, as the amount of air that

**Below** *Sniff lightly and long, with the nose slightly below the rim of the glass.*

**Above** *When opening sparkling wines, control the release of the cork.*

gets at the wine through the top of the bottle is minimal, unless the wine is decanted into a jug (pitcher) or carafe, merely opening the bottle normally has very little effect.

## Decanting

This involves pouring wine off the sediment that has formed in the bottle. Leave the bottle to stand upright undisturbed overnight so that all the sediment sinks to the bottom. Open the bottle gently and pour the wine into the decanter in a slow steady

**Below** *A foil cutter removes a neat circle from the seal over the cork.*

**Above** *This type of corkscrew requires the minimum of effort.*

stream, keeping the bottle at a minimum angle the whole time to retain the sediment in the bottom. Keep your eye on the sediment and stop pouring as soon as it reaches the neck of the bottle. If there is more than half a glass of wine left, strain it through muslin.

## Opening

Sparkling wine or chilled champagne will not go off like a cannon if properly opened, providing it has not been vigorously moved or shaken.

Have the glasses ready. Remove the foil and wire, holding the cork firmly in place. Hold the cork with one hand and the bottom part of the bottle with the other. Keep a firm hold on the cork. Concentrate on twisting the bottle, not the cork, until you feel the cork beginning to yield. Once it begins to go, the cork will push itself out, so the aim is to control its exit rather than leaving go and letting it pop out. The cork often needs a slight twist to help it on its way – just help it to move gently in the opposite direction to the bottle.

Pour a third to half a glass first to prevent the sparkling wine or champagne from overflowing, then go round again topping up the glasses when the first foam has subsided.

# Organizing Drinks, Glasses and Quantities

If you intend making an open offer of drinks, make sure guests know what is available. Tell them or display the bottles on a table or set up a bar.

As a rule, include gin, vodka, whisky, sherry and dry white vermouth as a basic selection. Rum, Campari, red vermouth and sweet white vermouth are other options. Pimm's is a favourite summer drink. Tonic, American dry ginger ale, lemonade, cola and soda water are the usual mixers; Russian is a pomegranate-flavoured mixer that goes well with vodka. Have plenty of ice cubes and sliced lemons to hand.

After-dinner drinks may include a selection of liqueurs, Cognac, brandy and port.

### Alcohol-free drinks

Have a plentiful supply of non-alcoholic drinks chilled. Still and sparkling mineral waters and jugs (pitchers) of tap water with ice and lemon are essential. Orange or tomato juice are

*Below Offer a selection of spirits for pre-dinner drinks.*

basic options, while apple, pineapple, exotic fruit and cranberry juices are popular. Alcohol-free beer is an acceptable alternative to beer.

• Add a generous dash of bitters to sparkling mineral water.

• Serve a squeeze of lime juice, lime slices and mint sprigs in tonic.

### Beer

While beer is traditionally associated with informal barbecues and student parties, it is also an excellent drink to offer as an alternative to wine at drinks parties or as a pre-dinner drink on more formal occasions.

There is a vast choice of bottled beers available in most supermarkets. Coming from all over the world, they range from some light in colour and flavour to others that are dark, malty with a rich deep flavour. Fruit-flavoured beers are also popular. Colour and flavour are not necessarily related to strength – something to be especially aware of at parties – and some of the paler, light and fizzy beers are extremely strong.

Make the most of any specialist local breweries that offer particularly good or unusual beers not readily available outside the area. As well as selling live beer on its yeasty sediment, in casks or by the bottle, or bottled "bright" beer without the same level of active yeast (and therefore to be consumed within a couple of days), specialist breweries usually prepare seasonal beers. For example, for a limited period they may offer refreshing summer brews or warming winter ales. When buying a cask, always take advice from the brewery on the delivery and setting up of the barrel or storing the beer before the party, if appropriate.

When beer is offered as an alternative to wine, a light, lager-type brew that is thirst quenching and not too strong usually appeals to most tastes. This type of beer is good for barbecues, homely cooking (such as pasta dishes and meat sauces) and spicy meals (Mexican or Indian dishes, for example).

Fruit-flavoured beers are a good choice for drinks parties. The rich ales and very dark beers – such as British stout or the famous Irish Guinness – are a good alternative to red wine with robust, hard cheeses, such as mature (sharp) Cheddar. They are also excellent with meaty stews and casseroles and are popular instead of wine for informal lunches and suppers.

Light beers should be served well chilled. Darker beers are usually served cool – at cellar or cool room temperature – rather than chilled. However, this is a matter for personal preference and many prefer dark beers lightly chilled. Tall, slim lager glasses or large, stemmed balloon glasses are ideal for light beers. Larger tankards are traditional for the darker beers but they are not necessarily ideal for parties, when tall tumblers are much more practical.

## Glasses

Disposable cups may be cheap and good for avoiding washing up but they do absolutely nothing for any drink, wine, spirits or otherwise. Even the most humble wine tastes better from a decent glass and a pleasing glass is one that is well balanced to hold, sturdy enough to feel safe but not chunky, and with a fine rim from which to sip. The bowl should be big and it should taper in towards the mouth to capture the aromas given off by the wine.

Conventionally, white wine glasses are smaller than red, which was thought to have more aroma and body to occupy a part-filled glass, but there is no good reason for this as whites are just as pleasing to swirl and sniff before sipping. The best solution for dinner parties is to have large white wine glasses and extra-large glasses for red.

Champagne and sparkling wines should be served in tall, slim, straight-sided flutes. These are designed to hold the bubbles, or mousse, of the wine for as long as possible, keeping it sparkling down to the last sip. The champagne saucers of the Sixties – wide and shallow glasses – allow all the bubbles to escape from the large surface area of the wine.

Fortified wines are served in smaller quantities, so smaller glasses are used, but they should still be large enough for the aroma and substance of the wine to be appreciated. Old-fashioned sherry glasses and even smaller liqueur glasses are sad receptacles.

## Tumblers and tankards

In addition to wine glasses, medium to large plain tumblers (250ml/8fl oz/ 1 cup to 300ml/½ pint/1¼ cups) are basic, ideally the smaller ones for shorts and mixed drinks and the larger for water, soft drinks, juices, cider or beer. Large-bowled wine glasses with sturdy stems are excellent for light beers, cider

**Above** *Wine glasses are a preferable option to disposable cups.*

and substantial soft drinks. Tall, larger glasses are good for light beers, retaining the fizz and being well balanced to hold. Straight-sided glasses holding 600ml/1 pint/2½ cups are preferred for larger quantities of beer; jugs (pitchers) with handles or tankards are also satisfying for large drinks.

## Quantities

A bottle of wine yields six average glasses. The amount consumed at a dinner party depends entirely on the company, ambience and attitude. It is always better to have more wine than needed and more than one bottle of each type than too little. When serving a selection of wines, remember that some guests may prefer to drink all white or all red rather than change with the courses. One bottle provides sufficient wine for two non-drivers.

When catering for a large gathering, calculate the number of glasses based on six from a bottle. When serving sparkling wine as an introductory drink, allow extra unless the wine will not be served until everyone is gathered, as those who arrive first will probably consume slightly more. When selecting

**Above** *Serve beer in tall tumblers, pint glasses or tankards.*

special wines, such as good champagne for a large special-occasion party, it can be worth buying from a supplier offering sale or return. Even in grown-up society, it is normal for guests to bring a bottle to large informal parties.

**Below** *One bottle of wine will provide around six average glasses.*

# Classic Cocktails

The cocktail party can be a fun occasion for a Twenties or Thirties theme or a sophisticated contemporary gathering. If you are planning a fancy dress party, write fun invitations and ask guests to dress in style. Go to town on decorative, colourful cocktails, with novelty cocktail sticks, swizzle sticks and straws. Follow the theme through with music from the era and encourage guests to dance. Conversely, adopt a stylishly understated approach to a contemporary cocktail party, with smart drinks, canapés and nibbles. Keep the music low and lighting discreet, and concentrate on circulating and instigating stimulating conversation.

## The cocktail bar

Invite guests to join in the mixing and shaking at a fun party, with the bar working from the kitchen. For more sophisticated gatherings, arrange a trolley or small table from which to shake, stir and pour, then use the kitchen as back-up. Hiring a good bartender will be worth every penny as long as the cocktail list, numbers and shopping list are discussed and agreed in advance.

*Below Cool and refreshing long cocktails are ideal on a hot day.*

*Above The choice of equipment is vast but you only need a few essentials.*

Whether the party is fun or formal, focus on a few cocktails based on a limited number of drinks, and stick to that list. Have a recipe sheet and all decorations or accessories ready. Include a number of alcohol-free drinks.

## Cocktail equipment

Bar measures and a small measuring jug (pitcher) are useful. The traditional single measure is 25ml/¾fl oz/1½ tbsp and the double is 45ml/1½fl oz/3 tbsp. If you do not have specialist measures, use a small sherry glass or similar. A set of measuring spoons is also essential.

**Shaker**: you will need several cocktail shakers for a party. Look out for those that have integral strainers. Make sure the shakers have tight-fitting tops and that they pour well.

**Mixing jug (pitcher)**: use for drinks that are stirred not shaken – look for one with a good pouring spout.

**Blender**: a goblet blender is useful for frothy cocktails. Do not crush ice in the blender, as this will blunt the blade.

**Strainer**: for straining mixed drinks into glasses.

**Muddler**: a long stirring stick with a bulbous end, which is used for crushing sugar or mint leaves.

**Mini-whisk**: a long-handled balloon whisk with a small balloon for whisking and frothing drinks.

**Citrus squeezer**: look for one with a deep container underneath and a good strainer to keep out the pips (seeds).

Zester and cannelle knife: these are usually combined in the one implement. Use for paring fine shreds of rind from citrus fruit. The cannelle knife cuts individual, slightly larger but thin strips and can be used to mark a pattern in the fruit rind. When sliced the rind forms a decorative edge.

Nutmeg grater: a small, fine grater for grating fresh nutmeg.

Straws, swizzle sticks and decorative cocktail sticks: just some of the finishing touches for decorating drinks.

## Glasses

Cocktail or martini glass: the classic V-shaped cocktail glass keeps warm hands away from cool drinks. This holds about 100ml/3½fl oz/½ cup.

Collins glass: the tallest of tumblers with narrow, straight sides, this holds about 250ml/8fl oz/1 cup.

Old-fashioned glass: the classic whisky tumbler, this is wide and short and it is referred to as a 175ml/6oz/¾ cup tumbler.

Highball glass: this is a 250ml/8fl oz/1 cup tumbler.

Liqueur glass: the smallest of glasses, this holds about 50ml/2fl oz/¼ cup.

*Below A wide variety of different shaped glasses are suitable for cocktails.*

Above *Small whole fruit, such as cherries or strawberries, can be used as decorations.*

Brandy balloon or snifter: the rounded shape is designed to be cupped in the hands to warm the contents while the narrow rim traps the aroma of the drink.

Large cocktail goblets: these vary in size and shape. Designed for serving longer or frothy drinks, these glasses have wide rims.

Champagne glasses: either saucers or tall narrow flutes. The flute is the best for sparkling wine and champagne cocktails; the saucer can be used for a variety of cocktails or drinks.

Red wine balloon: holding 250ml/8fl oz/1 cup, this should be filled about half-full to allow room for swirling the wine and releasing its aroma.

White wine glass: a long-stemmed glass held by the stem, so that warm hands keep away from chilled wine.

Pousse-café: a thin and narrow glass with a short stem, this is used for layered and floating cocktails.

Below *Slices of lemon or lime add colour and flavour to many cocktails such as a Moscow Mule.*

# Drinks Checklist

Familiarize yourself with the flavours before writing your cocktail menu. The following is a basic guide:

**Brandy**: Cognac and Armagnac are the two French brandies. Fruit brandies or eaux-de-vie include peach, cherry and apricot brandy.

**Champagne**: dry (brut) champagne features in many cocktails. Champagne has the best mousse for making excellent fizzy cocktails, but less expensive sparkling wines, such as Spanish Cava, can be used instead.

**Gin**: familiar as an aperitif with tonic, gin is used in a variety of cocktails. It is flavoured with juniper berries.

**Rum**: dark rum is punchy but light rum is clear; this type is used for cocktails.

**Tequila**: a powerful Mexican spirit distilled from the juice of the agave cactus. Used in a variety of cocktails.

**Vermouth**: dry white, sweet white or red, or bittersweet rosé, there are many brands of these herb-flavoured aperitifs. The more expensive brands are generally better quality.

**Vodka**: as well as the basic, slightly peppery strong spirit, there are many varieties of flavoured vodkas, some subtle with herbs or spices, others distinct with fruit. A good quality plain vodka is useful for most cocktails.

**Whisky**: basic whisky is good enough for cocktails rather than masking the flavour of a long-matured single malt.

## Liqueur flavours

**Amaretto di Sarone**: a sweet almond-flavoured liqueur.

**Anisette**: aniseed-flavoured liqueurs include French Pernod, Italian sambuca and Spanish anis.

**Bénédictine**: made by Benedictine monks of Fécamp in Normandy, this golden liqueur is flavoured with myrrh, honey and herbs.

**Chartreuse**: originally made by Carthusian monks at La Grande

Chartreuse monastery. This brandy-based liqueur is available as a green or yellow drink. Herbs, honey and spices flavour the liqueur. Yellow Chartreuse is flavoured with orange and myrtle.

**Cointreau**: orange liqueur.

**Crème de cacao**: cocoa-flavoured liqueur.

**Crème de cassis**: blackcurrant-flavoured liqueur – add a little to chilled dry white wine to make kir or use it to flavour champagne for kir royale.

**Crème de menthe**: mint liqueur.

**Curaçao**: orange-flavoured liqueur that is available coloured blue, clear or orange-brown.

**Drambuie**: malt whisky liqueur with herbs, honey and spices.

**Galliano**: golden liqueur flavoured with herbs, liquorice and aniseed.

**Grand Marnier**: French Curaçao, flavoured with bitter bergamot, orange and brandy.

**Kahlúa**: Mexican coffee-based liqueur with a rich flavour.

**Southern Comfort**: sweet fruity liqueur based on bourbon whisky.

**Above** *Strawberry and banana daiquiris are popular cocktails.*

## Crushing ice

In the absence of an ice-crushing machine, lay out a clean dishtowel and cover half with ice cubes. Fold the other half of the cloth over, and then use a rolling pin or mallet to crush the ice fairly coarsely. Store in plastic bags in the freezer. If necessary, crush the ice finely just before using it.

**Below** *Crushed ice can be prepared in advance and frozen until ready to use.*

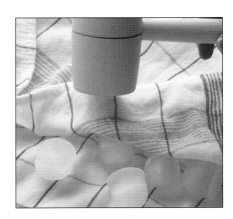

## Making decorative ice cubes

These are particularly good for enlivening simple cocktails and mixed soft drinks.

**1** Half-fill ice cube trays with water and freeze until firm.

**2** Dip pieces of fruit, olives, citrus rind, edible flowers or mint leaves in cold water, then place in the ice cube trays.

**3** Top up the trays with water and freeze until hard.

**Below** *Ice cubes with edible flowers.*

## Frosting glasses

This simple technique adds a decorative and/or flavoured edge to the glass. Instead of sugar, the rim can be dipped into celery salt, grated coconut, grated chocolate, coloured sugar or cocoa powder. The flavouring depends on the type of drink you intend to serve. Place the frosted glass in the refrigerator until it is required.

**1** Hold the glass upside down so that the juice does not run down the outside when you wet it. Rub the rim of the glass with the cut surface of a lemon, lime or orange.

**2** Keep the glass upside down, then lightly dip it in a shallow saucer of sugar, coconut, salt or celery salt. Re-dip the glass, if necessary, so that the rim is well coated.

**3** Turn the glass the right way up and leave to stand for a while until the rim has dried. Chill in the refrigerator before pouring the drink into the middle of the glass.

## Basic sugar syrup

Some cocktails include sugar syrup. This can be made in advance and stored in a sterilized airtight bottle in the refrigerator for up to 1 month.

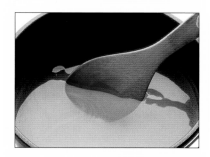

**1** Mix 175g/6oz/scant 1 cup sugar and 600ml/1 pint/2½ cups water in a heavy pan. Heat gently, stirring, until the sugar has dissolved.

**2** Brush the inside of the pan with cold water to clean any splashes of sugar that may crystallize.

**3** Stop stirring and boil for 3–5 minutes. Skim off any scum and, when it stops forming, remove from the heat. Pour the cooled syrup into sterilized bottles.

# Traditional Cocktails

Knowledge of a good selection of classic cocktails is essential, and some favourites are given here, but you may also enjoy creating your own.

**Black Velvet**: combine equal parts Guinness and champagne.

**Bloody Mary**: mix 1 part vodka with 2 parts tomato juice. Stir in a dash of Worcestershire sauce or Tabasco and add a squeeze of lemon.

**Brandy Alexander**: shake together 1 part brandy, 1 part crème de cacao and 1 part double (heavy) cream. Serve dusted with freshly grated nutmeg.

**Buck's Fizz:** serve 1 part freshly squeezed orange juice topped up with 1 part champagne.

**Daiquiri**: shake 15ml/1 tbsp lime juice with 45ml/3 tbsp white rum and 5ml/

*Below Bloody Mary served with celery, olives and cherry tomatoes.*

1 tsp sugar on crushed ice. Pour into a sugar-frosted glass. Add fruit if desired, such as banana or strawberry.

**Dry Martini**: shake 2 parts gin with 1 part dry white vermouth. Pour into a glass and add a stuffed green olive. Some prefer to reverse the quantities, with 1 part gin to 2 parts vermouth.

**Harvey Wallbanger**: place some ice in a tall glass and add 2 parts vodka and 6 parts orange juice, then float 1 part Galliano on the surface.

**Long Island Iced Tea**: Mix equal parts vodka, gin, light rum, and tequila (optional) and lemon. Sweeten with a little sugar syrup and top up with cola. Serve on ice.

**Manhatten**: Mix 1 part each of dry and sweet vermouth with 4 parts bourbon or whisky.

**Margarita**: shake 1 part Curaçao, 4 parts tequila and 1 part lime juice. Serve in a salt-frosted glass.

**Above** *Brandy Alexander.*

**Above** *Martini with olives and chillies*

**Below** *Strawberry Daiquiri.*

**Above** *Harvey Wallbanger with orange.*

**Above** *Long Island Iced Tea with mint.*

**Below** *Perfect Manhatten.*

**Above** *Margarita with lime.*

**Below** *Blushing Pina Colada.*

**Pina Colada**: shake 3 parts white rum with 4 parts pineapple juice, 2 parts coconut cream, 30ml/2 tbsp grenadine and 15ml/1 tbsp sugar syrup. Serve decorated with pineapple and a maraschino cherry.

**Pink Gin**: add a dash of Angostura bitters to a gin and tonic.

**Rusty Nail**: stir 2 parts whisky with 1 part Drambuie and serve on ice.

**Tequila Sunrise**: mix 1 part tequila with 2 parts orange juice. Pour 5ml/ 1 tsp grenadine into a glass and add ice, then carefully pour in the orange mix.

**Whisky Sour**: shake 1 measure whisky with the juice of ½ lemon and 5ml/ 1 tsp sugar on crushed ice. Pour into a tumbler.

# Punches and Cups

Warming mulled wine, heady punches or delicate fruit cups are excellent welcome drinks for medium to large parties. Most well-seasoned party givers have their favourite recipes for a summer punch and a warming winter wine cup. The following are basic recipes to tempt you into experimenting further.

**Mulled Wine**: the classic Christmas drink for complementing melt-in-the-mouth mince pies. Stud 1 orange with 8 cloves and place it in a pan. Add 1 cinnamon stick and 60ml/4 tbsp sugar. Pour in a bottle of fruity red wine and add 150ml/¼ pint/⅔ cup brandy or rum. Cover and place over very gentle heat for 30 minutes. The wine should be just hot and aromatic. Taste and add more sugar if required. Serve hot.

**Honey Glühwein**: mix a handful each of raisins and blanched almonds with 1 lemon studded with 4 cloves, 1 cinnamon stick, 150ml/¼ pint/⅔ cup rum, 30ml/2 tbsp honey and 1 bottle red wine in a pan. Cover and heat very gently for about 30 minutes, or until the wine is just hot. Taste for sweetness and add more honey as required.

**White Wine Cup**: place 150ml/ ¼ pint/⅔ cup brandy in a bowl. Add ½ sliced orange, ¼ sliced cucumber and some mint sprigs. Cover and leave to macerate for several hours – this can

be left overnight. Add 1 well-chilled bottle dry white wine and top up with 900ml/1½ pints/3¾ cups chilled tonic water or lemonade.

**Elderflower Strawberry Cup**: rinse 4 elderflower heads and place in a bowl with 50g/2oz/½ cup halved strawberries. Add 750ml/1¼ pints/ 3 cups sparkling mineral water and 60ml/4 tbsp sugar. Stir well, crushing the elderflowers slightly and pressing

*Below Cider punch with lemon rind.*

*Above Serve refreshing white wine cup with ice and garnish with borage.*

the strawberries without crushing them. Cover and leave to stand overnight, then chill well. Strain the mineral water into a bowl. Add 175g/6oz/1½ cups sliced strawberries and a bottle of chilled sparkling white wine. Taste for sweetness and decorate the bowl with washed elderflowers before serving.

**Cider Punch**: place 1 sliced lemon, 1 sliced orange, 1 quartered, cored and sliced apple and several mint sprigs in a bowl. Pour in 300ml/½ pint/1¼ cups medium-dry sherry. Cover and leave to macerate for several hours or overnight. Add 1 litre/1¾ pints/4 cups well-chilled dry (hard) cider and top up with 1 litre/ 1¾ pints/4 cups sparkling mineral water.

**Sangria**: slice 2 oranges and 2 lemons and place in a jug (pitcher) with 150ml/ ¼ pint/⅔ cup brandy or Grand Marnier. Add 1 bottle red wine, cover and leave to macerate for several hours. Add 2 cored and sliced apples and top up

*Below Warming mulled wine.*

with 1 litre/1⅓ pints/4 cups lemonade and 600ml/1 pint/2½ cups orange juice, soda water, or sparkling mineral water (alternatively, use all lemonade).

## Alcohol-free drinks

Although there is a wide choice of commercial soft drinks, there are many home-made cold drinks that are a real summer's treat for picnics or garden parties. Here is a selection:

**Lemonade**: grate the rind of 4 lemons and squeeze their juice. Place the rind and juice in a bowl and add 175g/6oz/scant 1 cup sugar. Add 600ml/1 pint/2½ cups boiling water, stir well and cover. Leave to stand overnight. Stir in a further 600ml/ 1 pint/2½ cups water, add 1 lemon cut into slices and some ice cubes. For picnics, carry the chilled lemonade in a bottle in a chiller bag.

**Above** *Sangria is a cool summer drink.*

**Ice Cream Soda**: place a scoop of good quality vanilla ice cream in a tall glass. Slowly add lemonade or soda water (lemonade is sweeter and tastes better

**Above** *Thirst-quenching St. Clements.*

even though soda water is correct), allowing the ice cream to froth up before filling the glass more than half-full. Decorate with berries, add a straw and long spoon and serve immediately.

**Strawberry Banana Shake**: purée 115g/4oz/1 cup hulled strawberries and 1 banana with 50g/2oz/¼ cup caster (superfine) sugar in a blender. Gradually add 600ml/1 pint/2½ cups chilled milk with the motor running. Pour into four glasses, add a large scoop of vanilla ice cream to each and decorate with fresh strawberries. For picnics, carry the chilled shake in a vacuum flask and omit the ice cream.

**Mango and Lime Smoothie**: peel, stone (pit) and dice 1 ripe mango, then purée it with the grated rind and juice of 1 lime. Add 600ml/1 pint/2½ cups chilled natural (plain) yogurt and whizz for a few seconds. Sweeten to taste with honey and serve immediately. For picnics, carry the chilled drink in a vacuum flask.

**St. Clements**: top up orange juice with an equal quantity of lemonade and serve with crushed ice.

**Left** *Old-fashioned lemonade is great at summer barbecues and picnics.*

# welcome nibbles

Stylish snacks and little bites set every gathering off to the right start. Choose a variety of different tastes and textures to complement the drinks you serve.

# Tortilla Chips

A useful and quick-to-prepare appetizer, tortilla chips or totopos as they are also known are excellent for scooping up a salsa or dip. They can also be sprinkled with a little grated cheese and grilled until golden, then served with a selection of other nibbles. Use corn tortillas that are a few days old; fresh tortillas will not crisp up so well.

**Makes 48**

8 corn tortillas
oil, for frying
salt

### COOK'S TIP

The oil needs to be very hot for cooking the tortillas chips – test it first by carefully adding one of the wedges to the frying pan. It should float and begin to bubble in the oil immediately.

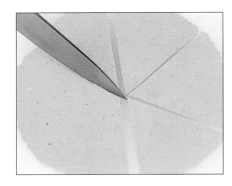

**1** Cut each corn tortilla into six triangular wedges. Pour oil into a large, heavy bottomed frying pan to a depth of 1cm/½ in, place the pan over a medium heat and heat until very hot (see Cook's Tip).

### VARIATION

To give a spicy flavour to the chips, prepare a mixture of garlic salt, paprika and a pinch of mace. Sprinkle over the freshly drained tortilla chips while they are still hot.

**2** Fry the tortilla wedges in the hot oil in small batches until they turn golden and are crisp. This will only take a few moments. Remove with a slotted spoon and drain on kitchen paper. Sprinkle with salt.

**3** The tortillas should be served warm. They can be cooled completely and stored in an airtight container for a few days, but will need to be reheated in a microwave or a warm oven before being served.

# Pepitas

These crunchy, spicy and slightly sweet pumpkin seeds are absolutely irresistible, especially if you use hot and tasty chipotle chillies to spice them up. Their smoky flavour is the perfect foil for the nutty taste of the pumpkin seeds and the hint of sweetness provided by the sugar. Serve pepitas with pre-dinner drinks and cocktails as an alternative to nuts.

**Makes 2 bowls**

250g/9oz/2 cups pumpkin seeds
8 garlic cloves, crushed
2.5ml/½ tsp salt
20ml/4 tsp crushed dried chillies
10ml/2 tsp caster (superfine) sugar
2 wedges of lime

**1** Heat a small, heavy frying pan, add the pumpkin seeds and dry fry for a few minutes, stirring constantly as they swell.

### COOK'S TIPS

• It is important to keep the pumpkin seeds moving as they cook. Watch them carefully and do not let them burn, or they will taste bitter.
• Chipotle chillies are smoke-dried jalapeño chillies.

**2** When all the seeds have swollen, add the garlic and cook for a few minutes more, stirring constantly. Add the salt and the crushed chillies and stir to mix. Turn off the heat, but keep the pan on the stove. Sprinkle the sugar over the seeds and shake the pan to ensure that they are all coated.

**3** Tip the pepitas into a bowl and serve with the wedge of lime for squeezing over the seeds. If the lime is omitted, the seeds can be cooled and stored in an airtight container for serving cold or reheating later, but they are best served fresh and warm.

### VARIATION

If you are using the pepitas cold, they can be mixed with cashew nuts and dried cranberries to make a spicy and fruity bowl of nibbles.

# Tapas of Almonds, Olives and Cheese

These three simple ingredients are lightly flavoured to create a Spanish tapas medley that is perfect to serve with pre-dinner drinks.

**Serves 6 to 8**

For the marinated olives
2.5ml/½ tsp coriander seeds
2.5ml/½ tsp fennel seeds
5ml/1 tsp chopped fresh rosemary
10ml/2 tsp chopped fresh parsley
2 garlic cloves, crushed
15ml/1 tbsp sherry vinegar
30ml/2 tbsp olive oil
225g/8oz/1⅓ cup black and green
    pitted or stuffed olives

For the marinated cheese
150g/5oz goat's cheese
90ml/6 tbsp olive oil
15ml/1 tbsp white wine vinegar
5ml/1 tsp black peppercorns
1 garlic clove, sliced
3 fresh tarragon or thyme sprigs
tarragon sprigs, to garnish

For the salted almonds
1.5ml/¼ tsp cayenne pepper
30ml/2 tbsp sea salt
25g/1oz/2 tbsp butter
60ml/4 tbsp olive oil
200g/7oz/1¾ cups blanched almonds

**1** To marinade the olives, crush the coriander and fennel seeds. Mix with the rosemary, parsley, garlic, vinegar and oil and pour over the olives in a bowl. Cover and chill for up to 1 week.

**2** To make the marinated cheese, cut the cheese into bitesize pieces, leaving the rind on. Mix together the oil, vinegar, peppercorns, garlic and herb sprigs and pour over the cheese in a bowl. Cover and chill for up to 3 days. Use a spoon and fork to turn the cheese cubes in the marinade.

**3** To make the salted almonds, mix together the cayenne pepper and salt in a bowl. Melt the butter with the olive oil in a frying pan. Add the almonds to the pan and fry, stirring for 5 minutes, or until the almonds are golden.

**4** Tip the almonds out of the frying pan, into the salt mixture and toss together until the almonds are coated. Leave to cool, then store them in a jar or airtight container for up to 1 week.

**5** To serve the tapas, arrange in small, shallow serving dishes. Use fresh sprigs of tarragon to garnish the cheese and scatter the almonds with a little more salt, if you like.

# Spicy Potato Wedges with **Chilli Dip**

These dry-roasted potato wedges with crisp spicy crusts are delicious with the chilli dip. They make a tasty appetizer or can be served with other dishes as part of a barbecue or informal buffet supper.

### Serves 6

*4 baking potatoes, about 225g/*
  *8oz each*
*60ml/4 tbsp olive oil*
*4 garlic cloves, crushed*
*10ml/2 tsp ground allspice*
*10ml/2 tsp ground coriander*
*30ml/2 tbsp paprika*
*salt and ground black pepper*

For the dip
*30ml/2 tbsp olive oil*
*2 small onions, finely chopped*
*2 garlic clove, crushed*
*400g/14oz can chopped tomatoes*
*2 fresh red chillies, seeded and*
  *finely chopped*
*30ml/2 tbsp balsamic vinegar*
*30ml/2 tbsp chopped fresh coriander*
  *(cilantro), plus extra to garnish*

**1** Preheat the oven to 200°C/400°F/ Gas 6. Cut the potatoes in half, then into eight wedges.

**2** Add the wedges to a large pan of cold water. Bring to the boil, reduce the heat and simmer for 10 minutes or until the wedges have softened but the flesh has not started to disintegrate. Drain well and pat dry on kitchen paper.

**3** Mix the olive oil, garlic, allspice, coriander and paprika in a roasting pan. Add salt and pepper to taste. Add the potatoes to the pan and shake to coat them thoroughly. Roast for 20–25 minutes, until the wedges are browned, crisp and fully cooked. Turn the potato wedges occasionally during the roasting time.

**4** Meanwhile, make the chilli dip. Heat the oil in a small pan, add the onion and garlic, and cook for 5–10 minutes until soft.

**5** Tip in the chopped tomatoes, with any juice. Stir in the chilli and vinegar. Cook gently for 10 minutes until the mixture has reduced and thickened, then taste and check the seasoning. Stir in the chopped fresh coriander.

**6** Pile the spicy potato wedges on a plate, garnish with the extra coriander and serve with the chilli dip.

**VARIATION**
Instead of balsamic vinegar, try brown rice vinegar, which has a mellow flavour.

# Party Eggs

Hard-boiled eggs make perfect party food. Use a variety of fillings for a stunning centrepiece. Double the quantities if you are making larger batches.

**Each variation fills 6 eggs**

### EGGS WITH CAVIAR

*6 eggs, hard-boiled*
*4 spring onions (scallions), trimmed and very finely sliced*
*30ml/2 tbsp sour cream*
*5ml/1 tsp lemon juice*
*25g/1oz/2 tbsp caviar*
*salt and ground black pepper*
*lemon rind and caviar, to garnish*

Mix all the ingredients with the egg yolks, spoon back into the egg whites and garnish with lemon rind and caviar.

### PRAWN AND CUCUMBER EGGS

*6 eggs, hard-boiled*
*75g/3oz/scant 1 cup cooked peeled prawns (shrimp), reserving 12 for garnish and the rest chopped*
*25g/1oz cucumber, peeled and diced*
*5ml/1 tsp tomato ketchup*
*15ml/1 tbsp lemon mayonnaise*
*salt and ground black pepper*
*fennel sprigs, to garnish*

Mix all the ingredients with the egg yolks, spoon back into the egg whites and garnish with prawns and fennel.

### NUTTY DEVILLED EGGS

*6 eggs, hard-boiled*
*40g/1½oz cooked ham, chopped*
*4 walnut halves, very finely chopped*
*15ml/1 tbsp Dijon mustard*
*15ml/1 tbsp mayonnaise*
*5ml/1 tsp white wine vinegar*
*few large pinches of cayenne pepper*
*salt and ground black pepper*
*paprika and gherkins, to garnish*

Mix together all the ingredients with the egg yolks, spoon into the whites and garnish with paprika and gherkin slices.

### GARLIC AND GREEN PEPPERCORN EGGS

*5ml/1 tsp garlic purée or 1 large garlic clove, crushed*
*45ml/3 tbsp crème fraîche*
*6 eggs, hard-boiled*
*salt and ground black pepper*
*2.5ml/½ tsp green peppercorns, crushed, to garnish*

Mix the garlic, crème fraîche, egg yolks and seasoning. Place in a piping bag and pipe into the egg whites. Sprinkle with a few crushed peppercorns.

# Bitesize Cheese Brioches

These mouthfuls of golden, buttery dough have a surprise in the middle: a nugget of melting cheese, so be sure to serve them warm to enjoy them at their best.

### Makes about 40

*450g/1lb/4 cups plain (all-purpose) or*
*    strong white bread flour, plus extra*
*    for dusting*
*5ml/1 tsp salt*
*5ml/1 tsp ground turmeric*
*1 sachet easy-blend (rapid-rise)*
*    dried yeast*
*150ml/¼ pint/⅔ cup warm milk*
*2 eggs, plus 2 egg yolks*
*75g/3oz/6 tbsp butter, melted*
*    and slightly cooled*
*50g/2oz/½ cup grated Cheddar cheese*
*oil, for greasing*
*50g/2oz/½ cup cubed cheese, such as*
*    Cheshire, Gouda or Port Salut*

**1** Sift the dry ingredients into a large bowl with the yeast and make a hollow in the middle. Mix the milk, eggs and one yolk with the butter and Cheddar.

**2** Pour the liquid into the bowl of dry ingredients and blend with a fork to bring the mixture together. Continue mixing in the bowl or in a food processor with a dough blade, until it is evenly mixed. Turn out the mixture on to a lightly floured surface and knead, working in as little flour as possible, until the surface of the mixture becomes smooth and dry.

**3** Place the dough in a lightly oiled bowl. Lightly oil the top of the dough, cover with a clean cloth and leave in a warm place for at least 1 hour, until the dough has doubled in bulk.

**4** Turn out on to a floured surface and knead the dough until it becomes firm and elastic again.

**5** Divide the dough into four batches, then divide each batch into eight to ten pieces. Knead each piece until smooth.

### COOK'S TIP

For a special party, use gold petits fours cases; they are firmer and give more support, and they look smart and elegant.

**6** Press a cube of cheese into the middle of each piece of dough, then shape into a round and place in paper sweet (candy) cases. Place the paper cases in mini muffin trays to support the soft dough during baking or, alternatively, put the dough in doubled paper cases. Set the brioches aside in a warm place until they are well risen and have almost doubled in size.

**7** Preheat the oven to 200°C/400°F/ Gas 6. Mix the remaining yolk with 15ml/1 tbsp water and glaze the brioches with the mixture, using a pastry brush. Bake for about 15 minutes, or until golden brown, well-risen and firm underneath if tapped.

# Stilton Croquettes

These are perfect little party bites, which you can make in advance and reheat at the last minute. For a really crisp result, double coat the croquettes in breadcrumbs.

**Makes about 20**

350g/12oz floury potatoes, cooked
75g/3oz/¾ cup creamy Stilton
 cheese, crumbled
3 eggs, hard-boiled, peeled
 and chopped
few drops of Worcestershire sauce
plain (all-purpose) flour, for coating
1 egg, beaten
45–60ml/3–4 tbsp fine, dry
 breadcrumbs
vegetable oil, for deep-frying
salt and ground black pepper
dipping sauce or salsa, to serve

**1** Mash the potatoes until they are quite smooth. Work in the crumbled Stilton cheese, chopped egg and Worcestershire sauce. Add salt and ground black pepper to taste.

**2** Divide the potato and cheese mixture into about 20 portions. Dust your hands lightly with flour and shape the pieces into small sausage shapes, no longer than 2.5cm/1in in length.

**3** Coat in flour, then dip into the beaten egg and coat evenly in breadcrumbs. Reshape, if necessary. Chill for about 30 minutes then deep-fry, seven to eight at a time, in hot oil turning frequently until they are golden brown all over. Drain on kitchen paper, transfer to a serving dish and keep warm for up to 30 minutes. Serve with a dipping sauce such as soy sauce or a tomato salsa.

# Cheese and Potato Bread Twists

These individual "ploughman's lunch" twists have the cheese cooked in the bread. They can be filled with smoked salmon seasoned with lemon juice after cooking to make them extra special.

**Makes 12**

*225g/8oz potatoes, diced*
*225g/8oz/2 cups strong white bread*
  *flour, plus extra for dusting*
*5ml/1 tsp easy-blend (rapid-rise)*
  *dried yeast*
*150ml/¼ pint/⅔ cup lukewarm water*
*175g/6oz/1½ cups finely grated red*
  *Leicester cheese*
*10ml/2 tsp olive oil, for greasing*
*salt*

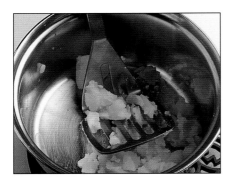

**1** Cook the potatoes in a large pan with plenty of lightly salted boiling water for 20 minutes, or until tender. Drain through a colander and return to the pan. Mash until smooth and set aside to cool.

**2** Meanwhile, sift the flour into a large bowl and add the yeast and a good pinch of salt. Stir in the mashed potatoes and rub with your fingers to form a crumb consistency.

**VARIATION**
Any hard, well-flavoured cheese can be used. Mature (sharp) Cheddar is the traditional choice for a ploughman's lunch, or you could try a smoked cheese or a variety with added herbs.

**3** Make a well in the centre of the dough and pour in the lukewarm water. Start by bringing the mixture together with a round-bladed knife then use your hands. Knead for 5 minutes on a well-floured surface. Return the dough to the bowl. Cover with a damp cloth and leave the dough to rise in a warm place for 1 hour or until doubled in size.

**4** Turn the dough out and knock back (punch down) the air bubbles. Knead again for a few seconds.

**5** Divide the dough into 12 even pieces and shape into rounds.

**6** Sprinkle the cheese over a baking sheet. Take each ball of dough and roll it in the cheese.

**7** Roll each cheese-covered roll on a dry surface to form a long sausage shape. Fold the two ends together and twist the bread. Lay the bread twists on an oiled baking sheet.

**8** Cover with a damp cloth and leave the bread to rise in a warm place for 30 minutes. Preheat the oven to 220°C/425°F/Gas 7. Bake the bread for 10–15 minutes. These bread twists stay moist and fresh for up to 3 days if stored in airtight food bags.

# **Potato** and **Onion Tortilla** with **Broad Beans**

This Spanish omelette, which includes herbs and broad beans, is ideal for a summer party when cut into pieces and served as a tapa.

### **Serves 8 to 10**

*45ml/3 tbsp olive oil*
*2 Spanish onions, thinly sliced*
*300g/11oz waxy potatoes, cut into*
*   1cm/½in dice*
*250g/9oz/1½ cups shelled broad*
*   (fava) beans*
*5ml/1 tsp chopped fresh thyme or*
*   summer savory*
*6 large (US extra large) eggs*
*45ml/3 tbsp mixed chopped chives*
*   and chopped flat leaf parsley*
*salt and ground black pepper*

**1** Heat 30ml/2 tbsp of the oil in a 23cm/9in deep non-stick frying pan. Add the onions and potatoes and stir to coat. Cover and cook gently, stirring frequently, for 20–25 minutes, or until the potatoes are cooked and the onions collapsed. Do not let the vegetables turn brown.

**2** Meanwhile, cook the beans in salted boiling water for 5 minutes. Drain well and set aside to cool.

**3** When the beans are cool enough to handle, peel off the grey outer skins. Add the beans to the frying pan, together with the thyme or savory and season with salt and pepper to taste. Stir well and cook for 2–3 minutes.

**4** Beat the eggs with salt and pepper to taste, add the mixed herbs, then pour over the potatoes and onions and increase the heat slightly. Cook gently until the egg on the bottom sets and browns, gently pulling the omelette away from the sides of the pan and tilting it to allow the uncooked egg to run underneath.

**5** Invert the tortilla on to a plate. Add the remaining oil to the pan and heat until hot. Slip the tortilla back into the pan, uncooked side down, and cook for another 3–5 minutes to allow the underneath to brown.

**6** Slide the tortilla out on to a clean plate. Use a sharp knife to cut the tortilla into eight to ten pieces or small squares and serve warm.

### **COOK'S TIP**
Cook the tortilla very gently once the eggs have been added to the pan – trying to speed up the cooking process by raising the temperature browns the underneath much too soon, before the egg has time to set.

# finger food and light bites

Standing-and-eating food has to be easy to eat

and sufficiently satisfying to keep everyone

munching through hours of chatting.

# Little Onions Cooked with Wine, Coriander and Olive Oil

If you can find the small, flat Italian cipolla or borettane onions, they are excellent in this recipe – otherwise use pickling onions, small red onions or shallots.

**Serves 6**

*105ml/7 tbsp olive oil*
*675g/1½ lb small onions, peeled*
*150ml/¼ pint/⅔ cup dry white wine*
*2 bay leaves*
*2 garlic cloves, bruised*
*1–2 small dried red chillies*
*15ml/1 tbsp coriander seeds, toasted*
  *and lightly crushed*
*2.5ml/½ tsp sugar*
*a few fresh thyme sprigs*
*30ml/2 tbsp currants*
*10ml/2 tsp chopped fresh oregano*
*5ml/1 tsp grated lemon rind*
*15ml/1 tbsp chopped fresh flat*
  *leaf parsley*
*30–45ml/2–3 tbsp pine nuts, toasted*
*salt and ground black pepper*

**1** Place 30ml/2 tbsp olive oil in a wide pan. Add the onions and cook gently over a medium heat for about 5 minutes, or until they begin to colour. Remove from the pan and set aside.

**2** Add the remaining oil, the wine, bay leaves, garlic, chillies, coriander seeds, sugar and thyme to the pan. Bring to the boil and cook briskly for 5 minutes. Return the onions to the pan.

**3** Add the currants, reduce the heat and cook gently for 15–20 minutes, or until the onions are tender but not falling apart. Use a slotted spoon to transfer the onions to a serving dish.

**4** Boil the liquid over a high heat until it reduces considerably. Taste and adjust the seasoning, if necessary, then pour the reduced liquid over the onions. Sprinkle the oregano over the onions, set aside to cool and then chill.

**5** Just before serving stir in the grated lemon rind, chopped flat leaf parsley and toasted pine nuts.

**COOK'S TIP**
Serve this dish with other small dishes such as an antipasto, or with some thinly sliced prosciutto or other air-dried ham.

# Quesadillas

These cheese-filled tortillas are the Mexican equivalent of toasted sandwiches. Serve them hot or they will become chewy. If you are making them for a crowd, fill and fold the tortillas ahead of time, but only cook them to order.

**Serves 8**

*400g/14oz mozzarella, Monterey Jack or mild Cheddar cheese*
*2 fresh fresno chillies (optional)*
*16 wheat flour tortillas, about 15cm/6in across*
*onion relish or tomato salsa, to serve*

**1** If using mozzarella cheese, it must be drained thoroughly and then patted dry and sliced into thin strips. Monterey Jack and Cheddar cheese should both be coarsely grated, as finely grated cheese will melt and ooze away when cooking. Set the cheese aside in a bowl.

**2** If using the chillies, spear them on a long-handled metal skewer and roast them over the flame of a gas burner until the skin blisters and darkens. Do not let the flesh burn. Place the roasted chillies in a strong plastic bag and tie the top to keep the steam in. Set aside for 20 minutes for the skin to loosen.

**VARIATIONS**
Try spreading a thin layer of your favourite salsa on the tortillas before adding the cheese, or add some cooked chicken or prawns (shrimp) before folding the tortillas.

**3** Remove the roasted chillies from the bag and carefully peel off the skin. Cut off the stalk, then slit the chillies and scrape out all the seeds. Cut the flesh into 16 even-sized thin strips.

**4** Warm a large frying pan or griddle. Place one tortilla on the pan or griddle at a time, sprinkle about one sixteenth of the cheese on to one half and add a strip of chilli, if using. Fold the tortilla over the cheese and press the edges together gently to seal. Cook the filled tortilla for 1 minute, then turn over and cook the other side for 1 minute.

**5** Remove the filled tortilla from the pan or griddle, cut it into three triangles or four strips and serve immediately while it still hot, with the onion relish or tomato salsa.

# Mozzarella and Tomato Skewers

Stacks of flavour – layers of oven-baked mozzarella, tomatoes, basil and bread. These colourful kebabs will be popular with children and adults alike, so make plenty for everyone to enjoy.

**Serves 10 to 12**

*24 slices white country bread, each
   about 1cm/½ in thick*
*90ml/6 tbsp olive oil*
*250g/9oz mozzarella cheese, cut into
   5mm/¼ in slices*
*6 ripe plum tomatoes, cut into
   5mm/¼ in slices*
*25g/1oz/1 cup fresh basil leaves,
   plus extra to garnish*
*salt and ground black pepper*
*60ml/4 tbsp chopped fresh flat leaf
   parsley, to garnish*

**1** Preheat the oven to 220°C/425°F/ Gas 7. Trim the crusts from the bread and cut each slice into four equal squares. Arrange on baking sheets and brush with half the olive oil. Bake for 3–5 minutes until the squares are a pale golden colour.

**2** Remove the bread squares from the oven and place them on a chopping board with the other ingredients.

**3** Make 32 stacks, each starting with a square of bread, then a slice of the mozzarella cheese topped with a slice of tomato and a basil leaf. Sprinkle with salt and pepper, then repeat, ending with a piece of bread. Push a skewer through each stack and place on the baking sheets. Drizzle with the remaining oil and bake for 10–15 minutes until the cheese begins to melt. Garnish with basil and parsley.

# Mussels in Black Bean Sauce

The large green-shelled mussels from New Zealand are perfect for this delicious dish. Buy the cooked mussels on the half-shell – it is an elegant way to serve them.

**Makes 20**

*15ml/1 tbsp vegetable oil*
*2.5cm/1in piece of fresh root ginger, finely chopped*
*2 garlic cloves, finely chopped*
*1 fresh red chilli, seeded and chopped*
*15ml/1 tbsp black bean sauce*
*15ml/1 tbsp dry sherry*
*5ml/1 tsp granulated sugar*
*5ml/1 tsp sesame oil*
*10ml/2 tsp dark soy sauce*
*20 cooked New Zealand green-shelled mussels*
*2 spring onions (scallions), 1 shredded and 1 cut into fine rings*

**1** Heat the vegetable oil in a pan or wok. Fry the ginger, garlic and chilli with the black bean sauce for a few seconds, then add the sherry and sugar and cook for 30 seconds more, stirring with cooking chopsticks or a wooden spoon to ensure the sugar is dissolved.

**2** Remove from the heat, stir in the oil and soy sauce. Mix thoroughly.

**COOK'S TIP**
Provide cocktail sticks (toothpicks) for spearing the mussels and removing them from their half-shells.

**3** Have ready a bamboo steamer or a medium pan holding 5cm/2in of simmering water, and fitted with a metal trivet. Place the mussels in layers on a heatproof plate that will fit inside the steamer or pan. Spoon the prepared sauce evenly over the half-shell mussels.

**4** Sprinkle all the spring onions over the mussels. Place in the steamer or cover the plate tightly with foil and place it on the trivet in the pan. It should be just above the level of the water. Cover and steam over a high heat for about 10 minutes or until the mussels have heated through. Serve immediately.

# Futo-Maki

Thick-rolled sushi, such as futo-maki, is a fashionable and attractive food to serve as canapés with drinks.

**Makes 16**

*2 nori sheets*

**For the su-meshi (vinegared rice)**
*200g/7oz/1 cup short grain rice*
*275ml/9fl oz/scant 1¼ cups water*
*45ml/3 tbsp rice vinegar*
*37.5ml/7½ tsp sugar*
*10ml/2 tsp salt*

**For the omelette**
*2 eggs, beaten*
*25ml/1½ tbsp second dashi stock*
*10ml/2 tsp sake*
*2.5ml/½ tsp salt*
*vegetable oil, for frying*

**For the fillings**
*4 dried shiitake mushrooms,*
  *soaked in water overnight*
*120ml/4fl oz/½ cup second dashi stock*
*15ml/1 tbsp shoyu*
*7.5ml/1½ tsp sugar*
*5ml/1 tsp mirin*
*6 raw king prawns (jumbo shrimp),*
  *heads and shells removed*
*4 asparagus spears, boiled and cooled*
*10 chives, about 23cm/9in long*
*salt*
*wasabi, gari and soy sauce, to serve*

**1** To make the su-meshi, wash the rice in cold water, drain and set aside for one hour. Put the rice into a pan and add the water. Cover and boil for 5 minutes, then simmer until the water has been absorbed. Remove from the heat and set aside for 10 minutes.

**2** Mix the rice vinegar with the sugar and salt. Tip the rice into a bowl and sprinkle with the vinegar mixture. Fold into the rice with a spatula, but do not stir. Cool the su-meshi before shaping.

**3** For the omelette, mix the beaten eggs, dashi stock, sake and salt in a bowl. Heat a little oil in a frying pan on a medium-low heat. Pour in just enough egg mixture to cover the base of the pan. As soon as the mixture sets, fold the omelette in half towards you and wipe the space left with a little oil. With the first omelette still in the pan, repeat until all the mixture is used.

**4** Each new omelette is laid on to the first to form a multi-layered omelette. Slide the layered omelette on to a chopping board. When cool, cut lengthways into 1cm/½ in wide strips.

**5** Put the shiitake mushrooms and the water, stock, shoyu, sugar and mirin in a small pan. Bring to the boil, then reduce the heat to low. Cook for 20 minutes, or until half of the liquid has evaporated. Drain the shiitake mushrooms, remove and discard the stalks, and slice the caps thinly. Squeeze out any excess liquid, then dry on kitchen paper. Discard the liquid.

**6** Make three cuts in the belly of each of the prawns to stop them curling up, and boil in salted water for 1 minute, or until they turn bright pink. Drain and cool, then remove the vein using a cocktail stick (toothpick).

**COOK'S TIP**
If you make the rolled sushi ahead, wrap each roll in clear film (plastic wrap) until ready to slice and serve the rolls.

**7** Place a nori sheet, rough side up, at the front edge of a sushi rolling mat. Scoop up half of the su-meshi and spread it on the nori. Leave a 1cm/½ in margin at the side nearest you, and 2cm/¾ in at the side furthest from you. Make a shallow depression lengthways across the centre of the rice. Fill this with half the omelette strips and half the asparagus. Place half the prawns along the egg and asparagus. Top with five chives and half the shiitake slices.

**8** Lift the mat with your thumbs while pressing the filling with your fingers. Roll the mat up gently. When completed, gently roll the mat to firm it up. Unwrap and set the futo-maki aside. Repeat to make another roll.

**9** Cut each futo-maki into eight pieces, using a very sharp knife. Wipe the knife with a clean dishtowel dampened with rice vinegar after each cut.

**10** Line up all the pieces on a large tray or serving platter. Serve with small dishes of wasabi, gari and soy sauce for dipping.

# Crab Egg Rolls

These wonderful crab rolls are similar to authentic Chinese spring rolls. They are made with wafer-thin pancakes, which provide the very crisp case for the filling. If you prefer a softer version the rolls can be steamed – they are equally delicious and quite light. These are ideal for buffets, children's parties and summer picnics.

**Makes about 12**

*3 eggs*
*450ml/¾ pint/scant 2 cups water*
*175g/6oz/1½ cups plain*
*(all-purpose) flour*
*2.5ml/½ tsp salt*
*oil, for deep-frying*
*lime wedges, to serve*
*45ml/3 tbsp light soy sauce mixed with*
*5ml/1 tsp sesame oil, for dipping*

For the filling
*225g/8oz/1⅓ cups white crab meat*
*or small prawns (shrimp)*
*3 large spring onions*
*(scallions), shredded*
*2.5cm/1in piece of fresh root*
*ginger, grated*
*2 large garlic cloves, chopped*
*115g/4oz bamboo shoots, chopped,*
*or beansprouts*
*15ml/1 tbsp soy sauce*
*10–15ml/2–3 tsp cornflour (cornstarch)*
*blended with 15ml/1 tbsp water*
*1 egg, separated*
*salt and ground black pepper*

**1** Lightly beat the eggs and gradually stir in the water. Sift the flour and salt into another bowl and work in the egg mixture. Blend to a smooth batter, then remove any lumps if necessary. Leave to rest for 20 minutes.

**2** When ready to use, lightly whisk the batter and stir in 15ml/1 tbsp cold water to thin it slightly if necessary.

**3** Lightly grease a 25cm/10in non-stick frying pan and heat gently. To make smooth, pale wrappers for the egg rolls, the frying pan must be hot enough to set the batter, but should not be hot enough for the batter to brown, bubble or develop holes. Pour in about 45ml/3 tbsp batter and swirl round the pan to spread evenly and very thinly. Cook for 2 minutes, or until loose underneath. There is no need to cook the pancake on the other side.

**4** Make a further 11 pancakes. Stack the pancakes, cooked side upwards, between sheets of baking parchment. Set aside until ready to use.

**5** To make the filling, combine the crab or prawns, spring onions, ginger, garlic, bamboo shoots or beansprouts, soy sauce, cornflour and water, egg yolk and seasoning.

**6** Lightly beat the egg white. Place a spoonful of filling in the middle of each pancake, brush the edges with egg white and fold into neat parcels, tucking in the ends well.

**7** Heat the oil in a deep-frying pan and when a cube of bread turns light golden in 1 minute carefully add four of the parcels, fold side downwards. Cook for 1–2 minutes, or until golden and crisp. Remove with a slotted spoon and place on kitchen paper. Keep warm in the oven while you cook the remaining egg rolls. Alternatively, using a stacking bamboo steamer, arrange four parcels in each layer, cover with a lid and steam for 30 minutes.

**8** Serve with the soy sauce and sesame oil dipping sauce and wedges of lime.

# Tortilla Cones with Smoked Salmon and Soft Cheese

These simple yet sophisticated wraps are a must for serving with drinks or as part of a buffet.

**Makes 8**

*115g/4oz/½ cup soft white
  (farmer's) cheese
30ml/2 tbsp roughly chopped fresh dill
juice of 1 lemon
1 small red onion
15ml/1 tbsp drained bottled capers
30ml/2 tbsp extra virgin olive oil
30ml/2 tbsp roughly chopped fresh flat
  leaf parsley
115g/4oz smoked salmon
8 small wheat flour tortillas
salt and ground black pepper
lemon wedges, for squeezing*

**3** Cut the smoked salmon into short, thin strips and add to the red onion mixture. Toss to mix. Season to taste with plenty of pepper.

**COOK'S TIP**
You can use salted capers in this dish instead of the unsalted variety, but rinse them thoroughly before using.

**4** Spread a little of the soft cheese mixture on each tortilla and top with the smoked salmon mixture.

**5** Roll up the tortillas into cones and secure with wooden cocktail sticks (toothpicks). Arrange on a serving plate and add some lemon wedges, for squeezing. Serve immediately.

**1** Place the soft cheese in a bowl and mix in half the chopped dill. Add a little salt and pepper and a dash of the lemon juice to taste. Reserve the remaining lemon juice in a separate mixing bowl.

**2** Finely chop the red onion. Add the onion, capers and olive oil to the lemon juice in the mixing bowl. Add the chopped flat leaf parsley and the remaining dill and gently stir.

**VARIATION**
Tortilla cones can be filled with a variety of ingredients. Try soft cheese with red pesto and chopped sun-dried tomatoes, or mackerel pâté with slices of cucumber.

# Tunisian Brik

You can make these little parcels into any shape you like, but the most important thing is to encase the egg white quickly before it starts to escape.

**Makes 6**

*45ml/3 tbsp butter, melted*
*1 small red onion, finely chopped*
*150g/5oz chicken or turkey*
*    fillet, minced (ground)*
*1 large garlic clove, crushed*
*juice of ½ lemon*
*30ml/2 tbsp chopped fresh parsley*
*12 sheets of filo pastry, each about*
*    15 x 25cm/6 x 10in, thawed if frozen*
*6 small (US medium) eggs, such as*
*    bantam, pheasant or guinea fowl*
*oil, for deep-frying*
*salt and ground black pepper*

**1** Heat half the butter in a pan and sauté the onion for 3 minutes. Add the chicken or turkey, garlic, lemon juice, parsley and seasoning, and cook, stirring, for 2–3 minutes, or until the meat is just cooked. Set aside to cool.

**COOK'S TIP**
If you prefer to cook these pastries in the oven, preheat it to 220°C/425°F/Gas 7. Brush the pastries with butter or beaten egg and cook for 8–10 minutes.

**2** Place one sheet of pastry lengthways on the work surface and brush with melted butter; top with a second sheet. Brush the edges with butter and place one-sixth of the mixture about 2.5cm/1in from the bottom left-hand side of the pastry sheet. Flatten the filling, making a slight hollow in it.

**3** Carefully crack an egg into the hollow and fold up the pastry immediately so the egg white does not run out. Lift the right-hand edge and fold it over to the left edge to enclose the filling and seal quickly. Fold the bottom left-hand corner straight up and then fold the bottom left corner up to the right edge, forming a triangle.

**4** Use the remaining pastry sheets and filling to make another five parcels, then heat the oil in a frying pan until a cube of bread turns golden in about 1½ minutes. Cook the pastries, two to three at a time, until golden. Lift them out of the pan with a slotted spoon and drain on kitchen paper. Serve hot or cold.

# Mini Ham, Roasted Pepper and Mozzarella Ciabatta Pizzas

These quick ciabatta pizzas are eye-catching with their bright pepper topping and great for children.

**Serves 8**

2 red (bell) peppers
2 yellow (bell) peppers
1 loaf ciabatta bread
8 slices prosciutto or other thinly-sliced
   ham, cut into thick strips
150g/5oz mozzarella cheese
ground black pepper
tiny basil leaves, to garnish

**1** Preheat a grill (broiler), Grill the peppers, skin sides uppermost, until they are black. Place them in a bowl, cover and leave for 10 minutes. Peel off the skins.

**2** Cut the bread into eight thick slices and toast both sides until golden.

**3** Cut the roasted peppers into thick strips and arrange them on the toasted bread with the strips of prosciutto or other ham.

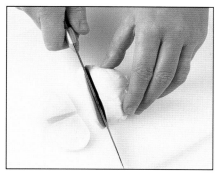

**4** Thinly slice the mozzarella cheese and arrange on top. Grind over plenty of black pepper. Place under a hot grill for 2–3 minutes until the cheese is bubbling.

**5** Arrange the fresh basil leaves on top and to serve transfer to a serving dish or platter. Allow the cheese to cool for a few minutes, if serving the mini-pizzas to children.

# Prosciutto and Mozzarella Parcels on Frisée Salad

Italian prosciutto crudo is a delicious raw smoked ham. Here it is baked with melting mozzarella in a light, crisp pastry case, making it an ideal finger food or as a first course with a fresh frisée salad.

**Serves 6**

*a little hot chilli sauce*
*6 prosciutto crudo slices*
*200g/7oz mozzarella cheese, cut into*
*  6 slices*
*6 sheets filo pastry, each measuring*
*  45 x 28cm/18 x 11in, thawed if frozen*
*50g/2oz/¼ cup butter, melted*
*150g/5oz frisée lettuce, to serve*

**1** Preheat the oven to 200°C/400°F/ Gas 6. Sprinkle a little of the chilli sauce over each slice of prosciutto crudo. Place a slice of mozzarella on each slice of prosciutto, then fold it around the cheese. The cheese should be enclosed by the ham.

**2** Brush a sheet of filo pastry with melted butter and fold it in half to give a double-thick piece measuring 23 x 14cm/9 x 5½ in. Place a prosciutto and mozzarella parcel in the middle of the pastry and brush the remaining pastry with a little butter, then fold it over to enclose the prosciutto and mozzarella in a neat parcel. Place on a baking sheet with the edges of the pastry underneath and brush with a little butter. Repeat with the remaining parcels and sheets.

**3** Bake the filo parcels for 15 minutes, or until the pastry is crisp and evenly golden. Arrange the salad on six plates and add the parcels. Serve immediately.

# Smoked Chicken with Peach Mayonnaise in Filo Tartlets

These tartlets require the minimum of culinary effort because smoked chicken is widely available ready cooked. The filling can be prepared a day in advance and chilled overnight but do not fill the pastry cases until you are ready to serve them or they will become soggy.

**Makes 12**

*25g/1oz/2 tbsp butter, melted*
*3 sheets filo pastry, each measuring*
*  45 x 28cm/18 x 11in, thawed if frozen*
*2 skinless cooked smoked chicken*
*  breast fillets, finely sliced*
*150ml/¼ pint/⅔ cup mayonnaise*
*grated rind of 1 lime*
*30ml/2 tbsp lime juice*
*2 ripe peaches, peeled, stoned (pitted)*
*  and chopped*
*salt and ground black pepper*
*fresh tarragon sprigs, lime slices and*
*  salad leaves, to garnish*

**1** Preheat the oven to 200°C/400°F/ Gas 6. Brush 12 small individual tartlet tins (muffin pans) with a little of the melted butter. Cut each sheet of filo pastry into 12 equal rounds large enough to line the tins, allowing just enough to stand up above the tops of the tins.

**2** Place a round of pastry in each tin and brush with a little butter, then add another round of pastry. Brush each with more butter and add a third round of pastry.

### COOK'S TIP
To peel peaches, place them in a bowl and pour in freshly boiled water to cover. Leave to stand for 30–60 seconds (the riper the peaches, the quicker their skins loosen). Use a slotted spoon to remove 1 peach from the water. Working quickly, slit the skin with the point of a knife then slip it off. Repeat with the remaining peaches.

**3** Bake the tartlets for 5 minutes, or until the pastry is golden brown. Leave in the tins for a few moments before transferring to a wire rack to cool.

**4** In a mixing bowl combine the chicken, mayonnaise, lime rind and juice, peaches and salt and pepper. Chill the mixture for at least 30 minutes, or up to 12 hours overnight. When you are ready to serve the tartlets, spoon the chicken mixture into the filo tartlets. Garnish with the fresh tarragon sprigs, lime slices and salad leaves.

# dips and dippers

Smooth or slightly chunky, luscious or refreshing, dips and dippers are ideal for large gatherings or instead of a formal appetizer for supper with friends.

# Walnut and Garlic Dip, Salsa Verde and Yogurt with Garlic, Cucumber and Mint

Full-flavoured classic sauces and salsas make terrific dips.

### WALNUT AND GARLIC DIP

#### Serves 4

*2 x 1cm/¹⁄₂ in slices white bread*
*60ml/4 tbsp milk*
*150g/5oz/1¹⁄₄ cups shelled walnuts*
*4 garlic cloves, chopped*
*120ml/4fl oz/¹⁄₂ cup mild olive oil*
*15–30ml/1–2 tbsp walnut oil*
  *(optional)*
*juice of 1 lemon*
*salt and ground black pepper*
*walnut or olive oil, for drizzling*
*paprika, for dusting (optional)*

**1** Remove the crusts of the white bread, and soak the slices in the milk for 5 minutes, then process with the walnuts and chopped garlic in a food processor or blender, to make a rough paste.

**2** Gradually add the olive oil to the paste with the motor still running, until the mixture forms a smooth thick sauce. Blend in the walnut oil, if using.

**3** Scoop the sauce into a bowl and add lemon juice to taste, season with salt and pepper and beat well.

**4** Transfer to a serving bowl, drizzle over a little more walnut or olive oil, then dust lightly with paprika, if using.

### SALSA VERDE

#### Serves 4

*1–2 garlic cloves, finely chopped*
*25g/1oz/1 cup flat leaf parsley leaves*
*15g/¹⁄₂oz/¹⁄₂ cup fresh basil, mint*
  *or coriander (cilantro) or a mixture*
  *of fresh herbs*
*15ml/1 tbsp chopped chives*
*15ml/1 tbsp salted capers, rinsed*
*5 anchovy fillets in olive oil, drained*
  *and rinsed*
*10ml/2 tsp French mustard (tarragon or*
  *fines herbes mustard are both good)*
*120ml/4fl oz/¹⁄₂ cup extra virgin olive oil*
*grated lemon rind and juice (optional)*
*ground black pepper*

**1** Process the garlic, parsley, basil, mint or coriander, chives, capers, anchovies, mustard and 15ml/1 tbsp of the oil in a blender or food processor.

**2** Gradually add the remaining oil in a thin stream with the motor running.

**3** Transfer to a bowl and adjust the seasoning to taste – there should be enough salt from the capers and anchovies. Add a little lemon juice and rind if you like. Serve immediately.

### VARIATIONS
Substitute fresh chervil, tarragon, dill or fennel, for the basil, mint or coriander to make a dip for prawns (shrimp).

### YOGURT WITH GARLIC, CUCUMBER AND MINT

#### Serves 4

*15cm/6in piece cucumber*
*5ml/1 tsp sea salt*
*300ml/¹⁄₂ pint/1¹⁄₄ cups Greek*
  *(US strained plain) yogurt*
*3–4 garlic cloves, crushed*
*45ml/3 tbsp chopped fresh mint*
*ground black pepper*
*chopped fresh mint and/or ground*
  *toasted cumin seeds, to garnish*

**1** Slice, chop or grate the cucumber, place in a sieve and sprinkle with half the salt. Leave over a deep plate for 30 minutes to drip.

**2** Rinse the cucumber in cold water, pat dry and mix with the yogurt, garlic and mint. Season to taste. Leave for 30 minutes, stir and sprinkle with fresh mint and/or toasted cumin seeds.

### COOK'S TIP
To make a yogurt and garlic dressing, spoon 150ml/¹⁄₄ pint/²⁄₃ cup Greek yogurt into a bowl. Beat in 1 chopped garlic clove, 5ml/1 tsp French mustard and a pinch of sugar. Season. Beat in 15–30ml/1–2 tbsp olive oil and 15–30ml/1–2 tbsp chopped herbs.

Right, from top to bottom:
Walnut and Garlic Dip, Yogurt with Garlic, Cucumber and Mint, and Salsa Verde.

# Avocado Salsa

A popular chunky dip that is
excellent with tortilla chips.

**Makes 1 bowl**

*2 large ripe avocados*
*1 small red onion, very finely chopped*
*1 red or green chilli, seeded and very*
*    finely chopped*
*½–1 garlic clove, crushed (optional)*
*finely shredded rind of ½ lime and*
*    juice of 1–1½ limes*
*pinch of caster (superfine) sugar*
*225g/8oz tomatoes, seeded*
*    and chopped*
*30ml/2 tbsp roughly chopped fresh*
*    coriander (cilantro)*
*2.5–5ml/½–1 tsp ground cumin seeds*
*15ml/1 tbsp olive oil*
*15–30ml/1–2 tbsp sour cream (optional)*
*salt and ground black pepper*
*lime wedges dipped in sea salt, and*
*    fresh coriander sprigs, to garnish*

**1** Halve, stone (pit) and peel the
avocados. Set half the flesh aside and
roughly mash the remainder in a bowl
using a fork.

**COOK'S TIPS**
• Leaving some of the avocado in chunks
adds a slightly different texture, but if you
prefer a smoother salsa, mash all the
avocado together.
• Hard avocados will soften in a few
seconds in a microwave. Check frequently
until you get the softness that you like.

**2** Add the onion, chilli, garlic (if using),
lime rind, juice of 1 lime, sugar,
tomatoes and coriander. Add the
ground cumin, seasoning and more
lime juice to taste. Stir in the olive oil.

**3** Dice the remaining avocado and stir
into the avocado salsa, then cover and
leave to stand for 15 minutes so that
the flavour develops. Stir in the sour
cream, if using. Serve immediately with
lime wedges dipped in sea salt, and
fresh coriander sprigs.

# Aubergine and Lemon Dip

Here is a delicious velvet-textured dish that can either be eaten as a dip with pieces of warm pitta bread, breadsticks or tortilla corn chips, or spread on slices of bread.

### Makes 1 bowl

*1 large aubergine (eggplant)*
*1 small onion, finely chopped*
*2 garlic cloves, finely chopped*
*30ml/2 tbsp olive oil*
*45ml/3 tbsp chopped fresh parsley*
*75ml/5 tbsp crème fraîche*
*Tabasco sauce, to taste*
*juice of 1 lemon, to taste*
*salt and ground black pepper*
*toast or crusty white bread, to serve*

**1** Preheat the grill (broiler). Place the whole aubergine on a baking sheet and grill it for 20–30 minutes, turning occasionally, until the skin is blackened and wrinkled, and the aubergine feels soft when pressed with a fork.

**2** Cover the aubergine with a clean dishtowel and then set it aside to cool for 5 minutes.

**3** Heat the olive oil in a frying pan and cook the finely chopped onion and garlic for 5 minutes, or until softened but not browned.

### COOK'S TIP

The aubergine can also be roasted in the oven at 200°C/400°F/Gas 6 for 20 minutes.

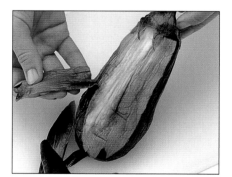

**4** Peel the skin from the aubergine. Mash the flesh into a pulpy purée.

**5** Stir in the onion mixture, parsley and crème fraîche. Add the Tabasco sauce, lemon juice and seasoning to taste. Serve on toast or crusty white bread or as a dip if you prefer.

# Taramasalata

This delicious smoked mullet roe speciality is perhaps one of the most famous Greek dips. It is ideal for a buffet table, or for handing round with drinks. Fingers of warm pitta bread, breadsticks or crispy crackers all make excellent dippers.

### Makes 1 bowl

*115g/4oz smoked mullet roe*
*2 garlic cloves, crushed*
*30ml/2 tbsp grated onion*
*60ml/4 tbsp olive oil*
*4 slices white bread, crusts removed*
*juice of 2 lemons*
*30ml/2 tbsp milk or water*
*ground black pepper*
*warm pitta bread, breadsticks or*
*   crackers, to serve*

**1** Place the smoked roe, garlic, onion, oil, bread and lemon juice in a blender or food processor and process briefly until just smooth.

### COOK'S TIP
Since the roe of grey mullet is expensive, smoked cod's roe is often used instead for this dish. It is paler than the burnt-orange colour of mullet roe but is still very good.

**2** Add the milk or water and process again for a few seconds. (This will give the taramasalata a creamier texture.)

**3** Pour the taramasalata into a serving bowl, cover with clear film (plastic wrap) and chill for 1–2 hours in the refrigerator before serving. Sprinkle the dip with freshly ground black pepper just before serving.

# Cheese-crusted Party Eggs

Similar to the popular Scotch egg, these whole small eggs are wrapped in a tasty herb-flavoured coating then deep-fried. Tiny bantam or quail's eggs will look dainty and are ideal for dipping into mayonnaise.

**Makes 12–20**

*225g/8oz/4 cups stale white breadcrumbs*
*1 small leek, very finely chopped*
*225g/8oz mild but tasty cheese, grated*
*10ml/2 tsp garlic and herb seasoning*
*60ml/4 tbsp chopped fresh parsley*
*10ml/2 tsp mild mustard*
*4 eggs, separated*
*60–90ml/4–6 tbsp milk*
*12–20 small spinach or sorrel leaves, stalks removed*
*12 very small eggs, such as bantam, guinea fowl, or 16–20 quail's eggs, hard-boiled and peeled*
*50–75g/2–3oz/½–⅔ cup flour, for coating, plus extra for dusting*
*50g/2oz/4 tbsp sesame seeds, for coating*
*oil, for deep-frying*
*salt and ground black pepper*
*mayonnaise, for dipping*

**1** Mix the breadcrumbs, leek, cheese, seasoning, parsley and mustard. Beat together the egg yolks and milk and blend into the mixture. Whisk two egg whites until stiff and gradually work sufficient stiff egg white into the breadcrumb mixture to give a firm, dropping consistency. Chill for 1 hour.

**2** Divide the mixture into 12 portions (or 16–20 if using the tiny eggs). Mould one portion in the palm of your hand, place a spinach leaf inside and then an egg and carefully shape the mixture around the egg to enclose it completely within a thin crust. Seal well and dust lightly with flour. Repeat with the remaining portions.

**3** Beat the remaining egg white with 30ml/2 tbsp water, then pour into a shallow dish. Mix the flour with salt and pepper and the sesame seeds and place in another shallow dish. Dip the eggs first in the beaten egg white, then in the sesame flour. Cover and chill for at least 20 minutes.

**4** Heat the oil in a pan until a crust of bread turns golden in about 1¼ minutes. Deep-fry the eggs in the hot oil, turning frequently, until they are golden brown all over. Remove the eggs with a slotted spoon, drain on kitchen paper and leave to cool completely. Serve the cooked eggs whole or sliced in half, with a bowl of good mayonnaise for dipping.

# Butterfly Prawn Spiedini with Chilli and Raspberry Dip

The success of this dish depends upon the quality of the prawns, so it is worthwhile getting really good ones, which have a good flavour and texture. A fruity, slightly spicy dip is such an easy, but fabulous, accompaniment.

### Makes 30

*30 raw king prawns (jumbo shrimp), peeled*
*15ml/1 tbsp sunflower oil*
*sea salt*

For the chilli and raspberry dip
*30ml/2 tbsp raspberry vinegar*
*15ml/1 tbsp sugar*
*115g/4oz/⅔ cup raspberries*
*1 large fresh red chilli, seeded and finely chopped*

**1** Soak 30 wooden skewers in cold water for 30 minutes. Make the dip by mixing the vinegar and sugar in a small pan. Heat gently until the sugar is dissolved, stirring, then add the raspberries.

**2** When the raspberry juices start to flow, tip the mixture into a sieve set over a bowl. Push the raspberries through the sieve using the back of a ladle. Discard the seeds. Stir the chilli into the purée. When the dip is cold, cover and place in a cool place until it is needed.

### COOK'S TIP
These mini kebabs also taste really delicious with a vibrant chilli and mango dip. Use 1 large, ripe mango in place of the raspberries.

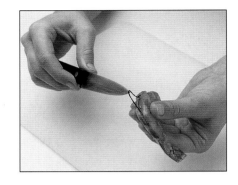

**3** Preheat the grill (broiler) or barbecue. Remove the dark spinal vein from the prawns using a small, sharp knife.

**4** Make an incision down the curved back and butterfly each prawn.

**5** Mix the sunflower oil with a little sea salt in a bowl. Add the prawns and toss to coat them completely.

**6** Thread the prawns on to the drained skewers, spearing them head first.

**7** Grill (broil) the prawns for about 5 minutes, depending on their size, turning them over once. Serve hot, with the chilli and raspberry dip.

### VARIATIONS
• Thin strips of chicken breast or turkey escalope (scallop) can be seasoned and threaded on to the skewers and grilled (broiled) instead of the prawns. They are delicious with the fruity dip.
• For a vegetarian version, grill chunks of halloumi cheese or firm tofu.

# Crisp-fried Crab Claws

Crab claws are readily available in the freezer cabinet in many Asian stores and supermarkets. Thaw out thoroughly and dry on kitchen paper before dipping in the batter. They are just the right size to munch on for a burst of flavour.

**Makes 12**

50g/2oz/¹/2 cup rice flour
15ml/1 tbsp cornflour (cornstarch)
2.5ml/¹/2 tsp sugar
1 egg
60ml/4 tbsp cold water
1 lemon grass stalk, root trimmed
2 garlic cloves, finely chopped
15ml/1 tbsp chopped fresh coriander
    (cilantro)
1–2 fresh red chillies, seeded and
    finely chopped
5ml/1 tsp fish sauce (nam pla)
vegetable oil, for frying
12 half-shelled crab claws
ground black pepper

**For the chilli vinegar dip**
45ml/3 tbsp sugar
120ml/4fl oz/¹/2 cup water
120ml/4fl oz/¹/2 cup red wine vinegar
15ml/1 tbsp fish sauce
2–4 fresh red chillies, seeded
    and chopped

**1** Combine the rice flour, cornflour and sugar in a bowl. Beat the egg with the cold water, then stir the egg and water mixture into the flour mixture and mix well until it forms a light batter.

**2** Cut off the lower 5cm/2in of the lemon grass stalk and chop it finely. Add the lemon grass to the batter, with the garlic, coriander, red chillies and fish sauce. Stir in pepper to taste.

**3** Make the chilli dip. Mix the sugar and water in a pan, stirring until the sugar has dissolved, then bring to the boil. Lower the heat and simmer for 5–7 minutes. Stir in the rest of the ingredients and set aside.

**4** Heat the vegetable oil in a wok or deep-fryer. Pat the crab claws dry and dip into the batter. Drop the battered claws into the hot oil, a few at a time. Fry until golden brown. Drain on kitchen paper and keep hot. Pour the chilli vinegar dip into a serving bowl and serve with the hot crab claws.

**VARIATION**
This Asian-style batter can also be used to coat king prawns (jumbo shrimp).

# Seafood Spring Onion Skewers
## with **Tartare Sauce**

Make these skewers quite small to serve as a canapé at a drinks party or before dinner, with the tartare sauce offered as a dip.

**Makes 9**

675g/1½lb monkfish, filleted, skinned
    and membrane removed
1 bunch thick spring onions (scallions)
75ml/5 tbsp olive oil
1 garlic clove, finely chopped
15ml/1 tbsp lemon juice
5ml/1 tsp dried oregano
30ml/2 tbsp chopped fresh flat
    leaf parsley
12–18 small scallops or raw king
    prawns (jumbo shrimp)
75g/3oz/1½ cups fine fresh
    breadcrumbs
salt and ground black pepper

### For the tartare sauce
2 egg yolks
300ml/½ pint/1¼ cups olive oil,
    or vegetable oil and olive oil mixed
15–30ml/1–2 tbsp lemon juice
5ml/1 tsp French mustard, preferably
    tarragon mustard
15ml/1 tbsp chopped gherkin or
    pickled cucumber
15ml/1 tbsp chopped capers
30ml/2 tbsp chopped fresh flat
    leaf parsley
30ml/2 tbsp chopped fresh chives
5ml/1 tsp chopped fresh tarragon

**1** Soak nine wooden skewers in water for 30 minutes to prevent them from scorching under the grill (broiler).

**2** To make the tartare sauce, whisk the egg yolks and a pinch of salt. Whisk in the oil, a drop at a time at first. When about half the oil is incorporated, add it in a thin stream, whisking constantly. Stop when the mayonnaise is thick.

**3** Whisk in 15ml/1 tbsp lemon juice, then a little more oil. Stir in all the mustard, gherkin or cucumber, capers, parsley, chives and tarragon. Add more lemon juice and seasoning to taste.

**4** Cut the monkfish into 18 pieces; cut the spring onions into 18 pieces about 5cm/2in long. In a bowl, mix the oil, garlic, lemon juice, oregano and half the parsley with seasoning. Add the seafood and the spring onions, then marinate for 15 minutes.

**5** Mix the breadcrumbs and remaining parsley together. Toss the seafood and spring onions in the mixture to coat.

**6** Preheat the grill. Drain the wooden skewers and thread the monkfish, scallops or prawns and spring onions on to them. Drizzle with a little marinade then grill (broil) for 5–6 minutes in total, turning once and drizzling with the marinade, until the fish is just cooked. Serve immediately with the tartare sauce.

# Stilton-stuffed Mushrooms Baked with Garlic Breadcrumbs

Serve these succulent stuffed mushrooms with warm bread.

### Serves 8

*900g/2lb chestnut mushrooms*
*6 garlic cloves, finely chopped*
*200g/7oz/scant 1 cup butter, melted*
*juice of 1 lemon*
*225g/8oz/2 cups Stilton cheese,*
*    crumbled*
*115g/4oz/1 cup walnuts, chopped*
*200g/7oz/3 cups white breadcrumbs*
*50g/2oz/⅔ cup Parmesan cheese*
*60ml/4 tbsp chopped fresh parsley*
*salt and ground black pepper*

### For the sauce
*225g/8oz/1 cup fromage frais or*
*    Greek (US strained plain) yogurt*
*1 bunch chopped fresh herbs*
*15ml/1 tbsp Dijon mustard*

**1** Preheat the oven to 200°C/400°F/ Gas 6. Place the mushrooms in an ovenproof dish and sprinkle half the garlic over them. Drizzle with 50g/ 2oz/¼ cup of the butter and the lemon juice. Season with salt and ground black pepper, and bake for 15–20 minutes. Leave to cool.

**2** Cream the crumbled Stilton with the chopped walnuts and mix in 30ml/2 tbsp of the breadcrumbs.

**3** Divide the Stilton mixture among the chestnut mushrooms.

**4** To make the sauce, mix the fromage frais or Greek yogurt with the chopped fresh herbs and the Dijon mustard until thoroughly combined.

**5** Preheat the grill (broiler). Mix the remaining garlic, breadcrumbs and melted butter together. Grate the Parmesan. Stir in the cheese and chopped, fresh parsley and season with plenty of ground black pepper. Cover the mushrooms with the breadcrumb mixture and grill for about 5 minutes, or until crisp and browned. Serve immediately with the sauce.

**VARIATION**
Use other types of mushrooms such as large flat mushrooms or ceps.

# Nonya Pork Satay

These skewers of tender pork with a spicy nut coating make tasty snacks for a drinks party.

**Makes 8 to 12**

450g/1lb pork fillet
15ml/1 tbsp light muscovado (brown) sugar
1cm/½in cube shrimp paste
1–2 lemon grass stalks
30ml/2 tbsp coriander seeds, dry-fried
6 macadamia nuts or blanched almonds
2 onions, roughly chopped
3–6 fresh red chillies, seeded and roughly chopped
2.5ml/½ tsp ground turmeric
300ml/½ pint/1¼ cups canned coconut milk
30ml/2 tbsp groundnut (peanut) oil or sunflower oil
salt

**1** Soak 8–12 bamboo skewers in water for at least 30 minutes to prevent them scorching when they are placed under the grill (broiler).

**2** Cut the pork into small, bitesize chunks, then spread it out in a single layer in a shallow dish. Sprinkle with the sugar, to help release the juices, and set aside.

**3** Fry the shrimp paste briefly in a foil parcel in a dry frying pan. Alternatively, warm the foil parcel on a skewer held over the gas flame.

**COOK'S TIP**
Nonya Pork Satay can be served either as part of a buffet or as a light party snack – in which case serve it with cubes of cooling cucumber, which contrast well with the spicy meat.

**4** Cut off the lower 5cm/2in of the lemon grass stalks and chop finely. Process the dry-fried coriander seeds to a powder in a food processor. Add the nuts and chopped lemon grass, process briefly, then add the onions, chillies, shrimp paste, turmeric and a little salt; process to a fine paste.

**5** Pour in the coconut milk and oil. Switch the machine on very briefly to mix. Pour the mixture over the pork and leave to marinate for 1–2 hours.

**6** Preheat the grill or prepare the barbecue. Thread three or four pieces of marinated pork on to each bamboo skewer and grill (broil) or cook on the barbecue for 8–10 minutes, or until tender, basting frequently with the remaining marinade. Serve the skewers immediately while hot.

# Yakitori Chicken

These Japanese-style kebabs are easy to eat and ideal for barbecues or parties.

**Makes 12**

6 boneless chicken thighs
1 bunch of spring onions (scallions)
shichimi (seven-flavour spice),
    to serve (optional)

**For the yakitori sauce**
150ml/¼ pint/⅔ cup Japanese
    soy sauce
90g/3½ oz/½ cup sugar
25ml/1½ tbsp sake or dry white wine
15ml/1 tbsp plain (all-purpose) flour

**1** Soak 12 wooden skewers in water for at least 30 minutes. Make the sauce. Stir the soy sauce, sugar and sake or wine into the flour in a small pan and bring to the boil, stirring. Lower the heat and simmer the mixture for 10 minutes, or until the sauce is reduced by a one-third. Set aside.

**2** Cut each chicken thigh into bitesize pieces and set aside.

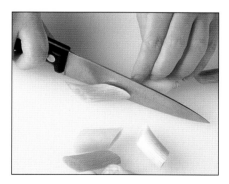

**3** Cut the spring onions into 3cm/1¼ in pieces. Preheat the grill (broiler) or prepare the barbecue.

**COOK'S TIP**
If shichimi is difficult to obtain, paprika can be used instead.

**4** Thread the chicken and spring onions alternately on to the drained skewers. Grill (broil) under a medium heat or cook on the barbecue, brushing generously several times with the sauce. Allow 5–10 minutes, or until the chicken is cooked but still moist.

**5** Serve with yakitori sauce, offering shichimi with the kebabs if available.

**VARIATION**
Bitesize chunks of turkey breast, lean boneless pork or lamb fillet can be used instead of chicken. Small, whole button (white) mushrooms are also delicious for a vegetarian alternative.

# brunches, lunches and fork suppers

Stylish dishes that are understated and easy to eat go down well for these light meal occasions, bringing a sophisticated touch to informal entertaining.

# Scrambled Eggs with Smoked Salmon

For a luxury brunch, you cannot beat this special combination. Try it with a glass of champagne or sparkling wine mixed with freshly squeezed orange juice.

**Serves 8**

8 slices of pumpernickel or wholemeal (whole-wheat) bread, crusts trimmed
115g/4oz/½ cup butter
250g/9oz thinly sliced smoked salmon
12 eggs
90–120ml/6–8 tbsp double (heavy) cream
120ml/8 tbsp crème fraîche
salt and ground black pepper
generous 120ml/8 tbsp lumpfish roe or salmon caviar and sprigs of dill, to garnish

**VARIATION**
Another real treat is to grate a little fresh truffle into the scrambled eggs.

**1** Spread the slices of bread with half of the butter and put on to eight individual plates. Arrange the smoked salmon on top and cut each slice in half. Set aside while you make the scrambled eggs.

**2** Lightly beat the eggs together and season with salt and freshly ground black pepper. Melt the remaining butter in a pan until it is sizzling, then quickly pour in the beaten eggs stirring vigorously with a wooden spoon all the time. Do not let the eggs burn.

**3** Stir constantly until the eggs begin to thicken. Just before they have finished cooking, stir in the cream.

**4** Remove the pan from the heat and stir in the crème fraîche, add more salt and ground black pepper to taste.

**5** Spoon the scrambled eggs on to the smoked salmon and bread on each plate. Top each serving with a spoonful of lumpfish roe or the salmon caviar and garnish with fresh sprigs of dill. Serve immediately.

# Egg Crostini with Rouille

Crostini are extremely quick to make so are perfect for breakfast or brunch. The rouille gives them a hint of a Mediterranean flavour and provides the perfect complement to lightly fried eggs.

**Serves 8**

8 slices of ciabatta bread
extra virgin olive oil, for brushing
90ml/6 tbsp home-made mayonnaise
10ml/2 tsp harissa
8 eggs
8 small slices smoked ham
watercress or salad leaves, to serve

**COOK'S TIP**
Harissa is a fiery North African chilli paste made from dried red chillies, cumin, garlic, coriander, caraway and olive oil.

**1** Preheat the oven to 200°C/400°F/ Gas 6. Use a pastry brush to lightly brush each slice of ciabatta bread with a little olive oil. Place the bread on a baking sheet and bake for 10 minutes, or until crisp and turning golden brown.

**VARIATION**
You can use 4 small portions of smoked haddock instead of ham and poach them for 5–7 minutes.

**2** Meanwhile, make the rouille. Put the mayonnaise and harissa in a small bowl and mix well together.

**3** Fry the eggs lightly in a little oil in a large non-stick frying pan.

**4** Top the baked bread with the ham, eggs and a small spoonful of rouille. Serve immediately with watercress or salad leaves.

# Polpettes

Little fried mouthfuls of potato and tangy-sharp Greek feta cheese, flavoured with dill and lemon juice are ideal to serve for lunch or supper.

**Makes 12**

500g/1¼lb floury potatoes
115g/4oz/1 cup feta cheese
4 spring onions (scallions), chopped
45ml/3 tbsp chopped fresh dill
1 egg, beaten
15ml/1 tbsp lemon juice
plain (all-purpose) flour, for dredging
45ml/3 tbsp olive oil
salt and ground black pepper
dill sprigs and shredded spring onions,
  to garnish
lemon wedges, to serve

**1** Cook the potatoes in their skins in boiling lightly salted water until soft. Drain and leave to cool, then chop them in half and peel while still warm.

### COOK'S TIP
To save time fry the polpettes in advance, cool and chill until required. Reheat in the oven before serving.

**2** Place the potatoes in a bowl and mash until smooth. Crumble the feta cheese into the potatoes and add the spring onions, dill, egg and lemon juice and season with salt and pepper. (The cheese is salty, so taste before you add salt.) Stir well, until combined.

**3** Cover and chill until firm. Divide the mixture into walnut-size balls, then flatten them slightly. Dredge with flour, shaking off the excess.

**4** Heat the oil in a large frying pan and fry the polpettes in batches until golden brown on both sides. Drain on kitchen paper and serve hot, garnished with spring onions and sprigs of dill, and serve with lemon wedges.

# Cheese and Leek Sausages with Chilli and Tomato Sauce

These popular vegetarian sausages served with a spicy sauce flavoured with chilli and balsamic vinegar are bound to be a hit for an informal lunch or supper.

**Makes 12**

*25g/1oz/2 tbsp butter*
*175g/6oz leeks, finely chopped*
*90ml/6 tbsp cold mashed potato*
*115g/4oz/2 cups fresh white*
*    breadcrumbs*
*150g/5oz/1¼ cups grated Caerphilly,*
*    Cheddar or Cantal cheese*
*30ml/2 tbsp chopped fresh parsley*
*5ml/1 tsp chopped fresh sage or*
*    marjoram*
*2 large (US extra large) eggs, beaten*
*good pinch of cayenne pepper*
*65g/2½oz/1 cup dry white*
*    breadcrumbs*
*oil, for shallow frying*
*salt and ground black pepper*

**For the sauce**
*30ml/2 tbsp olive oil*
*2 garlic cloves, thinly sliced*
*1 fresh red chilli, seeded and finely*
*    chopped, or a good pinch of dried*
*    red chilli flakes*
*1 small onion, finely chopped*
*500g/1¼lb tomatoes, peeled,*
*    seeded and chopped*
*a few fresh thyme sprigs*
*10ml/2 tsp balsamic vinegar or red*
*    wine vinegar*
*pinch of light muscovado*
*    (brown) sugar*
*15–30ml/1–2 tbsp chopped fresh*
*    marjoram or oregano*

**COOK'S TIP**
These sausages are also delicious when they are served with a fruity chilli salsa and a watercress salad.

**1** Melt the butter in a frying pan and fry the leeks for 4–5 minutes, or until softened but not browned. Mix with the mashed potato, fresh breadcrumbs, grated cheese, chopped parsley and sage or marjoram.

**2** Add sufficient beaten egg (about two-thirds of the quantity) to bind the mixture together. Season well and add the cayenne pepper to taste.

**3** Pat or roll the mixture between dampened hands to form 12 sausage shapes. Dip in the remaining egg, then coat in the dry breadcrumbs. Chill the coated sausages.

**4** Make the sauce. Heat the oil in a pan and cook the garlic, chilli and onion over a low heat for 3–4 minutes. Add the tomatoes, thyme and vinegar. Season with salt, pepper and sugar.

**5** Cook the sauce for 40–50 minutes, or until considerably reduced. Remove the thyme and purée the sauce in a food processor or blender. Reheat with the marjoram or oregano and then adjust the seasoning.

**6** Fry the sausages in shallow oil until golden brown on all sides. Drain on kitchen paper and serve with the sauce.

# Leek Roulade with Cheese, Walnut and Sweet Pepper Filling

This roulade is easy to prepare and is ideal for brunch or a vegetarian main course, served with home-made tomato sauce.

**Serves 6**

*butter or oil, for greasing*
*30ml/2 tbsp dry white breadcrumbs*
*75g/3oz/1 cup grated Parmesan cheese*
*50g/2oz/¼ cup butter*
*2 leeks, thinly sliced*
*40g/1½oz/⅓ cup plain*
  *(all-purpose) flour*
*250ml/8fl oz/1 cup milk*
*5ml/1 tsp Dijon mustard*
*1.5ml/¼ tsp freshly grated nutmeg*
*2 large (US extra large) eggs,*
  *separated, plus 1 egg white*
*2.5ml/½ tsp cream of tartar*
*salt and ground black pepper*
*rocket (arugula) and balsamic dressing,*
  *to serve*

### For the filling
*2 large red (bell) peppers*
*350g/12oz/1½ cups ricotta cheese,*
  *curd cheese or soft goat's cheese*
*90g/3½oz/scant 1 cup chopped walnuts*
*4 spring onions (scallions), chopped*
*15g/½oz fresh basil leaves*

**1** Grease and line a 30 x 23cm/12 x 9in Swiss roll tin (jelly roll pan) with baking parchment, then sprinkle with the breadcrumbs and 30ml/2 tbsp of the grated Parmesan. Preheat the oven to 190°C/375°F/Gas 5.

**2** Melt the butter in a pan and fry the leeks for 5 minutes, until softened.

**3** Stir in the flour and cook over a low heat, stirring constantly, for 2 minutes, then gradually stir in the milk. Cook for 3–4 minutes, stirring constantly to make a thick sauce.

**4** Stir in the mustard and nutmeg and season with salt and plenty of pepper. Reserve 30–45ml/2–3 tbsp of the remaining Parmesan, then stir the rest into the sauce. Cool slightly.

**5** Beat the egg yolks into the sauce. In a clean bowl, whisk the egg whites and cream of tartar until stiff. Stir 2–3 spoonfuls of the egg white into the leek mixture, then carefully fold in the remaining egg white.

**6** Pour the mixture into the tin and gently level it out using a spatula. Bake for 15–18 minutes, until risen and just firm to a light touch in the centre. If the roulade is to be served hot, increase the oven temperature to 200°C/400°F/Gas 6 after removing the roulade.

**7** Heat the grill (broiler). Halve and seed the peppers, grill (broil) them, skin sides uppermost, until black. Place in a bowl, cover and leave for 10 minutes. Peel and cut the flesh into strips. Mix the cheese, nuts and spring onions. Chop half the basil and stir into the mix.

**8** Sprinkle the remaining Parmesan on to a large sheet of baking parchment. Turn out the roulade on to it. Strip off the lining paper and allow the roulade to cool. Spread the cheese mixture over it and top with the red pepper strips. Sprinkle the remaining basil leaves over the top. Roll up the roulade and place on to a platter. If serving hot, roll it on to a baking sheet, cover with a tent of foil and bake for 15–20 minutes. Serve with rocket and drizzle with dressing.

# Potato and Red Pepper Frittata

For a light and easy-to-make lunch or a quick informal supper with plenty of flavour and colour this frittata will certainly fit the bill. Serve it with a mixed salad to complement the crisp flavours of the fresh mint sprigs and red peppers. You can also make this a day in advance to take to a picnic or serve at a barbecue.

### Serves 6 to 8

*900g/2lb small new or salad potatoes*
*12 eggs*
*60ml/4 tbsp chopped fresh mint*
*60ml/4 tbsp olive oil*
*2 onions, chopped*
*4 garlic cloves, crushed*
*4 red (bell) peppers, seeded and*
*roughly chopped*
*salt and ground black pepper*
*mint sprigs and crisp bacon, to garnish*

**1** Cook the potatoes in their skins in a large pan of lightly salted boiling water until they are just tender. Drain and leave to cool slightly, then cut the potaotes into thick slices.

**2** Whisk together half the eggs, mint and seasoning in a large bowl, then set aside. Heat 30ml/2 tbsp oil in a large frying pan that can be safely used under the grill (broiler).

**3** Add half the onion, garlic, peppers and potatoes to the pan and cook, stirring occasionally, for 5 minutes.

**4** Pour the egg mixture into the frying pan and stir gently. Gently push the mixture towards the centre of the pan as it cooks to allow the liquid egg to run on to the base and cook through completely. Meanwhile, preheat the grill (broiler).

**5** When the frittata is lightly set, place the pan under the hot grill for 2–3 minutes, or until the top is a light golden brown colour.

**6** Make another frittata with the other half of the ingredients.

**7** Serve hot or cold, cut into wedges piled high on a serving dish and garnished with mint and crisp bacon.

### VARIATIONS

Lightly cooked broccoli florets, cut quite small, are delicious with or instead of peppers in this frittata. Roughly chopped black olives also go well with both peppers and broccoli.

# Smoked Fish and Asparagus Mousse

This elegant mousse looks good with its studding of asparagus and smoked salmon. Serve a mustard and dill dressing separately if you like.

**Serves 8**

15ml/1 tbsp powdered gelatine
juice of 1 lemon
105ml/7 tbsp fish stock
50g/2oz/¼ cup butter, plus extra
    for greasing
2 shallots, finely chopped
225g/8oz smoked trout fillets
105ml/7 tbsp sour cream
225g/8oz/1 cup cream cheese or
    cottage cheese
1 egg white
12 spinach leaves, blanched
12 fresh asparagus spears,
    lightly cooked
115g/4oz smoked salmon, in strips
salt
shredded beetroot (beet) and beetroot
    leaves, to garnish

**1** Sprinkle the gelatine over the lemon juice and leave until spongy. In a small pan, heat the fish stock, then add the soaked gelatine and stir to dissolve completely. Set aside. Melt the butter in a pan, add the shallots and cook gently until softened but not coloured.

**2** Break up the smoked trout fillets and put them in a food processor with the shallots, sour cream, stock mixture and cream or cottage cheese. Whizz until smooth, then spoon into a bowl.

**3** In a clean bowl, beat the egg white with a pinch of salt to soft peaks. Fold into the fish. Cover the bowl; chill for 30 minutes, or until starting to set.

**4** Grease a 1 litre/1¾ pint/4 cup loaf tin (pan) or terrine with butter, then line it with the spinach leaves. Carefully spread half the trout mousse over the spinach-covered base, arrange the asparagus spears on top, then cover with the remaining trout mousse.

**5** Arrange the smoked salmon strips lengthways on the mousse and fold over the overhanging spinach leaves. Cover with clear film (plastic wrap) and chill for 4 hours, until set. To serve, remove the clear film, turn out on to a serving dish and garnish with the shredded beetroot and leaves.

**COOK'S TIP**
Use a serrated knife with a fine-toothed blade to cut the mousse into neat slices.

# Leek, Saffron and Mussel Tartlets

Serve these vividly coloured little tarts with cherry tomatoes and a few salad leaves, such as watercress, rocket and frisée.

**Makes 12**

*4 large yellow (bell) peppers, halved*
   *and seeded*
*2kg/4½lb mussels, scrubbed and*
   *beards removed*
*large pinch of saffron threads*
   *(about 30 strands)*
*30ml/2 tbsp hot water*
*4 large leeks, sliced*
*60ml/4 tbsp olive oil*
*4 large (US extra large) eggs*
*600ml/1 pint/2½ cups single*
   *(light) cream*
*60ml/4 tbsp finely chopped*
   *fresh parsley*
*salt and ground black pepper*
*salad leaves, to serve*

**For the pastry**
*450g/1lb/4 cups plain*
   *(all-purpose) flour*
*5ml/1 tsp salt*
*250g/8oz/1 cup butter, diced*
*30–45ml/2–3 tbsp water*

**1** To make the pastry, mix together the flour, salt and butter. Using your fingertips to rub the butter into the flour until the mixture resembles fine breadcrumbs. Mix in the water and knead lightly to form a firm dough. Wrap the dough in clear film (plastic wrap) and chill for 30 minutes.

**2** Grill (broil) the pepper halves, skin sides uppermost, until they are black. Place the peppers in a bowl, cover and leave for 10 minutes. When they are cool enough to handle, peel and cut the flesh into thin strips.

**3** Scrub the mussel shells with a brush and rinse in cold running water.

**4** Preheat the oven to 190°C/375°F/ Gas 5. Roll out the pastry and use it to line 12 x 10cm/4in tartlet tins, 2.5cm/ 1in deep. Prick the bases and then line the sides with strips of aluminium foil. Bake the pastry cases for 10 minutes. Remove the foil and bake for another 5–8 minutes, or until they are lightly coloured. Remove them from the oven. Reduce the oven temperature to 180°C/350°F/Gas 4.

**5** Soak the saffron in the hot water for 10 minutes. Fry the leeks in the oil over a medium heat for 6–8 minutes until beginning to brown. Add the pepper strips and cook for another 2 minutes.

**6** Bring 2.5cm/1in depth of water to a rolling boil in a large pan and add 10ml/2 tsp salt. Discard any open mussels that do not shut when tapped sharply, then throw the rest into the pan. Cover and cook over a high heat, shaking the pan occasionally, for 3–4 minutes, or until the mussels open. Discard any mussels that do not open. Shell the remainder.

**7** Beat the eggs, cream and saffron liquid together. Season and whisk in the parsley. Arrange the leeks, peppers and mussels in the pastry, add the egg mixture and bake for 20–25 minutes, until just firm. Serve with salad leaves.

# Roasted Vegetable and Garlic Sausage Loaf

Stuffed with cured meat and roasted vegetables, this crusty cob loaf makes a colourful centrepiece for a casual summer lunch or picnic. Serve with fresh green salad leaves.

### Serves 6

*1 large cob loaf*
*2 red (bell) peppers, quartered*
*   and seeded*
*1 large leek, sliced*
*90ml/6 tbsp olive oil*
*175g/6oz green beans, blanched*
*   and drained*
*75g/3oz garlic sausage, sliced*
*2 eggs, hard-boiled and quartered*
*115g/4oz/1 cup cashew nuts, toasted*
*75g/3oz/⅓ cup soft white (farmer's)*
*   cheese with garlic and herbs*
*salt and ground black pepper*

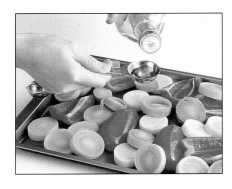

**1** Preheat the oven to 220°C/425°F/ Gas 7. Slice the top off the loaf using a large serrated knife and set it aside, then cut out the soft centre, leaving the crust intact. Stand the crusty shell on a baking sheet.

### COOK'S TIP

Do not throw away the soft centre of the loaf. It can be made into breadcrumbs and frozen for use in another recipe.

**2** Put the red peppers and sliced leek in a roasting pan with the olive oil and cook for 25–30 minutes, turning occasionally, or until the peppers have softened.

**3** Spoon half of the pepper and leek mixture into the bottom of the loaf shell, pressing it down well with the back of a spoon. Add the green beans, garlic sausage, eggs and cashew nuts, packing the layers down well. Season each layer with salt and ground black pepper before adding the next. Dot the soft cheese with garlic and herbs over the filling and top with the remaining pepper and leek mixture.

**4** Replace the top of the loaf and bake it for 15–20 minutes, or until the filling is warmed through. Serve, cut into wedges or slices.

### VARIATION

You can use a variety of different-shaped loaves, such as a large, uncut white or wholemeal (whole-wheat) sandwich loaf, for this recipe. Hollow out the loaf and fill as above, then cut into slices.

# Quiche Lorraine

This classic quiche from eastern France is perfect to serve at a relaxed lunch party. This recipe retains the traditional characteristics that are often forgotten in modern recipes, namely very thin pastry, a really creamy and light, egg-rich filling and smoked bacon.

## Serves 6 to 8

*175g/6oz/1½ cups plain (all-purpose) flour, sifted*
*pinch of salt*
*115g/4oz/½ cup unsalted (sweet) butter, at room temperature, diced*
*3 eggs, plus 3 yolks*
*6 smoked streaky (fatty) bacon rashers (strips), rinds removed*
*300ml/½ pint/1¼ cups double (heavy) cream*
*25g/1oz/2 tbsp unsalted (sweet) butter*
*salt and ground black pepper*

**1** Place the flour, salt, butter and 1 egg yolk in a food processor and process until blended. Tip out on to a floured surface and bring the mixture together into a ball. Leave to rest for 20 minutes.

**2** Lightly flour a deep 20cm/8in round flan tin, and place it on a baking tray. Roll out the pastry and use to line the tin, trimming off any overhanging pieces. Press the pastry into the corners of the tin. If the pastry breaks up just gently push it into shape. Chill for 20 minutes. Preheat the oven to 200°C/400°F/Gas 6.

**3** Meanwhile, cut the bacon into thin strips and grill (broil) until the fat runs. Arrange the bacon in the pastry case. Beat together the cream, the remaining eggs and yolks and seasoning, and pour into the pastry case.

**4** Bake for 15 minutes, then reduce the heat to 180°C/350°F/Gas 4 and bake for a further 15–20 minutes. When the filling is puffed up and golden brown and the pastry edge crisp, remove from the oven and top with knobs of butter. Stand for 5 minutes before serving.

# Chicken Fajitas with Grilled Onions

Classic fajitas are fun to eat with friends and make a good choice for an informal supper.

**Serves 6**

finely grated rind of 1 lime and the
    juice of 2 limes
120ml/4fl oz/½ cup olive oil
1 garlic clove, finely chopped
2.5ml/½ tsp dried oregano
good pinch of dried red chilli flakes
5ml/1 tsp coriander seeds, crushed
6 chicken breast fillets
3 Spanish onions, thickly sliced
2 large red, yellow or orange (bell)
    peppers, seeded and cut into strips
30ml/2 tbsp chopped fresh
    coriander (cilantro)
salt and ground black pepper

### For the tomato salsa

450g/1lb tomatoes, peeled, seeded
    and chopped
2 garlic cloves, finely chopped
1 small red onion, finely chopped
1–2 green chillies, seeded and chopped
finely grated rind of ½ lime
30ml/2 tbsp chopped fresh coriander
    (cilantro)
pinch of caster (superfine) sugar
2.5–5ml/½–1 tsp ground roasted
    cumin seeds

### To serve

12–18 soft flour tortillas
guacamole
120ml/4fl oz/½ cup sour cream
crisp lettuce leaves
coriander sprigs and lime wedges

**1** In an ovenproof dish, combine the lime rind and juice, 75ml/5 tbsp of the oil, the garlic, oregano, chilli flakes and coriander seeds and season. Slash the skin on the chicken breast fillets several times and turn them in the mixture, then cover and set aside to marinate for several hours.

**2** To make the salsa, combine the tomatoes, garlic, onion, chillies, lime rind and chopped coriander. Season to taste with salt, pepper, caster sugar and cumin seeds. Set aside for 30 minutes, then taste and adjust the seasoning, adding more cumin and sugar, if necessary.

**3** Heat the grill (broiler). Thread the onion slices on to a skewer or place them on a grill rack. Brush with 15ml/ 1 tbsp of the remaining oil and season. Grill (broil) until softened and slightly charred in places. Preheat the oven to 200°C/400°F/Gas 6.

**4** Cook the chicken breast fillets in their marinade, covered, in the oven for 20 minutes. Remove from the oven, then grill (broil) the chicken for 8–10 minutes, or until browned and fully cooked right through.

**5** Meanwhile, heat the remaining oil in a large frying pan and cook the peppers for about 10 minutes, or until softened and browned in places. Add the grilled onions and fry for 2–3 minutes.

**6** Add the chicken cooking juices and fry over a high heat, stirring frequently, until the liquid evaporates. Stir in the chopped coriander.

**7** Reheat the tortillas following the instructions on the packet. Using a sharp knife, cut the grilled chicken into strips and transfer to a serving dish. Place the onion and pepper mixture and the salsa in separate dishes.

**8** Serve the dishes of chicken, onions and peppers and salsa with the tortillas, guacamole, sour cream, lettuce and coriander for people to help themselves. Serve with lime wedges.

# Turkey Croquettes

Smoked turkey gives these crisp croquettes a distinctive flavour. Served with the tangy tomato sauce, crispy bread and salad they make a tasty fork supper.

**Makes 8**

450g/1lb maincrop potatoes, diced
3 eggs
30ml/2 tbsp milk
175g/6oz smoked turkey rashers
   (strips), finely chopped
2 spring onions (scallions), finely sliced
115g/4oz/2 cups fresh white
   breadcrumbs
vegetable oil, for deep fat frying
salt and ground black pepper

**For the sauce**
15ml/1 tbsp olive oil
1 onion, finely chopped
400g/14oz can tomatoes, drained
30ml/2 tbsp tomato purée (paste)
15ml/1 tbsp chopped fresh parsley

**1** Boil the potatoes until tender. Drain and return the pan to a low heat to make sure all the excess water evaporates.

**2** Mash the potatoes with two eggs and the milk. Season well with salt and pepper. Stir in the turkey rashers and spring onions. Chill for 1 hour.

**3** To make the sauce heat the oil in a frying pan and fry the onion until softened. Add the tomatoes and tomato purée, stir and simmer for 10 minutes. Stir in the parsley and season Keep the sauce warm until needed.

**4** Remove the potato mixture from the refrigerator and divide into eight pieces. Shape each piece into a sausage and dip in the remaining beaten egg and then the breadcrumbs.

**5** Heat the vegetable oil in a pan or deep-fat fryer to 190°C/375°F. Test this by dropping a cube of day-old bread into the hot oil, it should brown in 60 seconds. Deep-fry the croquettes for 5 minutes, or until they are golden and crisp. Reheat the sauce gently, if necessary, and serve with the freshly cooked croquettes.

# buffet
# centrepieces

These impressive buffet dishes will stand out among salads and accompaniments. They are fuss-free for self-service and delicious to eat.

# Potato and Leek Filo Pie

This filo pastry pie filled with a wonderful mixture of potatoes, leeks, cheese, cream and herbs, makes an attractive and unusual centrepiece for a vegetarian buffet. Serve it cold, together with a choice of different salads.

### Serves 8

800g/1¾ lb new potatoes, sliced
400g/14oz leeks (trimmed weight)
75g/3oz/6 tbsp butter
15g/½ oz/¼ cup finely chopped
    fresh parsley
60ml/4 tbsp chopped mixed fresh
    herbs, such as chervil, chives,
    a little tarragon and basil
12 sheets filo pastry, thawed if frozen
150g/5oz white Cheshire, Lancashire
    or Sonoma Jack cheese, sliced
2 garlic cloves, finely chopped
250ml/8fl oz/1 cup double
    (heavy) cream
2 large (US extra large) egg yolks
salt and ground black pepper

**1** Preheat the oven to 190°C/375°F/ Gas 5. Cook the potatoes in boiling, lightly salted water for 3–4 minutes, then drain and set aside.

**2** Thinly slice the leeks. Melt 25g/1oz/ 2 tbsp of the butter in a frying pan and fry the leeks gently over a low heat, stirring occasionally, until softened. Remove from the heat and season with pepper and stir in half the parsley and half the mixed herbs.

**3** Melt the remaining butter. Line a 23cm/9in loose-bottomed metal cake tin (pan) with six sheets of filo pastry, brushing each layer with butter. Allow the edges of the pastry to overhang the tin.

**4** Layer the potatoes, leeks and cheese in the tin, sprinkling a few herbs and the garlic between the layers. Season.

**5** Flip the overhanging pastry over the filling and cover with another two sheets of filo pastry, tucking in the sides to fit, and brush with melted butter as before. Cover the pie loosely with foil and bake for 35 minutes. (Keep the remaining pastry covered with a plastic bag and a damp cloth.)

**6** Meanwhile beat the cream, egg yolks and remaining herbs together. Make a hole in the centre of the pie and gradually pour in the eggs and cream.

**7** Arrange the remaining pastry on top, teasing it into swirls and folds, then brush with melted butter.

**8** Reduce the oven temperature to 180°C/350°F/Gas 4 and bake the pie for another 25–30 minutes, or until the top is golden and crisp. Allow to cool before serving.

### COOK'S TIP

Serve this pie with a spicy tomato sauce. Fry 1 chopped onion in 15ml/1 tbsp olive oil for 3 minutes, add 1 chopped garlic clove and cook for 2 minutes. Stir in 400g/14oz can chopped tomatoes and 5ml/1 tsp hot chilli powder. Simmer for 15–20 minutes or until thickened.

### VARIATIONS

• Reduce the quantity of leeks to 225g/8oz. Cook 1kg/2¼lb washed spinach in a covered pan over a high heat for 3–4 minutes, shaking the pan frequently. Drain, chop and mix with the cooked leeks.

• Reduce the quantity of leeks to 225g/8oz. Blanch 450g/1lb small broccoli florets in boiling water for 1 minute. Drain and add to the leeks.

• For a punchy flavour, use blue cheese, such as Stilton or Danish Blue, instead of white cheese. Crumble the cheese rather than slicing it.

# Baked Salmon with Watercress Sauce

A whole baked salmon makes a stunning centrepiece for a buffet. Baking it in foil is easier than poaching and yet the flesh has a similar melting quality. If you decorate the fish with thin slices of cucumber it will add a delicate touch to its appearance.

## Serves 6 to 8

2–3kg/4½–6½lb salmon, cleaned
   with head and tail left on
3–5 spring onions (scallions),
   thinly sliced
1 lemon, thinly sliced
1 cucumber, thinly sliced
fresh dill sprigs, to garnish
lemon wedges, to serve
salt and ground black pepper

### For the sauce
3 garlic cloves, chopped
200g/7oz watercress leaves,
   finely chopped
40g/1½oz/¾ cup finely chopped
   fresh tarragon
300g/11oz mayonnaise
15–30ml/1–2 tbsp freshly squeezed
   lemon juice
200g/7oz/scant 1 cup unsalted
   (sweet) butter

**1** Preheat the oven to 180°C/350°F/ Gas 4. Rinse the salmon and lay it on a large piece of foil. Stuff the fish with the sliced spring onions and layer the lemon slices inside and around the fish, then sprinkle with salt and pepper.

**2** Loosely fold the foil around the fish and fold the edges over to seal. Bake for about 1 hour.

**3** Remove the fish from the oven and leave it to stand, still wrapped in the foil, for about 15 minutes. Then unwrap the foil parcel and leave the salmon to cool.

**4** When the fish is cool, carefully lift it on to a large plate, still covered with lemon slices. Cover the fish tightly with clear film (plastic wrap) and chill for several hours in the refrigerator.

**5** Use a blunt knife to lift up the edge of the skin and carefully peel the skin away from the flesh, avoiding tearing the flesh. Pull out any fins at the same time. Carefully turn over the salmon and repeat on the other side. Leave the head on for serving, if you wish. Discard the skin.

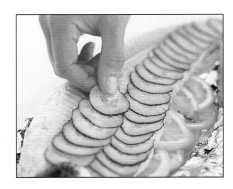

**6** Arrange the cucumber slices in overlapping rows along the length of the fish, so that they look like large fish scales.

**7** To make the sauce, put the garlic, watercress, tarragon, mayonnaise and lemon juice in a food processor or blender or a bowl, and process or mix to combine.

**8** Melt the butter, then add to the watercress mixture, a little at a time, processing or stirring, until the butter has been incorporated and the sauce is thick and smooth. Cover and chill before serving.

**9** Serve the fish, garnished with dill and lemon wedges, and the watercress sauce alongside.

### COOK'S TIP
Do not prepare the sauce more than a few hours ahead of serving as the watercress will discolour it.

### VARIATION
If you prefer to poach the fish rather than baking it you will need to use a fish kettle. Place the salmon on the rack, in the kettle. Cover with cold water and bring to a simmer, cook for 5–10 minutes per 450g/1lb until tender.

# Cider-glazed Ham

A succulent gammon joint with a sweet cider glaze that looks impressive and tastes wonderful. Served with a zesty cranberry sauce, it is ideal for a Christmas or Thanksgiving buffet, but is equally well suited to any festive occasion.

**Serves 8 to 10**

*2kg/4½ lb middle gammon joint*
*1 large or 2 small onions*
*about 30 whole cloves*
*3 bay leaves*
*10 black peppercorns*
*1.3 litres/2¼ pints/5⅔ cups*
*    medium-dry (hard) cider*
*45ml/3 tbsp soft light brown sugar*
*bunch of flat leaf parsley, to garnish*

**For the sauce**
*350g/12oz/3 cups cranberries*
*175g/6oz/¾ cup soft light brown sugar*
*grated rind and juice of 2 clementines*
*30ml/2 tbsp port*

**1** Weigh the gammon joint and calculate the cooking time at 20 minutes per 450g/1lb, then place it in a large casserole or pan. Stud the onion or onions with 5–10 of the cloves and add to the casserole or pan with the bay leaves and peppercorns.

**VARIATION**
Use clear honey in place of the soft brown sugar for the glaze and serve the ham with redcurrant sauce or jelly instead of the cranberry sauce.

**2** Add 1.2 litres/2 pints/5 cups of the cider and enough water to just cover the ham. Heat until simmering and then carefully skim off the scum that rises to the surface using a large spoon. Start timing the cooking from the moment the stock begins to simmer.

**3** Cover with a lid or foil and simmer gently for the calculated time. Towards the end of the cooking time, preheat the oven to 220°C/425°F/Gas 7.

**4** Heat the sugar and remaining cider in a pan; stir until the sugar has dissolved. Simmer for 5 minutes to make a dark, sticky glaze. Remove the pan from the heat and leave to cool for 5 minutes.

**COOK'S TIPS**
• A large stock pot or preserving pan can be used for cooking the ham.
• Leave the ham until it is just cool enough to handle before removing the rind. Snip off the string, then carefully slice off the rind, leaving a thin, even layer of fat. Use a narrow-bladed, sharp knife for the best results.

**5** Lift the ham out of the casserole or pan using a slotted spoon and a large fork. Carefully and evenly, cut the rind from the ham, then score the fat into a neat diamond pattern. Place the ham in a roasting pan or ovenproof dish.

**6** Press a clove into the centre of each diamond, then carefully spoon over the glaze. Bake for 20–25 minutes, or until the fat is brown, glistening and crisp.

**7** Simmer all the sauce ingredients in a heavy pan for 15–20 minutes, stirring frequently. Transfer the sauce to a jug.

**8** Serve the ham hot or cold, garnished with parsley and with the cranberry sauce accompaniment.

# Fillet of Beef with Ratatouille

This succulent beef is served cold with a colourful garlicky ratatouille.

**Serves 8**

675–900g/1½–2lb fillet of beef
45ml/3 tbsp olive oil
300ml/½ pint/1¼ cups aspic jelly, made
   up as packet instructions

**For the marinade**
30ml/2 tbsp sherry
30ml/2 tbsp olive oil
30ml/2 tbsp soy sauce
10ml/2 tsp grated fresh root ginger
   or 5ml/1 tsp ground ginger
2 garlic cloves, crushed

**For the ratatouille**
60ml/4 tbsp olive oil
1 onion, sliced
2–3 garlic cloves, crushed
1 large aubergine (eggplant), cubed
1 small red (bell) pepper, seeded
   and sliced
1 small green (bell) pepper, seeded
   and sliced
1 small yellow (bell) pepper, seeded
   and sliced
225g/8oz courgettes (zucchini), sliced
450g/1lb tomatoes, skinned
15ml/1 tbsp chopped fresh mixed herbs
30ml/2 tbsp French dressing
salt and ground black pepper

**1** Mix all the marinade ingredients together and pour over the beef. Cover the dish with clear film (plastic wrap) and leave for 30 minutes.

**2** Preheat the oven to 220°C/425°F/ Gas 7. Using a large slotted spoon, lift the fillet out of the marinade and pat it dry with kitchen paper. Heat the oil in a frying pan until smoking hot and then brown the beef all over to seal it.

**3** Transfer the beef to a roasting pan and roast for 10–15 minutes, basting it occasionally with the marinade. Lift the beef out on to a large plate and leave it to cool.

**4** Meanwhile, for the ratatouille, heat the oil in a large casserole and cook the onion and garlic over a low heat, until tender, without letting the onions become brown. Add the aubergine cubes to the casserole and cook for a further 5 minutes, until soft.

**5** Add the sliced peppers and the courgettes and cook for 2 minutes more. Then add the tomatoes and chopped herbs, and season well with salt and pepper. Cook for a few minutes longer. Turn the ratatouille into a dish and set aside to cool. Drizzle with a little French dressing.

**6** Slice the beef fillet and arrange overlapping slices on a large serving platter. Brush the slices of beef with a little cold aspic jelly that is just on the point of setting.

**7** Leave the aspic jelly to set completely, then brush the beef slices with a second coat. Spoon the cooled ratatouille around the beef slices on the platter and serve immediately.

**COOK'S TIP**

Ratatouille is a traditional French recipe that is at its best when made with the choicest fresh ingredients. It makes a wonderful side dish for a buffet or can be eaten as a snack, as a vegetarian filling for jacket potatoes.

**VARIATIONS**

• Instead of marinating the beef in soy sauce and ginger, add 15ml/1 tbsp chopped fresh marjoram to the mixture, increase the quantity of sherry to 60ml/ 4 tbsp and add 15ml/1 tbsp crushed juniper berries.

• Use pork instead of beef and increase the roasting time to 20–30 minutes.

# Rich Game Pie

Smart enough for a formal wedding buffet but also terrific for a stylish picnic, this rich game pie looks spectacular when baked in a fluted raised pie mould. Some specialist kitchen stores hire the moulds so you can avoid the expense of purchasing one; alternatively a 20cm/8in round deep, loose-bottomed tin can be used. Serve the pie garnished with salad leaves.

### Serves 10

25g/1oz/2 tbsp butter
1 onion, finely chopped
2 garlic cloves, finely chopped
900g/2lb mixed boneless game meat,
    such as skinless pheasant and/or
    pigeon breast, venison and
    rabbit, diced
30ml/2 tbsp chopped mixed fresh
    herbs, such as parsley, thyme
    and marjoram
salt and ground black pepper

### For the pâté

50g/2oz/¼ cup butter
2 garlic cloves, finely chopped
450g/1lb chicken livers, rinsed,
    trimmed and chopped
60ml/4 tbsp brandy
5ml/1 tsp ground mace

### For the pastry

675g/1½lb/6 cups strong plain
    (all-purpose) flour
5ml/1 tsp salt
115ml/3½fl oz/scant ½ cup milk
115ml/3½fl oz/scant ½ cup water
115g/4oz/½ cup white cooking
    fat, diced
115g/4oz/½ cup butter, diced
beaten egg, to glaze

### For the jelly

300ml/½ pint/1¼ cups game or
    beef consommé
2.5ml/½ tsp powdered gelatine

**1** Melt the butter in a small pan until foaming, then add the onion and garlic, and cook until softened but not coloured. Remove from the heat and mix with the diced game meat and the chopped mixed herbs. Season well, cover and chill.

**2** To make the pâté, melt the butter in a pan until foaming. Add the garlic and chicken livers and cook until the livers are just browned. Remove the pan from the heat and stir in the brandy and mace. Purée the mixture in a blender or food processor until smooth, then set aside and leave to cool completely.

**3** To make the pastry, sift the flour and salt into a bowl and make a well in the centre. Place the milk and water in a pan. Add the white cooking fat and butter and heat gently until melted, then bring to the boil and remove from the heat as soon as the mixture begins to bubble. Pour the hot liquid into the well in the flour and beat until smooth. Cover and leave until the dough is cool enough to handle.

**4** Preheat the oven to 200°C/400°F/Gas 6. Roll out two-thirds of the pastry and use to line a 23cm/9in raised pie mould. Press the pastry into the flutes in the mould and around the edge. Patch any thin areas with offcuts (scraps) from the top edge. Spoon in half the mixture and press it down evenly. Add the pâté and then top with the remaining game.

**5** Roll out the remaining pastry to form a lid. Brush the edge of the pastry lining the tin with a little water and cover the pie with the pastry lid. Trim off excess pastry from around the edge. Pinch the edges together to seal in the filling. Make two holes in the centre of the lid and glaze with egg. Use pastry trimmings to roll out leaves to garnish the pie. Brush with egg.

**6** Bake the pie for 20 minutes, then cover it with foil and cook for a further 10 minutes. Reduce the oven temperature to 150°C/300°F/Gas 2. Glaze the pie again with beaten egg and cook for a further 1½ hours, with the top covered loosely with foil.

**7** Remove the pie from the oven and leave it to stand for 15 minutes. Increase the oven temperature to 200°C/400°F/Gas 6. Stand the tin on a baking sheet and remove the sides. Quickly glaze the sides of the pie with beaten egg and cover the top with foil, then cook for a final 15 minutes to brown the sides. Leave to cool completely, then chill the pie overnight.

**8** To make the jelly, heat the game or beef consommé in a small pan until just beginning to bubble, whisk in the gelatine until dissolved and leave to cool until just setting. Using a small funnel, carefully pour the jellied consommé into the holes in the pie. Chill until set. This pie will keep in the refrigerator for up to 3 days.

# Turkey and Cranberry Pie

This is ideal for using up leftovers and the cranberries add a tart layer to this attractive pie. It needs to be made the day before, and it can even be frozen in advance.

### Serves 8

*450g/1lb pork sausage meat*
*  (bulk sausage)*
*450g/1lb/2 cups minced (ground) pork*
*15ml/1 tbsp ground coriander*
*15ml/1 tbsp mixed dried herbs*
*finely grated rind of 2 large oranges*
*10ml/2 tsp grated fresh root ginger or*
*  2.5ml/½ tsp ground ginger*
*450g/1lb turkey breast fillets, skinned*
*115g/4oz/1 cup fresh cranberries*
*salt and ground black pepper*

### For the pastry

*450g/1lb/4 cups plain (all-purpose) flour*
*5ml/1 tsp salt*
*150g/5oz/10 tbsp white cooking fat*
*150ml/¼ pint/⅔ cup mixed milk and*
*  water*

### To finish

*1 egg, beaten*
*300ml/½ pint/1¼ cups aspic jelly, made*
*  up as packet instructions*

**1** Preheat the oven to 180°C/350°F/ Gas 4. Place a large baking tray in the oven to preheat. In a large bowl, mix together the sausage meat, minced pork, coriander, mixed dried herbs, orange rind and ginger with plenty of salt and ground black pepper.

**2** To make the pastry, put the flour into a large bowl with the salt. Heat the fat in a small pan with the milk and water until just beginning to boil. Set aside and allow to cool slightly.

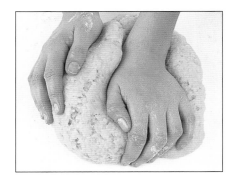

**3** Using a spoon, stir the liquid into the flour until a stiff dough forms. Turn on to a worksurface and knead until smooth. Cut one-third off the dough for the lid, wrap it in clear film (plastic wrap), and keep it in a warm place.

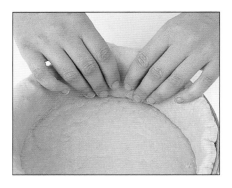

**4** Roll out the large piece of dough on a floured surface and line the base and sides of a well-greased 20cm/8in loose-bottomed, springform cake pan. Work the dough while it is warm, as it will crack and break if it is left to get cold.

**5** Thinly slice the turkey fillets and put between two pieces of clear film and flatten with a rolling pin to a 3mm/⅛in thickness. Spoon half the pork mixture into the base of the tin, pressing it well into the edges. Cover with half of the turkey slices and then the cranberries, followed by the remaining turkey and finally the rest of the pork mixture.

**6** Roll out the rest of the dough and cover the filling, trimming any excess and sealing the edges with beaten egg. Make a steam hole in the lid and decorate with pastry trimmings. Brush with beaten egg. Bake for 2 hours. Cover the pie with foil if it gets too brown. Place the pie on a wire rack to cool. When cold, use a funnel to fill the pie with aspic jelly. Allow to set for a few hours before unmoulding the pie.

### COOK'S TIPS

• Stand the springform pan on a baking tray with a shallow rim to catch any juices that may seep from the pie during baking.
• Leave the pie to cool in the pan until the pastry has firmed up slightly before transferring it to a wire rack.

# big dishes

Sharing a large dish with a few accompaniments or dipping into a classic one-pot meal is a sure way of having a memorable no-fuss meal with friends.

# Tofu and Vegetable Thai Curry

Traditional Thai ingredients –
chillies, galangal, lemon grass
and kaffir lime leaves – give this
vegetarian curry a wonderfully
fragrant aroma. It makes an
excellent main course when
served with boiled jasmine rice
or noodles.

**Serves 8**

*350g/12oz tofu, drained*
*90ml/6 tbsp dark soy sauce*
*30ml/2 tbsp sesame oil*
*10ml/2 tsp chilli sauce*
*5cm/2in piece fresh root ginger,*
*    finely grated*
*450g/1lb cauliflower*
*450g/1lb broccoli*
*60ml/4 tbsp vegetable oil*
*2 onions, peeled and sliced*
*750ml/1¼ pints/3 cups coconut milk*
*300ml/½ pint/1¼ cups water*
*2 red (bell) peppers, seeded*
*    and chopped*
*350g/12oz green beans, halved*
*225g/8oz/3 cups shiitake or button*
*    (white) mushrooms, halved*
*shredded spring onions (scallions),*
*    to garnish*
*boiled jasmine rice or noodles,*
*    to serve*

For the curry paste
*4 chillies, seeded and chopped*
*2 lemon grass stalks, chopped*
*5cm/2in piece fresh galangal, chopped*
*4 kaffir lime leaves*
*20ml/4 tsp ground coriander*
*a few sprigs fresh coriander (cilantro),*
*    including the stalks*

**1** Cut the drained tofu into 2.5cm/1in
cubes and place in an ovenproof dish.
Mix together the soy sauce, sesame oil,
chilli sauce and ginger and pour over
the tofu. Toss gently then marinate for
at least 2 hours or overnight, turning
and basting the tofu occasionally.

**2** To make the curry paste, blend the
chopped chillies, lemon grass, galangal,
kaffir lime leaves, ground and fresh
coriander in a food processor for a few
seconds. Add 90ml/6 tbsp water and
process to a thick paste.

**3** Preheat the oven to 190°C/375°F/
Gas 5. Using a sharp knife cut the
cauliflower and broccoli into florets
and cut any stalks into thin slices.

**4** Heat the vegetable oil in a frying pan,
add the sliced onions and gently fry for
about 8 minutes, or until soft and
lightly browned. Stir in the prepared
curry paste and the coconut milk. Add
the water and bring to the boil.

**5** Stir in the red peppers, green beans,
cauliflower and broccoli. Transfer to a
casserole. Cover and place in the oven.

**6** Stir the tofu and marinade, then place
the dish in the top of the oven and cook
for 30 minutes. Add the marinade
mixture and mushrooms to the curry.
Reduce the oven temperature to 180°C/
350°F/Gas 4 and cook for about 15
minutes, or until the vegetables are
tender. Garnish the curry with
shredded spring onions. Serve with
boiled jasmine rice or noodles.

# Swiss Cheese Fondue with Vegetables

This classic, richly flavoured fondue is traditionally served with cubes of bread, but here it is updated with herby vegetable dippers and toasted garlic croûtes.

### Serves 4 to 6

*2 French batons or 1 baguette*
*1–2 garlic cloves, halved*
*1 small head broccoli, divided*
  *into florets*
*1 small head cauliflower, divided*
  *into florets*
*200g/7oz mangetouts (snow peas)*
  *or green beans, trimmed*
*115g/4oz baby carrots, trimmed,*
  *or 2 medium carrots, cut into wedges*
*250ml/8fl oz/1 cup dry white wine*
*115g/4oz/1 cup grated Gruyère cheese*
*250ml/8fl oz/2¼ cups grated*
  *Emmenthal cheese*
*15ml/1tbsp cornflour (cornstarch)*
*30ml/2tbsp Kirsch*
*freshly grated nutmeg*
*salt and ground black pepper*

### For the dressing
*30ml/2 tbsp extra virgin olive oil*
*rind and juice of 2 lemons*
*25g/1oz/½ cup chopped fresh parsley*
*25g/1oz/½ cup chopped fresh mint*
*1 red chilli, seeded and finely chopped*

**1** Cut the batons or baguette on the diagonal into 1cm/½in slices, then toast on both sides. Rub one side of each slice with the cut side of a garlic clove, if you like, and transfer to a platter.

**2** Blanch all the vegetables for 2 minutes in a large pan of salted boiling water, then place them in a large bowl. While they are hot, add all the dressing ingredients, season, and toss together.

**3** Rub the inside of the fondue pot with the cut side of a garlic clove. Pour in the white wine and heat gently on the stove. Gradually add the grated cheeses to the pot, stirring constantly until melted. Mix the cornflour with the Kirsch and add, then stir until thickened.

**4** Season with salt, ground black pepper and grated nutmeg to taste. When the fondue is hot and smooth, but not boiling, transfer to a burner at the table.

**5** Each diner dips the vegetables and toasted bread into the fondue.

### VARIATIONS
• Use fresh chopped basil instead of mint.
• Use crunchy, fresh vegetables such as pink radishes, mushrooms, baby corn and red or yellow (bell) peppers.

# Seafood Laksa

A laksa is a Malaysian stew of fish, poultry, meat or vegetables with noodles. Authentic laksas are often very hot, and cooled by coconut milk and the noodles. If you prefer a hot and spicy version, add a little chilli powder instead of some of the paprika.

**Serves 8 to 10**

4 medium-hot fresh red chillies, seeded
6–8 garlic cloves
10ml/2 tsp mild paprika
20ml/4 tsp fermented shrimp paste
45ml/3 tbsp chopped fresh root
   ginger or galangal
500g/1¼ lb small red shallots
50g/2oz fresh coriander (cilantro),
   preferably with roots
90ml/6 tbsp groundnut (peanut) oil
10ml/2 tsp fennel seeds, crushed
4 fennel bulbs, cut into thin wedges
1.2 litres/2 pints/5 cups fish stock
600g/1 lb 6oz thin vermicelli
   rice noodles
900ml/1½ pints/3¾ cups coconut milk
juice of 2–4 limes
60–90ml/4–6 tbsp Thai fish sauce
   (nam pla)
900g/2lb firm white fish fillet, such as
   monkfish, halibut or snapper
900g/2lb large raw prawns (shrimp)
   (about 40), shelled and deveined
bunch of fresh basil
4 spring onions (scallions),
   thinly sliced

**1** Process the chillies, garlic, paprika, shrimp paste, ginger or galangal and four shallots to a paste in a food processor, blender or spice grinder. Remove the roots and stems from the coriander and add them to the paste; chop and reserve the coriander leaves. Add 30ml/2 tbsp of the groundnut oil to the paste and process again until fairly smooth.

**2** Heat the remaining oil in a large pan or stockpot. Add the remaining shallots, the fennel seeds and fennel wedges. Cook until lightly browned, then add 90ml/6 tbsp of the paste and stir-fry for about 2 minutes. Pour in the fish stock and bring to the boil. Reduce the heat and simmer for 8–10 minutes.

**3** Meanwhile, cook the vermicelli rice noodles according to the instructions on the packet. Drain and set aside.

**4** Pour the coconut milk into the pan of shallots, stirring continuously to prevent sticking, then add the juice of two limes, with 60ml/4 tbsp of the fish sauce. Stir well to combine. Bring to a simmer and taste, adding more of the curry paste, lime juice or fish sauce as necessary to taste.

**5** Cut the fish into chunks and add to the pan. Cook for 3–4 minutes, then add the prawns and cook until they turn pink. Chop most of the basil and add to the pan with the reserved chopped coriander leaves.

**6** Divide the noodles among 8–10 bowls, then ladle in the stew. Sprinkle with spring onions and the remaining whole basil leaves. Serve immediately.

# Tempura

This flavourful Japanese dish of crunchy battered vegetables and crispy squid rings is served with a piquant dipping sauce. Tempura can be cooked at the table over a special spillproof spirit burner making it ideal for a party.

### Serves 8 to 10

*2 medium aubergines (eggplant)*
*4 red (bell) peppers, seeded*
*500g/1¼ lb/5 cups plain (all-purpose)*
   *flour, plus extra for dusting*
*8 baby squid, cut into rings*
*400g/14oz green beans, trimmed*
*24 mint sprigs*
*oil, for deep-frying*
*4 egg yolks*
*1 litre/1¾ pints/4 cups iced water*
*10ml/2 tsp salt*
*gari (Japanese pickled ginger) or grated*
   *fresh root ginger, and grated daikon*
   *or pink radishes, to serve*

### For the dipping sauce
*400ml/14fl oz/1⅔ cups water*
*90ml/6 tbsp mirin or sweet sherry*
*20g/½oz bonito flakes (see Cook's Tip)*
*90ml/6 tbsp soy sauce*

**1** To make the dipping sauce, mix the sauce ingredients together in a pan, bring to the boil and then strain into serving saucers and leave to cool.

### COOK'S TIP
If you cannot get hold of bonito flakes, an acceptable substitute would be to use 200ml/7fl oz/scant 1 cup fish stock instead of the water to make the dipping sauce.

### VARIATIONS
• Any seafood is suitable for cooking in a tempura batter. Try mussels, clams, prawns (shrimp) or scallops, or slices of salmon, cod, tuna or haddock.
• Cauliflower, broccoli, and mangetouts (snow peas) work well, too.

**2** Cut the aubergine and peppers into fine julienne strips using a sharp knife or a mandolin. Put the flour for dusting into a plastic bag and add the squid. Shake the bag to coat the squid with a little flour, then place on a serving dish. Repeat with the vegetables and mint.

**3** Heat the oil for deep-frying in a wok or deep pan to 190°C/375°F. If you do not have a cook's thermometer, test by dropping a cube of day-old bread into the hot oil; it should brown in 30–60 seconds. Transfer to a burner at the table. Never leave it unattended.

**4** When ready to eat, beat the egg yolks and the iced water together. Tip in the flour and salt, and stir briefly. It is important that the tempura is lumpy and not mixed to a smooth batter.

**5** Each diner dips the food into the batter and then immediately into the hot oil using chopsticks, long fondue forks or wire baskets. Fry for 2 minutes, or until crisp.

**6** Serve the tempura dipped in the sauce and accompanied by gari or ginger and daikon or radishes.

# Celebration Paella

This paella is a marvellous mixture of some of the finest Spanish ingredients and makes a colourful one-pot party dish.

### Serves 6 to 8

6–8 large raw prawns (shrimp), peeled,
   or 12–16 smaller raw prawns
450g/1lb fresh mussels
90ml/6 tbsp white wine
150g/5oz green beans, cut into
   2.5cm/1in lengths
115g/4oz/1 cup frozen broad
   (fava) beans
6 small skinless chicken breast fillets,
   cut into large pieces
30ml/2 tbsp plain (all-purpose) flour,
   seasoned with salt and pepper
about 90ml/6 tbsp olive oil
150g/5oz pork fillet, cut into
   bitesize pieces
2 onions, chopped
2–3 garlic cloves, crushed
1 red (bell) pepper, seeded and sliced
2 ripe tomatoes, peeled, seeded
   and chopped
900ml/1½ pints/3¾ cups well-
   flavoured chicken stock
good pinch of saffron threads,
   dissolved in 30ml/2 tbsp hot water
350g/12oz/1¾ cups Spanish rice or
   risotto rice
225g/8oz chorizo, sliced
115g/4oz/1 cup frozen peas
6–8 stuffed green olives,
   thickly sliced
salt and ground black pepper

### COOK'S TIP

Ideally, you should use a paella pan for this recipe and the paella should not be stirred during cooking. However, you may find that the rice cooks in the centre but not around the outside. To make sure it cooks evenly stir occasionally, or cook the paella on the bottom of a hot 190°C/375°F/Gas 5 oven for about 15–18 minutes.

**1** Make a shallow cut down the centre of the curved back of each of the large prawns. Pull out the black veins with a cocktail stick (toothpick) or your fingers, then rinse the prawns thoroughly and set them aside.

**2** Scrub the mussels' shells with a stiff brush and rinse thoroughly under cold running water. Scrape off any barnacles and remove the "beards" with a small knife. Rinse well. Discard any mussels that are open and do not close when sharply tapped.

**3** Place the mussels in a large pan with the wine, bring to the boil, then cover the pan tightly and cook for 3–4 minutes, or until the mussels have opened, shaking the pan occasionally. Drain, reserving the liquid and discarding any mussels that remain closed.

**4** Briefly cook the green beans and broad beans in separate pans of boiling water for 2–3 minutes. Drain. As soon as the broad beans are cool enough to handle, pop the bright green inner beans out of their skins.

**5** Dust the chicken with the seasoned flour. Heat half the oil in a paella pan or frying pan and fry the chicken until browned all over. Transfer to a plate. Next, fry the prawns briefly, adding more oil if needed, use a slotted spoon to transfer them to a plate. Heat a further 30ml/2 tbsp of the oil in the pan and brown the pork. Transfer to a plate.

**6** Heat the remaining oil and fry the onions and garlic for 3–4 minutes, or until golden brown. Add the red pepper, cook for 2–3 minutes, then add the chopped tomatoes and cook until the mixture is fairly thick.

**7** Stir in the chicken stock, the reserved mussel liquid and the saffron liquid. Season well with salt and pepper and bring to the boil. When the liquid is bubbling, add the rice. Stir once, then add the chicken pieces, pork, prawns, beans, chorizo and peas. Cook over a moderately high heat for 12 minutes, then lower the heat and leave to cook for 8–10 minutes more, until all the liquid has been absorbed.

**8** Add the mussels and olives and continue cooking for a further 3–4 minutes to heat through. Remove the pan from the heat, cover with a clean damp dishtowel and leave the paella to stand for 10 minutes before serving from the pan.

# Mongolian Firepot

Cooking at the table in a firepot is a fun and sociable way to enjoy a meal with family or friends. It calls for plenty of participation on the part of the guests, who cook the assembled ingredients, dipping the meats in a variety of different sauces.

### Serves 6 to 8

*900g/2lb boned leg of lamb, preferably bought thinly sliced*
*225g/8oz lamb's liver and/or kidneys*
*900ml/1½ pints/3¾ cups lamb stock (see Cook's Tip)*
*900ml/1½ pints/3¾ cups chicken stock*
*1cm/½in piece fresh root ginger, peeled and thinly sliced*
*45ml/3 tbsp rice wine or medium-dry sherry*
*½ head Chinese leaves (Chinese cabbage), rinsed and shredded*
*few young spinach leaves*
*250g/9oz fresh firm tofu, diced (optional)*
*115g/4oz cellophane noodles*
*salt and ground black pepper*

### For the dipping sauce

*50ml/2fl oz/¼ cup red wine vinegar*
*7.5ml/1½ tsp dark soy sauce*
*1cm/½in piece fresh root ginger, peeled and finely shredded*
*1 spring onion (scallion), shredded*

### To serve

*bowls of tomato sauce, sweet chilli sauce, mustard oil and sesame oil*
*dry-fried coriander seeds, crushed*

### COOK'S TIP

To make lamb stock, place the leg bones in a large pan with water to cover. Bring to the boil and skim the surface. Add 1 peeled onion, 2 carrots, 1cm/½in piece of peeled and bruised ginger, 5ml/1 tsp salt and ground black pepper. Bring back to the boil, then simmer for about 1 hour. Strain, cool, then skim and use.

**1** When buying the lamb, ask your butcher to slice it thinly on a slicing machine, if possible. If you have had to buy the lamb in one piece, however, put it in the freezer for about an hour, so that it is easier to slice thinly.

**2** Trim the liver and remove the skin and core from the kidneys, if using. Place them in the freezer, too. If you managed to buy sliced lamb, keep it in the refrigerator until needed.

**3** Mix both types of stock in a large pan. Add the sliced ginger and rice wine or sherry, with salt and pepper to taste. Heat to simmering point; simmer for 15 minutes.

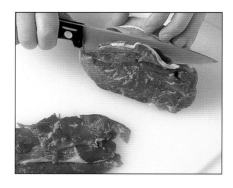

**4** Slice all the meats thinly and arrange them attractively on a large platter.

**5** Place the shredded Chinese leaves, spinach leaves and the diced tofu on a separate platter.

**6** Soak the noodles in warm or hot water, following the instructions given on the packet.

**7** Make the dipping sauce by mixing all the ingredients in a small bowl. The other sauces and the crushed coriander seeds should be spooned into separate small dishes and placed on a serving tray or on the table.

**8** When you are ready to eat, set the firepot on the dining table and light the burner. Fill the moat of the hotpot with the simmering stock. Alternatively, fill a fondue pot and place it over a burner. Remember never to leave the lighted burner unattended. Each guest selects a portion of meat from the platter and cooks it in the hot stock, using chopsticks, a little wire basket (usually sold alongside firepots) or a fondue fork. The meat is then dipped in one of the sauces and coated with the coriander seeds (if you like).

**9** When most of the meat has been eaten, top up the stock if necessary, then add the vegetables, tofu and drained noodles. Cook until the noodles are tender and the vegetables retain a little crispness. Serve the soup in warmed bowls.

# Beef Carbonade

This rich, dark stew of beef, cooked slowly with lots of onions, garlic and beer, is a classic one-pot casserole from the north of France and Belgium. Serve with roasted potatoes, if you like.

**Serves 6**

*45ml/3 tbsp vegetable oil or*
  *beef dripping*
*3 onions, sliced*
*45ml/3 tbsp plain (all-purpose) flour*
*2.5ml/½ tsp mustard powder*
*1kg/2¼lb stewing beef (shin or chuck),*
  *cut into large cubes*
*2–3 garlic cloves, finely chopped*
*300ml/½ pint/1¼ cups dark beer or ale*
*150ml/¼ pint/⅔ cup water*
*5ml/1 tsp dark brown sugar*
*1 fresh thyme sprig*
*1 fresh bay leaf*
*1 piece celery stick*
*salt and ground black pepper*

For the topping
*50g/2oz/½ cup butter*
*1 garlic clove, crushed*
*15ml/1 tbsp Dijon mustard*
*45ml/3 tbsp chopped fresh parsley*
*6–12 slices baguette or ficelle loaf*

**1** Preheat the oven to 160°C/325°F/ Gas 3. Heat 30ml/2 tbsp of the oil or dripping in a frying pan and cook the onions over a low heat until softened. Remove from the pan and set aside.

**2** Meanwhile, mix together the flour and mustard and season. Toss the beef in the flour. Add the remaining oil or dripping to the pan and heat over a high heat. Brown the beef all over, then transfer it to a casserole dish.

**COOK'S TIP**
When making more than double the quantity, limit the garlic cloves to 8 in total, otherwise the flavour is too strong.

**3** Reduce the heat and return the onions to the pan. Add the garlic, cook, then add the beer or ale, water and sugar. Tie the thyme and bay leaf together and add to the pan with the celery. Bring to the boil, stirring, then season.

**4** Pour the sauce over the beef and mix. Cover, then place in the oven for 2½ hours. Check the beef to make sure that it is not too dry, adding water, if necessary. Test for tenderness, allowing an extra 30–40 minutes' cooking time.

**5** To make the topping, cream the butter together with the garlic, mustard and 30ml/2 tbsp of the parsley. Spread the butter thickly over the bread.

**6** Increase the oven temperature to 190°C/375°F/Gas 5. Taste and season the casserole, then arrange the bread slices, buttered side uppermost, on top. Bake for 20–25 minutes, until the bread is browned. Sprinkle the remaining parsley over the top and serve.

# Moussaka

Layers of minced lamb, aubergines, tomatoes and onions are topped with a creamy yogurt and cheese sauce in this delicious, authentic eastern Mediterranean recipe. Serve with a simple, mixed leaf, green salad.

**Serves 8**

*900g/2lb aubergines (eggplant)*
*300ml/¹⁄₂ pint/1¹⁄₃ cups olive oil*
*2 large onions, chopped*
*4–6 garlic cloves, finely chopped*
*1.3kg/3lb lean minced (ground) lamb*
*30ml/2 tbsp plain (all-purpose) flour*
*2 x 400g/14oz cans chopped tomatoes*
*60ml/4 tbsp chopped mixed fresh*
   *herbs, such as parsley, marjoram*
   *and oregano*
*salt and ground black pepper*

**For the topping**
*600ml/1 pint/2¹⁄₂ cups natural (plain)*
   *yogurt*
*4 eggs*
*50g/2oz feta cheese, crumbled*
*50g/2oz/²⁄₃ cup grated Parmesan cheese*

**1** Cut the aubergines into thin slices and layer them in a colander, sprinkling each layer with salt.

**2** Cover the aubergines with a plate and a weight, then leave to drain for about 30 minutes. Drain and rinse well, then pat dry with kitchen paper.

**3** Heat 90ml/6 tbsp of the olive oil in a large, heavy pan. Fry the chopped onion and garlic until softened, but not coloured. Add the lamb and cook over a high heat, stirring often, until lightly browned.

**4** Stir in the flour until mixed, then stir in the tomatoes, herbs and seasoning. Bring to the boil, reduce the heat and simmer gently for 20 minutes.

**5** Meanwhile, heat a little of the remaining oil in a large frying pan. Add as many aubergine slices as can be laid in the pan, then cook until golden on both sides. Set the cooked aubergines aside. Heat more oil and continue frying the aubergines in batches, adding oil as necessary.

**6** Preheat the oven to 180°C/350°F/ Gas 4. Arrange half the aubergine slices in a large, shallow ovenproof dish or divide among two smaller dishes.

**7** Top the aubergine slices with about half of the meat and tomato mixture, then add the remaining aubergine slices. Spread the remaining meat mixture over the aubergines.

**8** Beat together the yogurt and eggs, mix in the feta and Parmesan cheeses, and spread the mixture over the meat.

**9** Transfer the moussaka to the oven and bake for 35–40 minutes, or until golden and bubbling.

# Lasagne with Three Cheeses

Mozzarella, ricotta and Parmesan cheeses make this lasagne rich and filling. Pasta meals such as these are always popular with adults and children alike so they make good fare for gatherings of family and friends.

**Serves 6 to 8**

25g/1oz/2 tbsp butter
15ml/1 tbsp olive oil
225–250g/8–9oz/2–2¼ cups button
 (white) mushrooms, quartered
30ml/2 tbsp chopped fresh flat
 leaf parsley
250–350ml/8–12fl oz/1–1½ cups
 hot beef stock
9–12 fresh or no pre-cook dried
 lasagne sheets
450g/1lb/2 cups ricotta cheese
1 large (US extra large) egg
3 x 130g/4½oz packets mozzarella
 cheese, drained and thinly sliced
115g/4oz/1¼ cups freshly grated
 Parmesan cheese
salt and ground black pepper

**For the bolognese sauce**
45ml/3 tbsp olive oil
1 onion, finely chopped
1 small carrot, finely chopped
1 celery stick, finely chopped
2 garlic cloves, finely chopped
400g/14oz minced (ground) beef
120ml/4fl oz/½ cup red wine
200ml/7fl oz/scant 1 cup passata
 (bottled, strained tomatoes)
15ml/1 tbsp tomato purée (paste)
5ml/1 tsp dried oregano
15ml/1 tbsp chopped fresh flat
 leaf parsley
350ml/12fl oz/1½ cups beef stock
8 baby Italian tomatoes (optional)
salt and ground black pepper

**VARIATION**
Grated mature (sharp) Cheddar cheese can be used instead of the grated Parmesan.

**1** Preheat the oven to 190°C/375°F/Gas 5. Melt the butter in the oil in a frying pan. Add the mushrooms, with salt and pepper to taste, and toss over a medium to high heat for 5–8 minutes, or until the mushrooms are tender and quite dry. Remove the pan from the heat and stir in the parsley.

**2** To make the bolognese sauce, heat the oil in a large pan, add the chopped vegetables and cook over a low heat, stirring frequently, for 5–7 minutes.

**3** Add the minced beef and cook for 5 minutes, stirring frequently. Stir in the wine and mix well.

**4** Cook for 1–2 minutes, then add the passata, tomato purée, herbs and 60ml/4 tbsp of the stock. Season with salt and pepper to taste. Stir well and bring to the boil.

**5** Cover the pan, and cook over a low heat for 30 minutes, stirring from time to time and adding more stock as necessary. Add the tomatoes, if using, and simmer for 5–10 minutes more.

**6** Stir in enough hot beef stock to make the sauce quite runny. (This is particularly important if using the no pre-cook sheets of dried lasagne).

**7** Stir in the mushroom and parsley mixture, then spread about a quarter of this sauce over the bottom of a baking dish. Cover with three or four sheets of lasagne.

**8** Beat together the ricotta and egg in a bowl, with salt and pepper to taste, then spread about a third of the mixture over the lasagne sheets. Cover with a third of the mozzarella slices, then sprinkle with about a quarter of the grated Parmesan.

**9** Repeat these layers twice, using half the remaining bolognese sauce each time, and finishing with the remaining Parmesan cheese.

**10** Bake the lasagne for 30–40 minutes, or until the cheese topping is golden brown and bubbling. Allow the lasagne to stand for about 10 minutes before serving.

# Red Chicken Curry with Bamboo Shoots

Bamboo shoots have a lovely crunchy texture and make a delightful, contrasting texture to the chicken in this Thai curry. It is perfect served with jasmine rice.

**Serves 6**

1 litre/1¾ pints/4 cups coconut milk
30ml/2 tbsp red curry paste
450g/1lb chicken breast fillets, skinned
    and cut into bitesize pieces
30ml/2 tbsp Thai fish sauce (nam pla)
15ml/1 tbsp sugar
225g/8oz canned whole bamboo
    shoots, rinsed, drained and sliced
5 kaffir lime leaves, torn
salt and ground black pepper
chopped fresh red chillies and kaffir
    lime leaves, to garnish

For the red curry paste
5ml/1tsp roasted coriander seeds
2.5ml/½ tsp roasted cumin seeds
6–8 fresh red chillies, seeded
    and chopped
4 shallots, thinly sliced
2 garlic cloves, peeled and chopped
15ml/1 tbsp fresh galangal, peeled
    and chopped
2 lemon grass stalks, chopped
4 fresh coriander (cilantro) roots
10 black peppercorns
pinch of ground cinnamon
5ml/1 tsp ground turmeric
2.5ml/½ tsp shrimp paste
5ml/1 tsp salt
30 ml/2 tbsp vegetable oil

**1** To make the red curry paste, put all the ingredients except the oil into a mortar or food processor and pound or process to a paste. Add the oil a little at a time, mixing or processing well after each addition. If you are not using the paste immediately, transfer it to a jar, and keep in the refrigerator until you are ready to use it. For a hotter paste, add a few chilli seeds.

**2** Pour half of the coconut milk into a wok or large pan over a medium heat. Bring to the boil, stirring constantly, with large cooking chopsticks or a spoon until it has separated.

**3** Add the red curry paste and cook the mixture for 2–3 minutes. Stir the paste constantly to prevent it from sticking to the base of the pan.

**4** Add the chicken pieces, fish sauce and sugar to the pan. Stir well, then cook for 5–6 minutes, or until the chicken changes colour and is cooked through. Continue to stir during cooking to prevent the mixture from sticking to the base of the pan and to ensure that the chicken cooks evenly.

**5** Pour the remaining coconut milk into the pan, then add the sliced bamboo shoots and torn kaffir lime leaves. Bring back to the boil over a medium heat, stirring constantly to prevent the mixture from sticking, then taste and add salt and pepper if necessary.

**6** To serve, spoon the curry into a warmed serving dish and garnish with chopped chillies and kaffir lime leaves.

**COOK'S TIP**
Preparing a double or larger quantity of paste in a food processor or blender makes the blending of the ingredients easier and the paste will be smoother. Store surplus curry paste in the freezer.

**VARIATIONS**
• For green curry paste, process 12–15 green chillies, 2 chopped lemon grass stalks, 3 sliced shallots, 2 garlic cloves, 15ml/1 tbsp chopped galangal, 4 chopped kaffir lime leaves, 2.5ml/½ tsp grated kaffir rind, 5ml/1 tsp each of chopped coriander root, salt, roasted coriander seeds, roasted cumin seeds and shrimp paste, 15ml/1 tbsp sugar, 6 black peppercorns and 15ml/1 tbsp vegetable oil until a paste forms.
• For yellow curry paste, process 6–8 yellow chillies, 1 chopped lemon grass stalk, 2 sliced shallots, 4 garlic cloves, 15ml/1 tbsp chopped fresh root ginger, 5ml/1 tsp ground cinnamon,15ml/1 tbsp light brown sugar and 30ml/2 tbsp vegetable oil until a paste forms.
• Use turkey or pork instead of chicken.

# dinner party soups and appetizers

These tempting first courses are all visually appealing and perfect for setting the right tone at the beginning of a special meal.

# Vichyssoise with Watercress Cream

Classic soups, such as this cold French version of leek and potato soup, will always remain firm favourites for dinner parties.

**Serves 6**

*50g/2oz/¼ cup butter*
*1 onion, sliced*
*450g/1lb leeks, sliced*
*225g/8oz potatoes, sliced*
*750ml/1¼ pints/3 cups chicken stock*
*300ml/½ pint/1¼ cups milk*
*45ml/3 tbsp single (light) cream*
*salt and ground black pepper*
*fresh chervil, to garnish*

**For the watercress cream**
*1 bunch watercress, about 75g/3oz,*
  *stalks removed*
*small bunch of fresh chervil,*
  *finely chopped*
*150ml/¼ pint/⅔ cup double*
  *(heavy) cream*
*pinch of freshly grated nutmeg*

**1** Melt the butter in a pan. Add the onion and leeks, cover and cook gently for 10 minutes, stirring occasionally, until softened. Stir in the potatoes and stock, and bring to the boil. Reduce the heat and simmer for 20 minutes, or until the potatoes are tender. Cool slightly.

**2** Process the soup in a food processor or blender until smooth, then press through a sieve into a clean pan.

**3** Stir in the milk and single cream. Season the soup well and chill for at least 2 hours.

**4** To make the watercress cream, process the watercress in a food processor or blender until finely chopped, then stir in the chervil and cream. Pour into a bowl and stir in the nutmeg with seasoning to taste.

**5** Ladle the vichyssoise into bowls and spoon the watercress cream on top. Garnish with chervil and serve.

**COOK'S TIP**
The soup is also delicious served hot in winter, especially sprinkled with a little grated nutmeg.

# Iced Melon Soup with Melon and Mint Sorbet

You can use different melons for the cool soup and ice sorbet to create a subtle contrast in flavour and colour. Try a combination of Charentais and Ogen or cantaloupe and Galia. This soup is refreshing and ideal for formal and informal summer dinner parties, and *al fresco* dining.

### Serves 6 to 8

*2.25kg/5lb very ripe melon*
*45ml/3 tbsp orange juice*
*30ml/2 tbsp lemon juice*
*mint leaves, to garnish*

For the melon and mint sorbet
*25g/1oz/2 tbsp sugar*
*120ml/4fl oz/½ cup water*
*2.25kg/5lb very ripe melon*
*juice of 2 limes*
*30ml/2 tbsp chopped fresh mint*

**1** To make the melon and mint sorbet, put the sugar and water into a pan and heat gently until the sugar dissolves. Bring to the boil and simmer for 4–5 minutes, then leave to cool.

**2** Halve the melon. Scrape out the seeds, then cut it into large wedges and cut the flesh out of the skin. It should weigh about 1.6kg/3½ lb.

**3** Purée the melon flesh in a food processor or blender with the cooled syrup and lime juice.

**4** If you are using an ice cream maker: stir in the mint and pour in the melon mixture. Churn, following the maker's instructions, or until the sorbet is smooth and firm. By hand: stir in the mint and pour the mixture into a freezer-proof container. Freeze until icy at the edges. Transfer to a food processor and process until smooth. Repeat this process until the mixture is smooth and holding its shape, then freeze until firm.

**5** To make the chilled melon soup, prepare the melon as in step 2 and purée until smooth in a food processor or blender. Pour the purée into a bowl and stir in the orange and lemon juice. Place the soup in the refrigerator for 30–40 minutes, but do not chill it for too long as this will dull its flavour.

**6** Ladle the soup into bowls and add a large scoop of the melon and mint sorbet to each. Garnish with mint leaves and serve immediately.

**COOK'S TIP**
The soup also looks impressive served in large wine glasses, with small balls of sorbet instead of large scoops. Keep the glasses cool by standing them in bowls filled with ice cubes.

# Cream of Mushroom Soup with Goat's Cheese Crostini

Classic cream of mushroom soup is still a firm favourite, especially with the addition of crisp and garlicky croûtes with tangy goat's cheese.

**Serves 6**

*25g/1oz/2 tbsp butter*
*1 onion, chopped*
*1 garlic clove, chopped*
*450g/1lb/6 cups chestnut or brown cap (cremini) mushrooms, some whole, some roughly chopped*
*15ml/1 tbsp plain (all-purpose) flour*
*45ml/3 tbsp dry sherry*
*900ml/1½ pints/3¾ cups vegetable stock*
*150ml/¼ pint/⅔ cup double (heavy) cream*
*salt and ground black pepper*
*fresh chervil sprigs, to garnish*

**For the crostini**
*15ml/1 tbsp olive oil, plus extra for brushing*
*1 shallot, chopped*
*115g/4oz/2 cups button (white) mushrooms, finely chopped*
*15ml/1 tbsp chopped fresh parsley*
*6 brown cap (cremini) mushrooms*
*6 slices baguette*
*1 small garlic clove*
*115g/4oz/1 cup soft goat's cheese*

**1** Melt the butter, cook the onion and garlic for 5 minutes. Add the mushrooms, cover, cook for 10 minutes.

**2** Stir in the flour and cook for 1 minute. Stir in the dry sherry and stock and bring to the boil, then simmer for 15 minutes. Cool slightly, then purée the mixture in a food processor or blender until smooth.

**3** Meanwhile, prepare the crostini. Heat the oil in a small pan. Add the shallot and button mushrooms, and cook for 8–10 minutes, until softened. Drain well and transfer to a food processor or blender. Add the fresh parsley and process the mushroom mixture until finely chopped.

**4** Preheat the grill (broiler). Brush the brown cap mushrooms with oil and grill (broil) for 5–6 minutes.

**5** Toast the slices of baguette, rub with the garlic and put a spoonful of cheese on each. Top the grilled mushrooms with the mushroom mixture and place on the crostini.

**6** Return the soup to the pan and stir in the cream. Season, then reheat gently. Ladle the soup into six bowls. Float a crostini in the centre of each and garnish with chervil.

# Cappuccino of Puy Lentils, Lobster and Tarragon

Here is a really impressive soup to start a dinner party with. Adding ice-cold butter a little at a time is the secret of whipping up the good froth that gives the soup its clever cappuccino effect.

**Serves 6**

*450–675g/1–1½ lb live lobster*
*150g/5oz/⅔ cup Puy lentils*
*1 carrot, halved*
*1 celery stick, halved*
*1 small onion, halved*
*1 garlic clove*
*1 bay leaf*
*large bunch of tarragon, tied firmly*
*1 litre/1¾ pints/4 cups fish stock*
*120ml/4fl oz/½ cup double*
  *(heavy) cream*
*25g/1oz/2 tbsp butter, finely diced and*
  *chilled until ice cold*
*salt and ground black pepper*
*fresh tarragon sprigs, to garnish*

**1** Bring a large stockpot of water to the boil. Lower the live lobster into the water and cover the pan. Cook for 15–20 minutes, then drain the lobster and leave to cool.

**2** Put the Puy lentils in a large pan and pour in enough cold water to cover. Add the carrot, celery, onion, garlic and herbs. Bring the water to the boil and simmer for 20 minutes.

**3** Drain the lentils and discard the herbs and vegetables. Purée the lentils in a food processor until smooth. Set aside.

**4** Break the claws off the lobster, crack them open and remove all the meat from inside. Break off the tail, split it open and remove the meat. Cut all the meat into bitesize pieces.

**5** Pour the fish stock into a large clean pan and bring to the boil. Lightly stir in the lentil purée and cream, but do not mix too much at this point otherwise you will not be able to create the frothy effect. The mixture should still be quite watery in places. Season well.

**6** Using either a hand-held blender or electric beater, whisk up the soup mixture, adding the butter one piece at a time, until it is very frothy.

**7** Divide the lobster meat among the bowls and carefully pour in the soup. Garnish with sprigs of tarragon and serve immediately.

**COOK'S TIP**
Instead of adding the live lobster to the pan, kill it first by freezing it overnight. Cook from frozen, allowing 30 minutes in the boiling water. The other way of killing lobster is by stabbing it in the back of the head, where the tail shell meets the head.

# Pancakes with Leek, Chicory and Squash Stuffing

Serve a chunky home-made tomato sauce and a crisp salad with these melt-in-the-mouth stuffed pancakes.

**Serves 8**

225g/8oz/2 cups plain
  (all-purpose) flour
115g/4oz/1 cup yellow corn meal
5ml/1 tsp salt
5ml/1 tsp chilli powder
4 large (US extra large) eggs
900ml/1½ pint/3¾ cups milk
50g/2oz/4 tbsp butter, melted
vegetable oil, for greasing

### For the filling
60ml/4 tbsp olive oil
900g/2lb butternut squash (peeled
  weight), seeded and diced
large pinch of dried red chilli flakes
4 large leeks, thickly sliced
5ml/1 tsp chopped fresh thyme
6 chicory heads, thickly sliced
225g/8oz goat's cheese, cut into cubes
200g/7oz walnuts, roughly chopped
60ml/4 tbsp chopped flat leaf parsley
50g/2oz Parmesan cheese, grated
90ml/6 tbsp melted butter or olive oil
salt and ground black pepper

**1** Sift the flour, corn meal, salt and chilli powder into a bowl and make a well in the centre. Add the eggs and a little milk. Whisk the eggs and milk, mixing the dry ingredients and adding more milk as the mixture comes together.

**2** When ready to cook the pancakes, whisk the melted butter into the batter. Heat a lightly greased or oiled 18cm/7in heavy frying pan or crêpe pan. Pour about 60ml/4 tbsp batter into the pan and cook for 2–3 minutes, until set and lightly browned underneath. Turn and cook the pancake on the second side for 2–3 minutes. Lightly grease the pan after every second pancake.

**3** To make the filling, heat the oil in a large frying pan. Add the squash and cook, stirring frequently, for 10 minutes, until almost tender. Add the chilli flakes and cook, stirring, for 1–2 minutes. Stir in the leeks and thyme and cook for another 4–5 minutes.

**4** Add the chicory and cook, stirring often, for another 4–5 minutes, until the leeks are cooked and the chicory is hot, but still has some bite to its texture. Cool slightly, then stir in the cheese, walnuts and parsley. Season the mixture.

**5** Preheat the oven to 200°C/400°F/ Gas 6. Lightly grease an ovenproof dish. Spoon 30–45ml/2–3 tbsp filling on to each pancake. Roll or fold each pancake to enclose the filling, then place in the prepared dish.

**6** Sprinkle the Parmesan over the pancakes and drizzle the melted butter or olive oil over. Bake for 10–15 minutes, until the cheese is bubbling. Serve hot.

# Coquilles St Jacques

A classic French first course that calls for the best quality scallops possible to ensure a truly wonderful result. Select firm, white shellfish and check that they have not previously been frozen before buying them to ensure they are not watery and flabby. You will need eight scallop shells to serve this dish.

**Serves 8**

*900g/2lb potatoes, chopped*
*115g/4oz/½ cup butter*
*8 large or 16 small scallops*
*250ml/8fl oz/1 cup fish stock*

**For the sauce**
*50g/2oz/4 tbsp butter*
*50g/2oz/½ cup plain (all-purpose) flour*
*600ml/1 pint/2½ cups milk*
*60ml/4 tbsp single (light) cream*
*250g/8oz/2 cups grated (sharp) mature*
  *Cheddar cheese*
*salt and ground black pepper*
*dill sprigs, to garnish*
*grilled (broiled) lemon wedges, to serve*

**1** Preheat oven to 200°C/400°F/Gas 6. Place the chopped potatoes in a large pan, cover with lightly salted water and boil for 15 minutes, or until tender. Drain and mash with the butter.

**2** Spoon the mixture into a piping (pastry) bag fitted with a star nozzle. Pipe the potatoes around the outside of a cleaned scallop shell. Repeat the process, making eight in total.

**3** Simmer the scallops in the fish stock for about 3 minutes, or until just firm. Do not allow the stock to boil but poach the scallops gently otherwise they will become tough and rubbery. Drain and slice the scallops finely. Set them aside.

**4** To make the sauce, melt the butter in a small pan, add the flour and cook over a low heat for a couple of minutes, gradually add the milk and cream, stirring constantly and cook until thickened.

**5** Stir in the cheese and cook until melted. Season to taste. Spoon a little sauce in the base of each shell. Divide the scallops between the shells and then pour the remaining sauce over the scallops.

**6** Bake the scallops for 10 minutes, or until golden. Garnish with dill and serve with grilled lemon wedges.

# Crab Salad with Rocket

Garnish these salads with strips of lemon rind, if you like.

**Serves 8**

*8 dressed crabs*
*2 red (bell) peppers, seeded*
  *and chopped*
*2 small red onions, finely chopped*
*60ml/4 tbsp fresh coriander (cilantro)*
*60ml/4 tbsp drained capers*
*grated rind and juice of 3 lemons*
*Tabasco sauce, to taste*
*salt and ground black pepper*

**For the salad**
*75g/3oz rocket (arugula) leaves*
*60ml/4 tbsp sunflower oil*
*30ml/2 tbsp fresh lime juice*

**1** Remove all the white and brown meat from the crab. Put it into a large mixing bowl with the chopped peppers, onions and coriander. Add the capers, lemon rind and juice, and toss gently to mix everything thoroughly together. Season with a few drops of Tabasco sauce, according to taste, and a little salt and pepper.

**2** To make the salad, wash the rocket leaves and pat them dry on kitchen paper. Divide between eight plates. Mix together the oil and lime juice in a small bowl. Dress the rocket leaves with the oil and lime juice.

**3** Pile the crab salad on top and serve garnished with lemon rind strips.

# Pork and Bacon Rillettes with Onion Salad

Rillettes is potted meat from pork and ham. This version makes a great appetizer or light meal.

**Serves 8**

1.8kg/4lb belly of pork, boned and cut into cubes (reserve the bones)
450g/1lb rindless streaky (fatty) bacon, finely chopped
5ml/1 tsp salt
1.5ml/¼ tsp freshly ground black pepper
4 garlic cloves, finely chopped
2 fresh parsley sprigs
1 bay leaf
2 fresh thyme sprigs
1 fresh sage sprig
300ml/½ pint/1¼ cups water
crusty French bread, to serve

For the onion salad
1 small red onion, halved and finely sliced
2 spring onions (scallions), cut into matchstick strips
2 celery sticks, cut into matchstick strips
15ml/1 tbsp freshly squeezed lemon juice
15ml/1 tbsp light olive oil
ground black pepper

**1** In a bowl, mix the pork, bacon and salt. Cover and leave for 30 minutes. Preheat the oven to 150°C/300°F/Gas 2. Stir the pepper and garlic into the meat. Tie the herbs together to make a bouquet garni and add to the meat.

**2** Spread the meat mixture in a roasting pan and pour in the water. Place the bones from the pork on top and cover tightly with foil. Cook for 3½ hours.

**3** Discard the bones and herbs, and ladle the meat mixture into a metal sieve set over a large bowl. Allow the liquid to drain through into the bowl, then turn the meat into a shallow dish. Repeat until all the meat is drained. Reserve the liquid. Use two forks to pull the meat apart into fine shreds.

**4** Line a 1.5 litre/2½ pint/6¼ cup terrine or deep, straight-sided dish with clear film (plastic wrap) and spoon in the shredded meat. Strain the reserved liquid through a sieve lined with muslin (cheesecloth) and pour it over the meat. Leave to cool. Cover and chill in the fridge for at least 24 hours, or until set.

**5** To make the onion salad, place the sliced onion, spring onions and celery in a bowl. Add the freshly squeezed lemon juice and light olive oil and toss gently. Season with a little freshly ground black pepper, but do not add any salt as the rillettes is well salted.

**6** Serve the rillettes, cut into thick slices, on individual plates with a little onion salad and thick slices of crusty French bread.

# Chicken Liver Pâté with Garlic

This smooth pâté is wickedly indulgent but absolutely delicious. Start preparation the day before so that the flavour can develop fully.

**Serves 6 to 8**

225g/8oz/1 cup unsalted (sweet) butter
400g/14oz chicken livers, chopped
45–60ml/3–4 tbsp Madeira
3 large shallots, chopped
2 large garlic cloves, finely chopped
5ml/1 tsp finely chopped fresh thyme
pinch of ground allspice
30ml/2 tbsp double (heavy)
    cream (optional)
salt and ground black pepper
small fresh bay leaves or fresh thyme
    sprigs, to garnish
toast and small pickled gherkins,
    to serve

**1** Melt 75g/3oz/6 tbsp butter in a small pan over a low heat, then allow it to bubble gently until it is clear. Pour off the clarified butter into a bowl.

**2** Melt 40g/1½oz/3 tbsp butter in a frying pan and fry the chicken livers for 4–5 minutes, or until browned. Stir frequently to ensure that the livers cook evenly. Do not overcook them or they will be tough.

**3** Add 45ml/3 tbsp Madeira and set it alight, then scrape the contents of the pan into a food processor or blender.

**4** Melt 25g/1oz/2 tbsp butter in the pan over a low heat and cook the shallots for 5 minutes, or until soft. Add the garlic, thyme and allspice and cook for another 2–3 minutes. Add this mixture to the livers with the remaining butter and cream, if using, then process until smooth.

**5** Add about 7.5ml/1½ tsp each of salt and black pepper and more Madeira to taste. Scrape the pâté into a serving dish and place a few bay leaves or thyme sprigs on top. Melt the clarified butter, if necessary, then pour it over the pâté. Cool and chill the pâté for 4 hours or overnight.

**VARIATIONS**
• Cognac, Armagnac or port can be used instead of the Madeira.
• Use duck livers instead of chicken and add 2.5ml/½ tsp grated orange rind.
• Use chopped fresh tarragon instead of the thyme.

# Prosciutto with Potato Rémoulade

Lime juice brings a contemporary twist to this cream-enriched version of the classic piquant rémoulade dressing. It is best made when the new season's asparagus is available.

### Serves 8

*4 potatoes, each weighing about*
*   350g/12oz, quartered lengthways*
*300ml/½ pint/1¼ cup mayonnaise*
*300ml/½ pint/1¼ cup double*
*   (heavy) cream*
*10–15ml/2–3 tsp Dijon mustard*
*juice of 1 lime*
*60ml/4 tbsp olive oil*
*24 prosciutto slices*
*900g/2lb asparagus spears, halved*
*salt and ground black pepper*
*50g/2oz wild rocket (arugula),*
*   to garnish*
*extra virgin olive oil, to serve*

**1** Put the potatoes in a pan. Add water to cover and bring to the boil. Add salt, then simmer for about 15 minutes, or until the potatoes are tender, but do not let them get too soft. Drain thoroughly and leave to cool and then cut into long, thin strips.

**2** Beat together the mayonnaise, cream, mustard, lime juice and seasoning in a large bowl. Add the potatoes and stir carefully to coat them with the dressing.

**3** Heat the oil in a griddle or frying pan and cook the prosciutto in batches until crisp and golden. Use a slotted spoon to remove, draining each piece well.

**4** Cook the asparagus in the fat remaining in the pan for 3 minutes, or until tender and golden.

**5** Put a generous spoonful of potato rémoulade on each plate and top with several slices of prosciutto. Add the asparagus and garnish with rocket. Serve immediately, offering olive oil to drizzle over.

### VARIATION
Use a mixture of potatoes and celeriac instead of all potatoes. For an inexpensive salad use mixed root vegetables and omit the asparagus, adding fresh or roasted cherry tomatoes instead.

# dinner party and festive main courses

Classic dishes are sure winners for dinner parties

and celebrations, especially with a clever twist

of seasoning or a contemporary garnish.

# Roasted Garlic and Aubergine Custards with Red Pepper Dressing

These make a splendid main course for a special vegetarian dinner. Serve fresh, warm bread and steamed broccoli as accompaniments.

**Serves 6**

*2 large heads of garlic*
*6–7 fresh thyme sprigs*
*60ml/4 tbsp extra virgin olive oil, plus extra for greasing*
*350g/12oz aubergines (eggplant), cut into 1cm/½in dice*
*2 large red (bell) peppers, halved and seeded*
*pinch of saffron threads*
*300ml/½ pint/1¼ cups whipping cream*
*2 large (US extra large) eggs*
*pinch of caster (superfine) sugar*
*30ml/2 tbsp shredded fresh basil leaves*
*salt and ground black pepper*

**For the dressing**
*90ml/6 tbsp extra virgin oil*
*15–25ml/1–1½ tbsp balsamic vinegar*
*pinch of caster (superfine) sugar*
*115g/4oz tomatoes, peeled, seeded and finely diced*
*½ small red onion, finely chopped*
*generous pinch of ground toasted cumin seeds*
*handful of fresh basil leaves*

**1** Preheat the oven to 190°C/375°F/ Gas 5. Place the garlic on a piece of foil with the thyme and sprinkle with 15ml/1 tbsp of the oil. Wrap the foil around the garlic and cook for 35–45 minutes, or until the garlic is soft. Cool slightly. Reduce the oven temperature to 180°C/350°F/Gas 4.

**2** Meanwhile, heat the remaining olive oil in a heavy pan. Add the diced aubergines and fry over a medium heat, stirring frequently, for 5–8 minutes, or until they are browned and cooked.

**3** Grill (broil) the peppers, skin sides uppermost, until they are black. Place the peppers in a bowl, cover and leave for 10 minutes.

**4** When the peppers are cool enough to handle, peel and dice them. Soak the saffron in 15ml/1 tbsp hot water for 10 minutes.

**5** Unwrap the roasted garlic and separate the cloves, then squeeze the flesh out of its skin into a blender or food processor. Discard the thyme sprigs. Add the oil from cooking the garlic, the cream and eggs to the garlic. Process until smooth. Add the soaked saffron with its liquid, and season well with salt, pepper and a pinch of sugar. Stir in half the diced red pepper and the shredded basil leaves.

**6** Lightly grease six large ovenproof ramekins (about 200–250ml/7–8fl oz/ 1 cup capacity) and line the base of each with a circle of baking parchment. Grease the baking parchment.

**7** Divide the aubergines among the dishes. Pour the egg mixture into the ramekins, then place them in a roasting pan. Cover each dish with foil and make a little hole in the centre of the foil to allow steam to escape. Pour hot water into the tin to come halfway up the outsides of the ramekins. Bake for 25–30 minutes, or until the custards are just set in the centre.

**8** Make the dressing while the custards are cooking. Whisk the oil and vinegar with salt, pepper and a pinch of sugar. Stir in the tomatoes, red onion, remaining red pepper and cumin. Set aside some of the basil leaves for garnishing, then chop the rest and add to the dressing.

**9** Leave the custards to cool for about 5 minutes. Slide a knife around the insides of the ramekins and invert the custards on to warmed serving plates. Spoon the dressing around the custards and garnish each with the reserved fresh basil leaves.

# Goat's Cheese Soufflé

The mellow flavour of roasted garlic pervades this simple, but elegant soufflé. Balance the rich soufflé with a crisp green salad, including peppery leaves.

**Serves 6 to 8**

*4 large heads of garlic*
*6 fresh thyme sprigs*
*30ml/2 tbsp olive oil*
*475ml/16fl oz/2 cups milk*
*2 fresh bay leaves*
*4 x 1cm/½ in thick onion slices*
*4 cloves*
*115g/4oz/½ cup butter*
*75g/3oz/⅔ cup plain (all-purpose)*
   *flour, sifted*
*cayenne pepper*
*6 eggs, separated, plus 1 egg white*
*300g/11oz goat's cheese, crumbled*
*115g/4oz/1¼ cups freshly grated*
   *Parmesan cheese*
*5–10ml/1–2 tsp chopped fresh thyme*
*5ml/1 tsp cream of tartar*
*salt and ground black pepper*

**1** Preheat the oven to 180°C/350°F/ Gas 4. Place the garlic and thyme sprigs on a piece of foil. Sprinkle with the oil and close the foil around the garlic, then bake for about 1 hour, until the garlic is soft. Leave to cool.

**2** Squeeze the garlic out of its skin. Discard the thyme and garlic skins, then purée the garlic flesh with the oil.

**3** Meanwhile, place the milk, bay leaves, onion slices and cloves in a medium pan. Bring to the boil, then remove from the heat. Cover and leave to stand for 30 minutes.

**4** Melt 75g/3oz/6 tbsp of the butter in another pan. Stir in the flour and cook gently for 2 minutes, stirring. Reheat and strain the milk, then slowly stir it into the flour and butter.

**5** Cook the sauce very gently for 10 minutes, stirring frequently. Season with salt, pepper and a pinch of cayenne. Cool slightly. Preheat the oven to 200°C/400°F/Gas 6.

**6** Beat the egg yolks into the sauce one at a time. Then beat in the goat's cheese, all but 30ml/2 tbsp of the Parmesan and the chopped thyme. Use the remaining butter to grease a large soufflé dish (1 litre/1¾ pints/4 cups) or eight ramekins (about 125ml/4fl oz/½ cup).

**7** Whisk the egg whites and cream of tartar in a scrupulously clean bowl until firm, but not dry. Stir 90ml/6 tbsp of the egg whites into the sauce, then gently, but thoroughly, fold in the remainder using a rubber spatula.

**8** Pour the mixture into the prepared dish or dishes. Run a knife around the edge of each dish, pushing the mixture away from the rim. Sprinkle with the reserved Parmesan.

**9** Place the dish or dishes on a baking sheet and cook for 25–30 minutes for a large soufflé or 20 minutes for small soufflés. The mixture should be risen and firm to a light touch in the centre; it should not wobble excessively when given a light push. Serve immediately.

**COOK'S TIP**
Whisked egg whites give a soufflé its characteristic airy texture. But the lightness can be destroyed if they are folded in too roughly. Fold whites in using a rubber spatula and a cutting and scooping action. Turn the bowl a little after each stroke.

# **Peppers** filled with **Spiced Vegetables**

Indian spices season the potato and aubergine stuffing in these colourful baked peppers. They are good with plain rice and a lentil dhal, or a salad, Indian breads and a cucumber or mint and yogurt raita.

**Serves 6**

*6 large evenly shaped red or yellow (bell) peppers*
*500g/1¼lb waxy potatoes*
*1 small onion, chopped*
*4–5 garlic cloves, chopped*
*5cm/2in piece fresh root ginger, chopped*
*1–2 fresh green chillies, seeded and chopped*
*105ml/7 tbsp water*
*90–105ml/6–7 tbsp groundnut (peanut) oil*
*1 aubergine (eggplant), cut into 1cm/½in dice*
*10ml/2 tsp cumin seeds*
*5ml/1 tsp kalonji (nigella) seeds*
*2.5ml/½ tsp ground turmeric*
*5ml/1 tsp ground coriander*
*5ml/1 tsp ground toasted cumin seeds*
*pinch of cayenne pepper*
*about 30ml/2 tbsp lemon juice*
*salt and ground black pepper*
*30ml/2 tbsp chopped fresh coriander (cilantro), to garnish*

**1** Cut the tops off the red or yellow peppers then remove and discard the seeds. Cut a thin slice off the base of the peppers, if necessary, to make them stand upright.

**2** Bring a large saucepan of lightly salted water to the boil. Add the peppers and cook for 5–6 minutes. Drain and leave the peppers upside down in a colander.

**3** Cook the potatoes in boiling, salted water for 10–12 minutes, until just tender. Drain, cool and peel, then cut into 1cm/½in dice.

**4** Put the onion, garlic, ginger and green chillies in a food processor or blender with 60ml/4 tbsp of the water and process to a purée.

**5** Heat 45ml/3 tbsp of the oil in a large, deep frying pan and cook the aubergine, stirring occasionally, until browned on all sides. Remove from the pan and set aside. Add another 30ml/2 tbsp of the oil to the pan and cook the potatoes until lightly browned. Remove from the pan and set aside.

**6** If necessary, add another 15ml/1 tbsp oil to the pan, then add the cumin and kalonji seeds. Fry briefly until the seeds darken, then add the turmeric, coriander and ground cumin. Cook for 15 seconds. Stir in the onion and garlic purée and fry, scraping the pan with a spatula, until it begins to brown.

**7** Return the potatoes and aubergines to the pan, season with salt, pepper and 1–2 pinches of cayenne. Add the remaining water and 15ml/1 tbsp lemon juice and then cook, stirring, until the liquid evaporates. Preheat the oven to 190°C/375°F/Gas 5.

**8** Fill the peppers with the potato mix and place on a lightly greased baking tray. Brush the peppers with a little oil and bake for 30–35 minutes, until the peppers are cooked. Allow to cool, then sprinkle with a little more lemon juice, garnish with the coriander and serve.

# Fillets of Sea Bream in Filo Pastry

Any firm fish fillets can be used for this dish. Each little parcel is a meal in itself and can be prepared several hours in advance, which makes them ideal for entertaining.

### Serves 8

*16 small waxy salad potatoes*
*400g/14oz sorrel, stalks removed*
*60ml/4 tbsp olive oil*
*32 sheets of filo pastry, thawed*
  *if frozen*
*8 sea bream fillets, about 175g/6oz*
  *each, scaled but not skinned*
*115g/4oz/½ cup butter, melted*
*250ml/8fl oz/1 cup fish stock*
*475ml/16fl oz/2 cups double*
  *(heavy) cream*
*salt and ground black pepper*
*finely diced red (bell) pepper, to garnish*

**1** Preheat the oven to 200°C/400°F/ Gas 6. Cook the salad potatoes in lightly salted boiling water for 15–20 minutes, or until just tender. Drain and set aside to cool.

**2** Shred half the sorrel leaves by piling up six or eight at a time, rolling them up like a fat cigar and cutting them with a sharp knife, into very fine slices: shake these out.

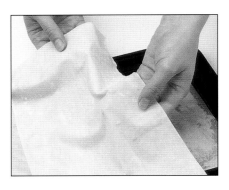

**3** Thinly slice the potatoes lengthways. Brush a baking tray with a little oil. Lay a sheet of filo pastry on the tray, brush it with oil then lay a second sheet crossways over the first. Repeat with two more sheets. Arrange one-eighth of the sliced potatoes in the centre of the pastry, season well and add one-eighth of the shredded sorrel. Lay a bream fillet on top, skin side up. Season to taste again.

**4** Loosely fold the filo pastry up and over to make a neat parcel. Make seven more parcels in the same way. Place on the baking tray and brush them with half the butter. Bake for 20 minutes, or until the filo has fully puffed up and is golden brown.

**5** Meanwhile, make the sorrel sauce. Heat the remaining butter in a small pan, add the reserved sorrel and cook until it wilts. Stir in the fish stock and cream. Heat almost to boiling point, stirring constantly. Season and keep hot. Serve the fish parcels garnished with red pepper and offer the sauce separately in its own bowl.

# Lobster Thermidor

One of the classic French dishes, lobster thermidor makes a little lobster go a long way. It is best to use large lobsters rather than small ones, as they will contain a higher proportion of flesh and the meat will be sweeter.

## Serves 6

3 large lobsters, about
    800g–1kg/1¾–2¼lb, boiled
120ml/4fl oz/½ cup brandy
75g/3oz/6 tbsp butter
6 shallots, finely chopped
350g/12oz/4½ cups button (white)
    mushrooms, thinly sliced
50ml/3 tbsp plain (all-purpose) flour
350ml/12fl oz/1½ cups fish stock
350ml/12fl oz/1½ cups double
    (heavy) cream
15ml/1 tbsp Dijon mustard
6 egg yolks, beaten
120ml/9 tbsp dry white wine
115g/4oz/1¼ cups freshly grated
    Parmesan cheese
salt, ground black pepper and
    cayenne pepper
steamed rice and salad leaves, to serve

**1** Split each lobster in half lengthways; crack the claws. Discard the stomach sac, and keep the coral for another dish. Keeping each half-shell intact, extract the meat from the tail and claws, then cut into large dice. Place in a shallow dish; sprinkle over the brandy. Cover and set aside. Wipe and dry the half-shells and set them aside.

**2** Melt the butter in a pan and cook the shallots over a low heat until soft. Add the mushrooms and cook until just tender, stirring constantly. Stir in the flour and a pinch of cayenne pepper; cook, stirring, for 2–3 minutes. Gradually add the stock, stirring until the sauce boils and thickens.

**3** Stir in the cream and mustard and continue to cook until the sauce is smooth and thick. Season to taste with salt, black pepper and cayenne. Pour half the sauce on to the egg yolks, stir well and return the mixture to the pan. Stir in the wine. Taste and adjust the seasoning, being generous with the cayenne pepper.

**4** Preheat the grill (broiler) to medium-high. Stir the diced lobster and the brandy into the sauce. Arrange the lobster half-shells in a grill pan and divide the mixture among them. Sprinkle with Parmesan and place under the grill until browned. Serve with the rice and salad leaves.

# Boeuf Bourguignonne

This classic French dish of beef cooked in Burgundy style with red wine, small pieces of bacon, baby onions and mushrooms, is a favourite choice for a dinner party.

## Serves 6

*175g/6oz rindless streaky (fatty) bacon*
*rashers (strips), chopped*
*900g/2lb lean braising steak, such as*
*top rump of beef or braising steak*
*30ml/2 tbsp plain (all-purpose) flour*
*45ml/3 tbsp sunflower oil*
*25g/1oz/2 tbsp butter*
*12 shallots*
*2 garlic cloves, crushed*
*175g/6oz/2⅓ cups mushrooms, sliced*
*450ml/¾ pint/scant 2 cups red wine*
*150ml/¼ pint/⅔ cup beef stock*
*or consommé*
*1 bay leaf*
*2 sprigs each of fresh thyme, parsley*
*and marjoram*
*salt and ground black pepper*
*creamed potatoes and celeriac, to serve*

**1** Preheat the oven to 160°C/325°F/ Gas 3. Heat a large flameproof casserole, then add the bacon and cook, stirring occasionally, until the fat runs and the cooked pieces are crisp and golden brown.

**2** Meanwhile, cut the meat into 2.5cm/1in cubes. Season the flour and use to coat the meat. Use a slotted spoon to remove the bacon from the casserole and set aside. Add and heat the oil, then brown the beef in batches and set aside with the bacon (cooking too much at once reduces the temperature of the oil drastically).

**3** Add the butter to the fat remaining in the casserole. Cook the shallots and garlic until just starting to colour, then add the mushrooms and cook for a further 5 minutes. Replace the bacon and meat, and stir in the wine and stock or consommé. Tie the bay leaf, thyme, parsley and marjoram together into a bouquet garni and add to the casserole.

**4** Cover and cook in the oven for 1½ hours, or until the meat is tender, stirring once or twice. Season to taste and serve the casserole with creamy mashed root vegetables, such as celeriac and potatoes.

# Beef Wellington

Tender fillet of beef baked in puff pastry makes a sophisticated main course for a formal dinner. Start preparing the dish well in advance to allow time for the meat to cool before it is wrapped in the pastry.

## Serves 6

1.5kg/3¼lb fillet of beef
45ml/3 tbsp sunflower oil
115g/4oz/1½ cups mushrooms, chopped
2 garlic cloves, crushed
175g/6oz smooth liver pâté
30ml/2 tbsp chopped fresh parsley
400g/14oz puff pastry
beaten egg, to glaze
salt and ground black pepper
fresh flat leaf parsley, to garnish

**1** Tie the fillet of beef at regular intervals with string so that it stays in a neat shape during cooking.

**2** Heat 30ml/2 tbsp of the sunflower oil in a large frying pan, and fry the beef over a high heat for about 10 minutes, until brown on all sides. Transfer to a roasting pan, bake for 20 minutes. Allow to cool.

**3** Heat the remaining oil in a frying pan and cook the mushrooms and garlic for about 5 minutes. Beat the mushroom mixture into the pâté with the parsley, season well. Set aside to cool.

**4** Roll out the pastry into a sheet large enough to enclose the beef, plus a strip to spare. Trim off the spare pastry, trim the other edges to neaten. Spread the pâté mix down the middle of the pastry. Untie the beef and lay it on the pâté.

**5** Preheat the oven to 220°C/425°F/Gas 7. Brush the edges of the pastry with beaten egg and fold the pastry over the meat to enclose it in a neat parcel. Place the parcel on a baking tray with the join in the pastry underneath. Cut leaf shapes from the reserved pastry. Brush the parcel with egg, garnish with pastry leaves. Chill for 10 minutes.

**6** Bake the Beef Wellington for 50–60 minutes, covering it loosely with foil after about 30 minutes to prevent the pastry from burning. Serve cut into thick slices garnished with parsley.

# Tagine of Lamb with Couscous

A tagine is a classic Moroccan stew which is traditionally served with couscous. Its warm and fruity flavourings create a rich and flavoursome sauce that is perfect for serving at winter-evening dinner parties.

**Serves 6**

1kg/2¼lb lean boneless lamb,
   such as shoulder or neck fillet
25g/1oz/2 tbsp butter
15ml/1 tbsp sunflower oil
1 large onion, chopped
2 garlic cloves, chopped
2.5cm/1in piece fresh root ginger,
   peeled and finely chopped
1 red (bell) pepper, seeded
   and chopped
900ml/1½ pints/3¾ cups lamb stock
   or water
250g/9oz/generous 1 cup
   ready-to-eat prunes
juice of 1 lemon
15ml/1 tbsp clear honey
1.5ml/¼ tsp saffron threads
1 cinnamon stick, broken in half
50g/2oz/½ cup flaked (sliced)
   almonds, toasted
salt and ground black pepper

**To serve**
450g/1lb/2⅔ cups couscous
25g/1oz/2 tbsp butter
30ml/2 tbsp chopped fresh
   coriander (cilantro)

**1** Trim the lamb and cut it into 2.5cm/1in cubes. Heat the butter and oil in a large flameproof casserole until foaming. Add the onion, garlic and ginger and cook, stirring occasionally, until softened but not coloured.

**2** Add the lamb and red pepper and mix well. (The meat is not sealed in batches over high heat for an authentic tagine.) Pour in the stock or water.

**3** Add the prunes, lemon juice, honey, saffron threads and cinnamon. Season to taste with salt and pepper and stir well. Bring to the boil, then reduce the heat and cover the casserole. Simmer for 1½–2 hours, stirring occasionally, or until the meat is melt-in-the-mouth tender.

**4** Meanwhile, cook the couscous according to packet instructions, usually by placing in a large bowl and pouring in boiling water to cover the "grains" by 2.5cm/1in. Stir well, then cover and leave to stand for 5–10 minutes. The couscous absorbs the water and swells to become tender and fluffy. Stir in the butter, chopped fresh coriander and seasoning to taste.

**5** Taste the stew for seasoning and add more salt and pepper if necessary. Pile the couscous into a large, warmed serving dish or on to individual warmed bowls or plates. Ladle the stew on to the couscous and sprinkle the toasted flaked almonds over the top.

# Medallions of Venison with Herby Horseradish Dumplings

Venison is lean and full-flavoured, and tastes great with these piquant dumplings. This recipe makes an attractive dinner party dish.

**Serves 8**

*1.2 litres/2 pints/5 cups venison stock*
*250ml/8fl oz/1 cup port*
*30ml/2 tbsp sunflower oil*
*8 medallions of venison, about*
  *175g/6oz each*
*chopped fresh parsley, to garnish*
*steamed baby vegetables, to serve*

**For the dumplings**
*150g/5oz/1¼ cup self-raising*
  *(self-rising) flour*
*75g/3oz beef suet (US grated shortening)*
*30ml/2 tbsp chopped mixed herbs*
*10ml/2 tsp creamed horseradish*
*90–120ml/6–8 tbsp water*

**1** First make the dumplings: mix the flour, suet and herbs and make a well in the middle. Add the horseradish and water, then mix to make a soft but not sticky dough. Shape the dough into walnut-sized balls and chill in the refrigerator for up to 1 hour.

**2** Boil the venison stock in a pan until reduced by half. Add the port and continue boiling until reduced again by half, then pour the reduced stock into a frying pan. Heat the stock until it is simmering and add the dumplings. Poach them for 5–10 minutes, or until risen and cooked through. Use a slotted spoon to remove the dumplings.

**COOK'S TIP**
Serve a variety of steamed vegetables with the venison such as carrots, courgettes (zucchini) and turnips.

**3** Smear the sunflower oil over a non-stick griddle, heat until very hot. Add the venison, cook for 2–3 minutes on each side. Place the venison medallions on warmed serving plates and pour the sauce over. Serve with the dumplings and vegetables, garnished with parsley.

**VARIATION**
Beef fillet medallions can be used instead of the venison. Replace the venison stock with beef stock.

# Herb-crusted Rack of Lamb with Puy Lentils

This roast is quick and easy to prepare, yet impressive when served: the perfect choice when entertaining.

### Serves 8

*4 × 6-bone racks of lamb, chined*
*115g/4oz/2 cups fresh white*
  *breadcrumbs*
*4 large garlic cloves, crushed*
*40g/1½ oz chopped mixed fresh herbs,*
  *such as rosemary, thyme, flat leaf*
  *parsley and marjoram, plus extra*
  *sprigs to garnish*
*115g/4oz/½ cup butter, melted*
*salt and ground black pepper*

### For the Puy lentils

*2 red onions, chopped*
*60ml/4 tbsp olive oil*
*2 x 400g/14oz cans Puy or green*
  *lentils, rinsed and drained*
*2 x 400g/14oz cans chopped tomatoes*
*60ml/4 tbsp chopped fresh parsley*

**1** Preheat the oven to 220°C/425°F/ Gas 7. Trim off any excess fat from the racks of lamb, and season well with salt and ground black pepper.

**2** Mix together the breadcrumbs, garlic, herbs and butter, and press on to the fat-sides of the lamb. Place in a roasting pan and roast for 25 minutes. Cover with foil; stand for 5 minutes before carving.

### COOK'S TIP
Boiled or steamed new potatoes and broccoli are good accompaniments.

**3** To make the Puy lentils, cook the onion in the olive oil until softened. Add the lentils and tomatoes and cook gently for 5 minutes, or until the lentils are piping hot. Stir in the parsley and season to taste.

**4** Cut each rack of lamb in half and serve with the lentils. Garnish with the extra herb sprigs.

### VARIATION
Add the grated rind of 1 lemon and 30ml/2 tbsp finely chopped walnuts to the crumb mixture.

# Glazed Poussins

Golden poussins make an impressive main course. Serve them with traditional roast accompaniments or a refreshing side salad.

### Serves 6

*75g/3oz/6 tbsp butter*
*15ml/1 tbsp mixed (pumpkin pie) spice*
*45ml/3 tbsp clear honey*
*grated rind and juice of 3 clementines*
*6 poussins, each weighing about*
  *450g/1lb*
*1 large onion, finely chopped*
*2 garlic cloves, chopped*
*25ml/1½ tbsp plain (all-purpose) flour*
*75ml/2½ fl oz/⅓ cup Marsala*
*450ml/¾ pint/scant 2 cups*
  *chicken stock*
*bunch of fresh coriander (cilantro),*
  *to garnish*

### VARIATION
You can stuff each poussin, before roasting, with a quartered clementine.

**1** Preheat the oven to 220°C/425°F/ Gas 7. To make the glaze, heat the butter, mixed spice, honey and clementine rind and juice until the butter has melted, stirring to mix well. Remove from the heat.

**2** Place the poussins in a large roasting pan, brush them with the glaze, then roast for 40 minutes. Brush with any remaining glaze and baste occasionally with the pan juices during cooking. Transfer the poussins to a serving platter, cover with foil and leave to stand for 10 minutes.

**3** Skim off all but 15ml/1 tbsp of the fat from the roasting pan. Add the onion and garlic to the juices in the pan and cook on the stove, stirring occasionally, until beginning to brown. Stir in the flour, then gradually pour in the Marsala, followed by the stock, whisking constantly. Bring to the boil and simmer for 3 minutes to make a smooth, rich gravy.

**4** Transfer the poussins to warm plates or leave on the serving platter and garnish with coriander. Serve at once, offering the gravy separately.

# Roast Goose with Caramelized Apples

Tender goose served with sweet apples makes this a perfect celebration main course.

**Serves 8**

4.5–5.5kg/10–12lb goose, with giblets, thawed, if frozen
salt and ground black pepper

**For the apple and nut stuffing**
225g/8oz/1 cup prunes
150ml/¼ pint/⅔ cup port or red wine
675g/1½lb cooking apples, peeled, cored and cubed
1 large onion, chopped
4 celery sticks, sliced
15ml/1 tbsp mixed dried herbs
finely grated rind of 1 orange
goose liver, chopped
450g/1lb pork sausage meat (bulk sausage)
115g/4oz/1 cup chopped pecan nuts
2 eggs

**For the caramelized apples**
50g/2oz/¼ cup butter
60ml/4 tbsp redcurrant jelly
30ml/2 tbsp red wine vinegar
9 small eating apples, peeled and cored

**For the gravy**
30ml/2 tbsp plain (all-purpose) flour
600ml/1 pint/2½ cups giblet stock
juice of 1 orange

**1** Soak the prunes in the port or red wine for 24 hours. Stone (pit) and cut each prune into four. Reserve the liquid.

**2** The next day, mix the prunes with all the remaining stuffing ingredients and season well. Moisten with half the reserved port or red wine.

**3** Preheat the oven to 200°C/400°F/ Gas 6. Stuff the neck-end of the goose, tucking the flap of skin under and securing it with a small skewer. Remove the excess fat from the cavity and pack it with the stuffing. Tie the legs together to hold them in place.

**4** Weigh the stuffed goose to calculate the cooking time: allow 15 minutes for each 450g/1lb plus 15 minutes over. Put the bird on a rack in a roasting pan and rub the skin with salt. Prick the skin all over to help the fat run out. Roast for 30 minutes, then reduce the heat to 180°C/350°F/Gas 4 and roast for the remaining cooking time. Occasionally check and pour off any fat produced during cooking into a bowl. The goose is cooked when the juices run clear when the thickest part of the thigh is pierced with a skewer. Pour a little cold water over the breast halfway through the cooking time to crisp up the skin.

**5** Meanwhile, prepare the apples. Melt the butter, redcurrant jelly and vinegar in a small roasting pan or a shallow ovenproof dish. Put in the apples, baste them well and cook in the oven for 15–20 minutes. Baste the apples halfway through the cooking time. Do not cover them or they will collapse.

**6** Lift the goose on to the serving dish and let it stand for 15 minutes before carving. Pour off the excess fat from the roasting pan, leaving any sediment in the bottom. Stir in the flour, cook gently until brown, and then blend in the stock. Bring to the boil, add the remaining reserved port, orange juice and seasoning. Simmer for 2–3 minutes. Strain into a gravy boat.

**7** Surround the goose with the caramelized apples and spoon over the redcurrant glaze. Serve with the gravy.

**COOK'S TIP**
Do not overestimate the yield from a goose – the bird often looks big but there is a lot of fat and not too much meat on it for its size.

# Roasted Stuffed Turkey

Serve this classic roast with stuffing balls, bacon rolls, roast potatoes, vegetables and gravy.

**Serves 8**

*4.5kg/10lb oven-ready turkey, with*
*  giblets, thawed, if frozen*
*1 large onion, peeled and studded*
*  with 6 whole cloves*
*50g/2oz/¼ cup butter, softened*
*10 chipolata sausages*
*salt and ground black pepper*

**For the stuffing**
*225g/8oz rindless streaky (fatty)*
*  bacon, chopped*
*1 large onion, finely chopped*
*450g/1lb pork sausage meat*
*  (bulk sausage)*
*25g/1oz/⅓ cup rolled oats*
*30ml/2 tbsp chopped fresh parsley*
*10ml/2 tsp dried mixed herbs*
*1 large (US extra large) egg, beaten*
*115g/4oz/1 cup ready-to-eat dried*
*  apricots, finely chopped*

**For the gravy**
*25g/1oz/¼ cup plain (all-purpose) flour*
*450ml/¾ pint/scant 2 cups giblet stock*

**1** Preheat the oven to 200°C/400°F/ Gas 6. To make the stuffing, cook the bacon and onion over a gentle heat in a frying pan until the bacon is crisp and the onion is tender but not browned. Transfer to a large bowl and add the remaining stuffing ingredients. Season well and mix to combine.

**2** Stuff the neck end of the turkey only, tucking the flap of skin under and securing it with a small skewer or stitching it in place with a thread. Do not overstuff the turkey or the skin will burst during cooking. Reserve any remaining stuffing and set aside.

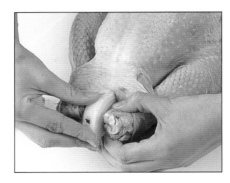

**3** Put the onion studded with cloves in the body cavity of the turkey and tie the legs together with string to hold them in place. Weigh the stuffed bird and calculate the cooking time: allow 15 minutes per 450g/1lb plus 15 minutes over. Place the turkey in a large roasting pan.

**4** Brush the turkey with the butter and season well with salt and pepper. Cover it loosely with foil and cook it for 30 minutes. Baste the turkey with the pan juices. Then lower the oven temperature to 180°C/350°F/Gas 4 and cook for the remainder of the calculated cooking time. Baste the turkey every 30 minutes or so and check for any small bubbles of fat, pricking them with a fork to release the fat from the skin.

**5** Remove the foil from the turkey for the last hour of cooking and baste. With wet hands, shape the remaining stuffing into small balls or pack it into a greased ovenproof dish. Cook in the oven for 20 minutes, or until golden brown and crisp. About 20 minutes before the end of cooking, put the chipolata sausages into an ovenproof dish and put them in the oven. The turkey is cooked if the juices run clear when the thickest part of the thigh is pierced with a skewer.

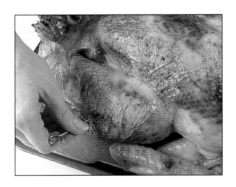

**6** Transfer the turkey to a serving plate, cover it with foil and let it stand for 15 minutes before carving. To make the gravy, spoon off the fat from the roasting pan, leaving the meat juices. Blend in the flour and cook for 2 minutes. Gradually stir in the stock and bring to the boil. Check the seasoning and pour into a sauce boat.

**7** To serve the turkey, remove the skewer and pour any juices into the gravy. Surround the turkey with chipolata sausages and stuffing and carve it at the table.

# **Duck** with **Plum Sauce**

This is an updated version of an old English dish, which is quite quick to prepare and cook, and ideal formal dinner party fare. Make it when plums are in season, when they will be ripe and juicy.

**Serves 8**

*8 duck quarters*
*2 large red onions, finely chopped*
*1kg/2¼lb ripe plums, stoned*
  *and quartered*
*60ml/4 tbsp redcurrant jelly*
*salt and ground black pepper*

**COOK'S TIP**
It is important that the plums used in this dish are very ripe, otherwise the mixture will be too dry and the sauce will be extremely tart.

**1** Prick the duck skin all over with a fork to release the fat during cooking and help give a crisp result, then place the portions in a heavy frying pan, skin sides down.

**2** Cook the duck pieces for 10 minutes on each side, or until golden brown and cooked right through. Remove the duck from the frying pan using a slotted spoon, and keep warm.

**3** Pour away all but 30ml/2 tbsp of the duck fat, then stir-fry the onion for 5 minutes, or until golden. Add the plums and cook for a further 5 minutes, stirring frequently. Add the redcurrant jelly and mix well.

**4** Replace the duck portions and cook for a further 5 minutes, or until thoroughly reheated. Season with salt and pepper to taste before serving.

# Wild Duck with Olives

Compared to farmed duck, wild duck, which has a brilliant flavour, is worth the extra expense for a special occasion meal. They are often quite small birds, so allow two pieces per portion. Mashed parsnips and green vegetables are good accompaniments.

**Serves 4**

*2 wild ducks, weighing about 1.5kg/*
*    3¼lb, each cut into 4 portions*
*2 onions, chopped*
*2 carrots, chopped*
*4 celery sticks, chopped*
*6 garlic cloves, sliced*
*2 bottles red wine*
*600ml/1 pint/2½ cups well-flavoured*
*    game stock*
*handful of fresh thyme leaves*
*5ml/1 tsp arrowroot*
*450g/1lb/4 cups pitted green olives*
*225g/8oz passata (bottled*
*    strained tomatoes)*
*salt and ground black pepper*

**1** Preheat the oven to 220°C/425°F/Gas 7. Season the duck portions generously with salt and ground black pepper and place them in a large flameproof casserole.

**2** Roast the duck portions for 25–30 minutes, then remove the casserole from the oven. Use a slotted spoon to remove the duck from the casserole, reserving the cooking fat, and set aside. Reduce the oven temperature to 160°C/325°F/Gas 3.

**3** Carefully transfer the casserole to the stove and heat the duck fat until it is sizzling. Add the chopped onions, carrots, celery sticks and garlic cloves, and cook for 10 minutes, or until the vegetables are softened. Pour in the red wine and boil until it has reduced by about half.

**4** Add the stock and thyme leaves, then replace the duck portions in the casserole. Bring to the boil, skim the surface, then cover the casserole and place in the oven for about 1 hour, or until the duck is tender. Remove the duck portions and keep warm.

**5** Skim the excess fat from the cooking liquid, strain it and return it to the casserole, then bring it to the boil. Skim the liquid again, if necessary.

**VARIATION**
Process 225g/8oz canned tomatoes in a blender and use instead of the passata.

**6** Mix the arrowroot to a thin paste with a little cold water and whisk it into the simmering sauce. Add the olives and passata and replace the duck, then cook, uncovered, for 15 minutes. Check the seasoning and serve.

# stylish salads

A repertoire of exciting salads is every cook's

standby for colourful first courses,

refreshing side dishes or buffet pizzazz.

# New York Deli Coleslaw

The key to a good coleslaw is a zesty dressing and an interesting selection of vegetables. Serve at barbecues, picnics or buffets.

**Serves 6 to 8**

1 large white or green cabbage, very
   thinly sliced
3–4 carrots, coarsely grated
½ red (bell) pepper, chopped
½ green (bell) pepper, chopped
1–2 celery sticks, finely chopped or
   5–10ml/1–2 tsp celery seeds
1 onion, chopped
2–3 handfuls of raisins or sultanas
   (golden raisins)
45ml/3 tbsp white wine vinegar or
   cider vinegar
60–90ml/4–6 tbsp sugar, to taste
175–250ml/6–8fl oz/¾–1 cup
   mayonnaise, to bind
salt and ground black pepper

**1** Put the cabbage, carrots, peppers, celery or celery seeds, onion, and raisins or sultanas in a salad bowl and mix to combine well. Add the vinegar, sugar, salt and ground black pepper and toss together. Leave to stand for about 1 hour.

### COOK'S TIP
The salad can be prepared beforehand to the end of step 1 and chilled overnight. Next day, it can be dressed with the mayonnaise before serving.

**2** Stir enough mayonnaise into the salad to lightly bind the ingredients together. Taste the salad for seasoning and sweet-and-sour flavour, adding more sugar, salt and pepper if necessary. Chill for about 1 hour.

**3** Drain off any excess liquid that has formed before serving.

### VARIATION
Use low-fat fromage frais or crème fraîche for a lighter dressing.

# Potato Salad with Egg, Mayonnaise and Olives

This version of potato salad includes a mustard mayonnaise, chopped eggs and green olives.

**Serves 6 to 8**

1kg/2¼lb waxy salad potatoes, cleaned
1 red, brown or white onion,
   finely chopped
2–3 celery sticks, finely chopped
60–90ml/4–6 tbsp chopped parsley
15–20 pimiento-stuffed olives, halved
3 hard-boiled eggs, chopped
60ml/4 tbsp extra virgin olive oil
60ml/4 tbsp white wine vinegar
15–30ml/1–2 tbsp mild or
   wholegrain mustard
celery seeds, to taste (optional)
175–250ml/6–8fl oz/¾–1 cup
   mayonnaise
salt and ground black pepper
paprika, to garnish

**1** Cook the potatoes in a pan of salted boiling water until tender. Drain, return to the pan and leave for 2–3 minutes to cool and dry a little.

**2** When the potatoes are cool enough to handle but still warm, cut them into chunks and place in a salad bowl.

### VARIATION
Instead of potatoes, use 400g/14oz cooked macaroni.

**3** Sprinkle the potatoes with salt and pepper, then add the onion, celery, parsley, olives and the chopped eggs to the salad bowl.

**4** In a jug (pitcher), combine the olive oil, vinegar, mustard and celery seeds, if using. Pour over the salad and toss to combine thoroughly. Add enough mayonnaise to bind the salad together. Chill for about 1 hour before serving, sprinkled with a little paprika.

# Peruvian Salad

This really is a spectacular-looking salad. If you serve it in a deep, glass salad bowl, the guests can then see the various layers of rice and green salad leaves, topped by the bright colours of the peppers, corn, eggs and olives.

**Serves 8**

*450g/1lb/4 cups cooked long grain
   brown or white rice
30ml/2 tbsp chopped fresh parsley
2 red (bell) peppers
2 onions, sliced
olive oil, for sprinkling
250g/9oz green beans, halved
115g/4oz/²⁄₃ cup baby corn
8 quail's eggs, hard-boiled
75g/3oz Spanish ham, cut into
   thin slices (optional)
2 small avocados
lemon juice, for sprinkling
150g/5oz mixed salad
30ml/2 tbsp capers
about 20 stuffed olives, halved*

### For the dressing
*2 garlic cloves, crushed
120ml/4fl oz/½ cup olive oil
90ml/6 tbsp sunflower oil
60ml/4 tbsp lemon juice
90ml/6 tbsp natural (plain) yogurt
5ml/1 tsp mustard
5ml/1 tsp granulated sugar
salt and ground black pepper*

**1** Make the dressing by placing all the ingredients in a bowl and whisking with a fork until smooth. Alternatively, shake the ingredients together in a screwtop jar.

### COOK'S TIP
To hard-boil quail's eggs, place them in a pan of simmering water, bring the water back to simmering point and cook for 4 minutes. Drain the eggs and rinse in cold water, then shell.

**2** Put the cooked rice into a large bowl and spoon in half the dressing. Add the chopped parsley, stir well and set aside.

**3** Cut the peppers in half, remove the seeds and pith, then place the halves, cut side down, in a small roasting pan. Add the onion rings. Sprinkle the onion with a little olive oil, place the pan under a hot grill (broiler) and grill (broil) for 5–6 minutes, or until the peppers blacken and blister and the onion turns golden. You may need to stir the onion once or twice so that it grills evenly.

**4** Stir the onion in with the rice. Put the pepper in a bowl, cover and leave until cool. Peel the peppers and cut the flesh into thin strips.

**5** Cook the green beans in boiling water for 2 minutes, then add the corn and cook for 1–2 minutes more, until tender. Drain both vegetables, refresh them under cold water, then drain again. Place in a large mixing bowl and add the red pepper strips, quail's eggs and ham, if using.

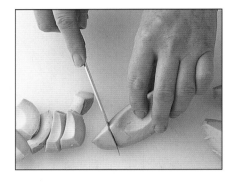

**6** Peel each avocado, remove the stone (pit), and cut the flesh into slices or chunks. Sprinkle with the lemon juice. Put the salad in a separate mixing bowl, add the avocado and mix lightly. Arrange the salad on top of the rice.

**7** Stir about 45ml/3 tbsp of the remaining dressing into the green bean and pepper mixture. Pile this on top of the salad.

**8** Sprinkle the capers and stuffed olives on top and serve the salad with the remaining dressing.

### VARIATION
Use couscous instead of rice. Place in a bowl and cover with 2.5cm/1in boiling water. Leave to stand for 10–15 minutes.

# Moroccan Orange, Onion and Olive Salad

This is a refreshing salad to add to a selection of buffet dishes.

**Serves 6**

*5 large oranges*
*90g/3½oz/scant 1 cup black olives*
*1 red onion, thinly sliced*
*1 large fennel bulb, thinly sliced,*
*    feathery tops reserved*
*15ml/1 tbsp chopped fresh mint, plus*
*    a few extra sprigs to garnish*
*15ml/1 tbsp chopped fresh coriander*
*    (cilantro), plus extra to garnish*
*60ml/4 tbsp olive oil*
*10ml/2 tsp lemon juice*
*2.5ml/½ tsp ground toasted*
*    coriander seeds*
*2.5ml/½ tsp orange flower water*
*salt and ground black pepper*

**1** Peel the oranges with a sharp knife, making sure you remove all the white pith, and cut them into 5mm/¼in slices. Remove any pips (seeds) and work over a bowl to catch all the orange juice. Set the juice aside for adding to the salad dressing.

**2** Stone (pit) the olives, if you like. In a bowl, toss the orange slices, onion and fennel together with the olives, chopped fresh mint and coriander.

**3** Make the dressing: in a bowl or jug (pitcher), whisk together the olive oil, 15ml/1 tbsp of the reserved fresh orange juice and the lemon juice. Add the ground toasted coriander seeds and season to taste with a little salt and pepper. Whisk thoroughly to mix.

**4** Toss the dressing into the salad, cover and leave to stand in a cool place for 30–60 minutes.

**5** To serve, drain off any excess dressing and place the salad in a serving dish or bowl. Sprinkle with the chopped herbs and reserved fennel tops, and sprinkle with the orange flower water.

# Tomato, Mozzarella and Red Onion Salad with Basil and Caper Dressing

Sweet tomatoes and the heady scent of basil capture the essence of summer in this simple salad.

**Serves 8**

*10 large ripe tomatoes*
*4 small packets buffalo mozzarella*
*    cheese, drained and sliced*
*2 small red onions, chopped*
*fresh basil and parsley sprigs, to garnish*

For the dressing
*1 small garlic clove, peeled*
*25g/1oz/1 cup fresh basil*
*60ml/4 tbsp chopped fresh flat*
*    leaf parsley*
*45ml/3 tbsp salted capers, rinsed*
*5ml/1 tsp mustard*
*150ml/¼ pint/⅔ cup extra virgin*
*    olive oil*
*15ml/1tbsp balsamic vinegar*
*salt and ground black pepper*

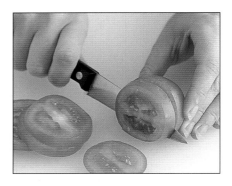

**1** First make the dressing. Put the garlic, basil, parsley, half the capers and the mustard in a food processor or blender and process briefly to chop. Then, with the motor running, gradually pour in the olive oil through the feeder tube to make a smooth purée with a dressing consistency. Add the balsamic vinegar to taste and season with ground black pepper. Alternatively, the dressing can be made by pounding the ingredients in a mortar and adding the oil by hand.

**2** Slice the tomatoes thinly. Arrange the tomato and mozzarella slices overlapping alternately on a large plate. Sprinkle the onion over the top and season with a little pepper.

**3** Drizzle the dressing over the salad, then sprinkle a few basil leaves, parsley sprigs and the remaining capers on top.

**4** Leave the salad to marinate for 10–15 minutes for the flavours to develop before serving.

# Country Pasta Salad

Colourful, tasty and nutritious, this is the ideal pasta salad for a picnic.

### Serves 6

*300g/11oz/2¾ cups dried fusilli*
*150g/5oz green beans, trimmed and*
*   cut into 5cm/2in lengths*
*1 potato, about 150g/5oz, diced*
*200g/7oz baby tomatoes, hulled*
*   and halved*
*2 spring onions (scallions), chopped*
*90g/3½oz/scant 1¼ cups Parmesan*
*   cheese, diced or coarsely shaved*
*6–8 pitted black olives, cut into rings*
*15–30ml/1–2 tbsp capers, to taste*

### For the dressing
*90ml/6 tbsp extra virgin olive oil*
*15ml/1 tbsp balsamic vinegar*
*15ml/1 tbsp chopped fresh flat*
*   leaf parsley*
*salt and ground black pepper*

**1** Cook the pasta according to the instructions on the packet. Drain it into a colander, rinse under cold running water until cold, then shake the colander to remove as much water as possible. Leave to drain and dry, shaking the colander occasionally so that it does not stick.

**2** Cook the beans and diced potato in a pan of salted boiling water for 5–6 minutes, or until tender. Drain and leave to cool.

**3** Make the dressing. Put all the ingredients in a large bowl with salt and pepper to taste and whisk well until thoroughly combined.

**4** Add the baby tomatoes, spring onions, Parmesan, olive rings and capers to the dressing, then the cold pasta, beans and potato. Toss well to mix all the ingredients. Cover the salad and leave to stand for about 30 minutes. Season to taste with salt and pepper before serving.

# Salad with Watermelon and Feta Cheese

The combination of sweet and juicy watermelon with salty feta cheese was inspired by the Turkish tradition of eating watermelon with salty white cheese in the hot summer months. It is ideal for barbecues and picnics.

**Serves 6 to 8**

*30–45ml/2–3 tbsp extra virgin olive oil*
*juice of ½ lemon*
*5ml/1 tsp vinegar of choice*
*sprinkling of fresh thyme*
*pinch of ground cumin*
*4 large slices of watermelon, chilled*
*1 frisée lettuce, core removed*
*130g/4½oz feta cheese, preferably
  sheep's milk feta, cut into
  bitesize pieces*
*handful of lightly toasted
  pumpkin seeds*
*handful of sunflower seeds*
*10–15 black olives*

**1** Pour the extra virgin olive oil, lemon juice and vinegar into a bowl or jug (pitcher). Add the fresh thyme and ground cumin, and whisk until well combined. Set the dressing aside until you are ready to serve the salad.

**2** Cut the rind off the watermelon and remove as many seeds as possible.

**COOK'S TIP**
Use plump black Mediterranean olives such as kalamata for this recipe or other shiny, dry-cured black olives.

**3** Cut the flesh into bitesize triangular-shaped chunks.

**4** Put the lettuce leaves in a bowl, pour over the dressing and toss together. Arrange the leaves on a serving dish or individual plates and add the watermelon, feta cheese, pumpkin and sunflower seeds and black olives. Serve the salad immediately.

**VARIATION**
Use Galia, cantaloupe or Charentais melon instead of the watermelon.

# eating outdoors

Discover great dishes for making barbecues
and *al fresco* eating as delicious and easy
as they are fun and informal.

# Summer Vegetables with Yogurt Pesto

Chargrilled summer vegetables make a meal on their own, or are delicious served as a Mediterranean-style accompaniment to grilled meats and fish.

**Serves 8**

*4 small aubergines (eggplant)*
*4 large courgettes (zucchini)*
*2 red (bell) peppers*
*2 yellow (bell) peppers*
*2 fennel bulbs*
*2 red onions*
*300ml/½ pint/1¼ cups Greek*
*   (US strained plain) yogurt*
*90ml/6 tbsp pesto*
*olive oil, for brushing*
*salt and ground black pepper*

**1** Cut the aubergines into 1cm/½in slices. Sprinkle with salt and leave to drain for about 30 minutes. Rinse well in cold running water and pat dry.

**2** Use a sharp kitchen knife to cut the courgettes in half lengthways. Cut the peppers in half, removing the seeds but leaving the stalks in place.

**3** Slice the fennel bulbs and the red onions into thick wedges, using a sharp kitchen knife.

**4** Prepare the barbecue. Stir the yogurt and pesto lightly together in a bowl, to make a marbled sauce. Spoon the yogurt pesto into a serving bowl and set aside.

**5** Arrange the vegetables on the hot barbecue, brush generously with olive oil and sprinkle with plenty of salt and ground black pepper.

**6** Cook the vegetables until golden brown and tender, turning occasionally. The aubergines and peppers will take 6–8 minutes to cook, the courgettes, onion and fennel 4–5 minutes. Serve the vegetables as soon as they are cooked, with the yogurt pesto.

**COOK'S TIP**
Baby vegetables are excellent for grilling whole on the barbecue, so look out for baby aubergines (eggplant) and (bell) peppers, in particular. There's no need to salt the aubergines if they are small.

# Moroccan Grilled Fish Brochettes

Serve these delicious skewers with strips of red peppers, potatoes and aubergine slices, which can also be cooked on the barbecue. Accompany them with warm, soft flour tortillas.

### Serves 6

*5 garlic cloves, chopped*
*2.5ml/½ tsp paprika*
*2.5ml/½ tsp ground cumin*
*2.5–5ml/½–1 tsp salt*
*2–3 pinches of cayenne pepper*
*60ml/4 tbsp olive oil*
*30ml/2 tbsp lemon juice*
*30ml/2 tbsp chopped fresh coriander*
  *(cilantro) or parsley*
*675g/1½lb firm-fleshed white fish,*
  *such as haddock, halibut, sea bass or*
  *snapper, cut into 2.5–5cm/*
  *1–2in cubes*
*3–4 green (bell) peppers, cut into*
  *2.5–5cm/1–2in pieces*
*2 lemon wedges, to serve*

**1** Put the garlic, paprika, cumin, salt, cayenne pepper, oil, lemon juice and coriander or parsley in a large bowl and mix together.

**2** Add the fish and toss to coat. Leave to marinate for at least 30 minutes, and preferably 2 hours, at room temperature, or chill overnight.

### COOK'S TIP
If you are using wooden skewers, soak them in cold water for 30 minutes before using to stop them burning.

**3** Thread the fish cubes and pepper pieces alternately on to six wooden or metal skewers.

**4** About 40 minutes before you are going to cook the brochettes, prepare and light the barbecue. It will be ready when the flames subside and the coals have turned white and grey.

**5** Grill the brochettes on the barbecue for 2–3 minutes on each side, or until the fish is tender and lightly browned. Serve with lemon wedges.

# Grilled Squid Stuffed with Feta Cheese

A large, fresh leafy salad or a vegetable dish, such as fresh green beans with tomato sauce could be served with the grilled squid.

**Serves 8**

*8 medium squid, total weight*
*about 900g/2lb*
*8–12 finger-length slices of feta cheese*
*175ml/6fl oz/¾ cup olive oil*
*4 garlic cloves, crushed*
*6–8 fresh marjoram sprigs, leaves*
*removed and chopped*
*salt and ground black pepper*
*lemon wedges, to serve*

**1** To prepare the squid: wash the squid carefully. If there is any ink on the body, rinse it off so that you can see what you are doing. Holding the body firmly, pull away the head and tentacles. If the ink sac is still intact, remove it. Either keep it for cooking or discard it.

**2** Pull out all the innards, including the long transparent stick or "pen". Peel off and discard the thin purple skin on the body, but keep the two small fins on the sides, if desired. Slice the head across just under the eyes, severing the tentacles. Discard the rest of the squid's head. Squeeze the tentacles at the head end to push out the round beak in the centre. Throw this away. Rinse the pouch inside and out and the tentacles very thoroughly under cold running water. Drain well and pat dry on kitchen paper.

**3** Lay the squid bodies and tentacles in a large shallow dish that will hold them in a single layer. Tuck the pieces of cheese between the squid.

**4** To make the marinade, pour the olive oil into a jug (pitcher) or bowl and whisk in the fresh garlic and marjoram sprigs. Season to taste with salt and pepper. Pour the marinade over the squid and the cheese, then cover with foil and leave in a cool place to marinate for 2–3 hours to allow the flavours to develop, turning once.

**5** Insert one or two pieces of cheese and a few bits of marjoram from the marinade into each squid and place them in a lightly oiled grill (broiler) pan or tray. Thread the tentacles on to wooden skewers that have been soaked in water for half an hour (this prevents them from burning).

**6** Preheat the grill to a low setting or prepare a barbecue. Grill the stuffed squid for about 6 minutes, then turn them over. Grill them for 1–2 minutes more, then add the skewered tentacles. Grill them for 2 minutes on each side, until they start to scorch. Serve the stuffed squid with the tentacles and serve with a few lemon wedges.

**COOK'S TIP**
Tentacles are often left whole for frying, but can be chopped into short lengths.

# Seared Tuna Steaks with Red Onion Salsa

Red onions are ideal for this salsa, not only for their mild and sweet flavour, but also because they look so appetizing. Salad, rice or bread and a bowl of thick yogurt flavoured with chopped fresh herbs are good accompaniments.

**Serves 8**

8 tuna loin steaks, about
    175–200g/6–7oz each
10ml/2 tsp cumin seeds, toasted
    and crushed
pinch of dried red chilli flakes
grated rind and juice of 2 limes
60–75ml/4–5 tbsp extra virgin
    olive oil
salt and ground black pepper
lime wedges and fresh coriander
    (cilantro) sprigs, to garnish

For the salsa
2 small red onions, finely chopped
400g/14oz red or yellow cherry
    tomatoes, roughly chopped
2 avocados, peeled, stoned, (pitted)
    and chopped
4 kiwi fruit, peeled and chopped
2 fresh red chillies, seeded and finely
    chopped
25g/1oz/½ cup chopped fresh
    coriander (cilantro)
12 fresh mint sprigs, leaves
    only, chopped
10–15ml/2–3 tsp Thai fish sauce
    (nam pla)
about 10ml/2 tsp muscovado
    (molasses) sugar

**1** Wash the tuna steaks and pat dry. Sprinkle with half the cumin, the dried chilli flakes, salt, pepper and half the lime rind. Rub in 60ml/4 tbsp of the oil and set aside in a dish for about 30 minutes.

**COOK'S TIP**
The spicy fruity salsa also goes well with barbecued salmon steaks.

**2** Meanwhile, make the salsa. Mix the onions, tomatoes, avocados, kiwi fruit, fresh chilli, chopped coriander and mint. Add the remaining cumin, the rest of the lime rind and half the lime juice. Add Thai fish sauce and sugar to taste. Set aside for 15–20 minutes, then add more Thai fish sauce, lime juice and olive oil if required.

**3** Heat a griddle. Cook the tuna, allowing about 2 minutes on each side for rare tuna or a little longer for a medium result.

**4** Serve the tuna steaks garnished with lime wedges and coriander sprigs. Serve the salsa separately or spoon it next to the tuna.

# Garlic and Chilli Marinated Beef with Corn-crusted Onion Rings

Fruity, smoky and mild Mexican chillies combine well with garlic in this marinade for grilled steak.

### Serves 8

*40g/1½oz large mild dried red chillies,*
*    such as mulato or pasilla*
*4 garlic cloves, plain or smoked,*
*    finely chopped*
*10ml/2 tsp ground toasted cumin seeds*
*10ml/2 tsp dried oregano*
*120ml/4fl oz/½ cup olive oil*
*8 beef steaks, rump or rib-eye (round),*
*    175–225g/6–8oz each*
*salt and ground black pepper*

### For the onion rings

*4 onions, sliced into rings*
*475ml/16fl oz/2 cups milk*
*175g/6oz/1½ cup coarse corn meal*
*5ml/1 tsp dried red chilli flakes*
*10ml/2 tsp ground toasted cumin seeds*
*10ml/2 tsp dried oregano*
*vegetable oil, for deep-frying*

**1** Cut the stalks from the chillies and discard the seeds. Toast the chillies in a dry frying pan for 2–4 minutes. Place them in a bowl, cover with warm water and leave to soak for 20–30 minutes. Drain and reserve the water.

**2** Process the chillies to a paste with the garlic, cumin, oregano and oil in a food processor. Add a little soaking water, if needed. Season with pepper.

**3** Wash and dry the steaks, drizzle the chilli paste all over them and leave to marinate for up to 12 hours.

**4** For the onion rings, soak the onions in the milk for 30 minutes. Mix the corn meal, chilli, cumin and oregano and season with salt and pepper.

**5** Heat the oil for deep-frying to 160–180°C/325–350°F, or until a cube of day-old bread turns brown in about 60 seconds.

**6** Drain the onion rings and dip each one into the corn meal mixture, coating it thoroughly. Fry for 2–4 minutes, or until browned and crisp. Do not overcrowd the pan, but cook in batches. Lift the onion rings out of the pan with a slotted spoon and drain on kitchen paper.

**7** Heat a barbecue or griddle. Season the steaks with salt and cook for about 4 minutes on each side for a medium result.

# Lamb Burgers with Red Onion and Tomato Relish

A sharp-sweet red onion relish works well with burgers based on Middle-Eastern style lamb. The burgers can be made a day ahead and chilled. Serve them with pitta bread and tabbouleh or a crisp green salad.

**Serves 8**

*50g/2oz/⅓ cup bulgur wheat*
*1kg/2¼lb lean minced (ground) lamb*
*2 small red onions, finely chopped*
*4 garlic cloves, finely chopped*
*2 green chillies, seeded and*
  *finely chopped*
*10ml/2 tsp ground toasted cumin seeds*
*5ml/1 tsp ground sumac*
*25g/1oz/½ cup chopped fresh flat*
  *leaf parsley*
*60ml/4 tbsp chopped fresh mint*
*olive oil, for frying*
*salt and ground black pepper*

**For the relish**
*4 red (bell) peppers, halved*
  *and seeded*
*4 red onions, cut into 5mm/¼in*
  *thick slices*
*150ml/¼ pint/⅔ cup olive oil*
*700g/1lb 9oz cherry tomatoes, chopped*
*1 fresh red or green chilli, seeded and*
  *finely chopped (optional)*
*60ml/4 tbsp chopped fresh mint*
*60ml/4 tbsp chopped fresh parsley*
*30ml/2 tbsp chopped fresh oregano*
  *or marjoram*
*5ml/1 tsp ground toasted cumin seeds*
*5ml/1 tsp ground sumac*
*juice of 1 lemon*
*caster (superfine) sugar, to taste*

**1** Pour 300ml/½ pint/1¼ cups hot water over the bulgur wheat in a bowl and leave to stand for 15 minutes, then drain in a sieve and squeeze out the excess moisture.

**2** Place the bulgur wheat in a bowl and add the minced lamb, onion, garlic, chilli, cumin, sumac, parsley and mint. Mix the ingredients thoroughly together by hand, then season with 10ml/2 tsp salt and plenty of black pepper and mix again. Form the mixture into 16 small burgers and set aside while you make the relish.

**3** Grill (broil) the peppers, skin side up, until the skin chars and blisters. Place in a bowl, cover and leave to stand until cool. Peel off the skin, dice the peppers finely and place in a bowl.

**4** Brush the onions with 30ml/2 tbsp oil and grill for 5 minutes on each side, until browned. Cool, then chop.

**5** Add the onions, tomatoes, chilli (if using) to taste, the mint, parsley, oregano or marjoram and half of the cumin and sumac to the peppers. Stir in the remaining oil and 30ml/2 tbsp of the lemon juice. Season with salt, pepper and sugar and allow to stand for 20–30 minutes.

**6** Prepare a barbecue or heat a heavy frying pan or griddle over a high heat and grease with olive oil. Cook the burgers for about 5–6 minutes on each side, or until just cooked at the centre.

**7** While the burgers are cooking, taste the relish and adjust the seasoning, adding more salt, pepper, sugar, chilli, cumin, sumac and lemon juice to taste. Serve the burgers as soon as they are cooked, with the relish.

# Barbecued Chicken

A fragrant marinade of Thai spices and coconut gives this barbecued chicken a superb flavour. It makes ideal party food for outdoor eating with a difference.

**Serves 6**

1 chicken, about 1.5kg/3¼lb, cut into
   8–10 pieces
lime wedges and fresh red chillies,
   to garnish

For the marinade
2 lemon grass stalks, roots removed
2.5cm/1in piece fresh root ginger,
   peeled and thinly sliced
6 garlic cloves, roughly chopped
4 shallots, roughly chopped
½ bunch coriander (cilantro)
   roots, chopped
15ml/1 tbsp palm sugar
120ml/4fl oz/½ cup coconut milk
30ml/2 tbsp Thai fish sauce (nam pla)
30ml/2 tbsp light soy sauce

**1** To make the marinade, cut off the lower 5cm/2in of both of the lemon grass stalks and chop them roughly. Put into a food processor or blender along with all the other marinade ingredients and process until the mixture has reached a smooth consistency.

**COOK'S TIP**
You can buy coconut milk fresh, in cans or cartons, or use 50g/2oz creamed coconut, available in packets, and dissolve in 120ml/4fl oz/½ cup warm water.

**2** Place the chicken pieces in a fairly deep dish, pour over the marinade and stir to mix well, turning the chicken pieces over. Cover the dish and leave in a cool place to marinate for at least 4 hours or place the dish in the refrigerator if you leave the chicken to stand overnight.

**3** Prepare the barbecue. Grill the chicken over the barbecue for 20–30 minutes, or until the pieces are cooked and golden brown. Turn the pieces and brush with the marinade once or twice during cooking. Transfer to a serving platter and garnish with lime wedges and red chillies to serve.

# Turkey Patties

Minced turkey makes deliciously light patties, which are ideal for summer meals. Serve the patties in split and toasted buns or between thick pieces of crusty bread, with chutney, salad leaves and chunky fries or potato wedges.

**Serves 6**

*675g/1½lb minced (ground) turkey*
*1 small red onion, finely chopped*
*grated rind and juice of 1 lime*
*small handful of fresh thyme leaves*
*15–30ml/1–2 tbsp olive oil*
*salt and ground black pepper*

**1** Mix together the turkey, onion, lime rind and juice, thyme and seasoning. Cover and chill for up to 4 hours to allow the flavours to infuse (steep), then divide the mixture into six equal portions and shape into round patties.

**2** Preheat a griddle. Brush the patties with oil, then place them on the griddle and cook for 10–12 minutes. Turn the patties over, brush with more oil and cook for 10–12 minutes on the second side, or until cooked through.

# Herbed Greek Pies

Mixed fresh herbs give these little pies a delicate flavour.

**Makes 8**

*45–60ml/3–4 tbsp tapenade or sun-*
*    dried tomato purée (paste)*
*1 large (US extra large) egg*
*100g/3¾oz/scant ½ cup thick Greek*
*    (US strained plain) yogurt*
*90ml/6 tbsp milk*
*1 garlic clove, crushed*
*30ml/2 tbsp chopped mixed herbs,*
*    such as thyme, basil and parsley*
*salt and ground black pepper*

**For the pastry**

*115g/4oz/1 cup plain (all-purpose) flour*
*50g/2oz/4 tbsp butter, diced*
*15–25ml/1–1½ tbsp water*

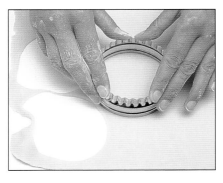

**1** To make the pastry, mix together the flour, a pinch of salt and the butter. Using the fingertips or a pastry cutter, rub the butter into the flour until the mixture resembles fine breadcrumbs. Mix in the water using a round-bladed knife and knead lightly to form a firm dough. Wrap the dough in clear film (plastic wrap) and chill in the refrigerator for 30 minutes.

**2** Preheat the oven to 190°C/375°F/Gas 5. Roll out the pastry thinly and cut out eight rounds using a 7.5cm/3in cutter. Line deep patty tins (muffin pans) with the pastry rounds, then line each one with a small piece of baking parchment. Bake blind for 15 minutes. Remove the baking parchment and cook for a further 5 minutes, or until the cases are crisp.

**3** Spread a little tapenade or tomato purée in the base of each pastry case. Whisk together the egg, yogurt, milk, garlic, herbs and seasoning. Spoon carefully into the pastry cases and bake for 25–30 minutes, or until the filling is just firm and the pastry golden. Allow the pies to cool slightly before carefully removing from the tins and serving.

# Tomato and Black Olive Tart

This delicious tart has a fresh, rich Mediterranean flavour and is ideal for picnics and buffets. Using a rectangular tin makes the tart easier to transport and divide into portions.

**Serves 8**

*3 eggs, beaten*
*300ml/½ pint/1¼ cups milk*
*30ml/2 tbsp chopped fresh herbs,*
*    such as parsley, marjoram or basil*
*6 firm plum tomatoes*
*75g/3oz ripe Brie*
*about 16 black olives, pitted*
*salt and ground black pepper*

**For the pastry**

*250g/9oz/1 cup plain (all-purpose)*
*    flour, plus extra for dusting*
*2.5ml/½ tsp salt*
*130g/4½oz/1 cup butter, diced*
*45ml/3 tbsp water*

**1** Preheat the oven to 190°C/375°F/ Gas 5. To make the pastry, mix together the flour, salt and butter. Using the fingertips or a pastry cutter, rub the butter into the flour until the mixture resembles fine breadcrumbs. Mix in the water and knead lightly to form a firm dough. Roll out the pastry thinly on a lightly floured surface. Line a 28 × 18cm/11 × 7in loose-based rectangular flan tin (quiche pan), trimming off any overhanging edges.

**2** Line the pastry case with baking parchment and baking beans, and bake blind for 15 minutes. Remove the baking parchment and baking beans and bake for a further 5 minutes, or until the base is crisp.

**VARIATION**
This tart is delicious made with other cheeses. Try slices of Gorgonzola or Camembert for a slightly stronger flavour.

**3** Meanwhile, beat the eggs with the milk, seasoning and herbs. Slice the tomatoes thinly, cube the cheese, and slice the olives. Place the prepared flan case on a baking tray, arrange the tomatoes, cheese and olives in the bottom of the case, then pour over the egg mixture.

**4** Transfer the tart carefully to the oven and bake for about 40 minutes, or until the filling is just firm and turning golden. Serve the tart warm or cold, cut into slices.

# Summer Herb Ricotta Flan

Infused with aromatic herbs, this flan makes a delightful picnic dish.

## Serves 8

*olive oil, for greasing and glazing*
*800g/1³/₄lb/3½ cups ricotta cheese*
*75g/3oz/1 cup grated Parmesan cheese*
*3 eggs, separated*
*60ml/4 tbsp torn fresh basil leaves*
*60ml/4 tbsp chopped fresh chives*
*45ml/3 tbsp fresh oregano leaves*
*2.5ml/½ tsp paprika*
*salt and ground black pepper*
*fresh herb leaves, to garnish*

### For the tapenade

*400g/14oz/3½ cups pitted black olives,*
*  rinsed and halved, reserving a few*
*  whole to garnish (optional)*
*5 garlic cloves, crushed*
*75ml/5 tbsp olive oil*

**1** Preheat the oven to 180°C/350°F/ Gas 4 and lightly grease a 23cm/9in springform cake tin (pan) with oil. Mix together the ricotta cheese, Parmesan and egg yolks in a food processor or blender. Add the herbs and seasoning, and blend until smooth and creamy.

**2** Whisk the egg whites in a large bowl until they form soft peaks. Gently fold the egg whites into the ricotta cheese mixture using a rubber spatula, taking care not to knock out too much air. Spoon the ricotta mixture into the prepared tin and smooth the top.

**3** Bake for 1 hour 20 minutes or until the flan is risen and the top is golden. Remove from the oven and brush lightly with olive oil, then sprinkle with paprika. Leave the flan to cool before removing from the pan.

**4** Make the tapenade. Place the olives and garlic in a food processor or blender and process until finely chopped. Gradually add the olive oil and blend to a coarse paste, then transfer to a serving bowl. Garnish the flan with fresh herbs leaves and serve with the tapenade.

**VARIATION**
Sprinkle 25g/1oz chopped, drained sun-dried tomatoes over the flan as a garnish.

# Red Onion and Goat's Cheese Pastries

These attractive little pastries are ideal for picnics and summer buffets and couldn't be easier to make. Serve simply with a mixed green salad dressed with balsamic vinegar and extra-virgin olive oil.

## Serves 8

*30ml/2 tbsp olive oil*
*900g/2lb red onions, sliced*
*60ml/4 tbsp fresh thyme or*
*  20ml/4 tsp dried*
*30ml/2 tbsp balsamic vinegar*
*850g/1lb 14oz ready-rolled puff pastry*
*225g/8oz/1 cup goat's cheese, cubed*
*2 eggs, beaten*
*salt and ground black pepper*
*fresh thyme sprigs, to garnish*
*  (optional)*
*mixed green salad leaves and*
*  cherry tomatoes, to serve*

**1** Heat the olive oil in a large heavy frying pan, add the sliced red onions and fry over a gentle heat for 10 minutes or until softened, stirring occasionally with a wooden spoon to prevent them browning.

**2** Add the thyme, seasoning and balsamic vinegar, and cook the onions for a further 5 minutes. Remove the frying pan from the heat and leave to cool.

**3** Preheat the oven to 220°C/425°F/ Gas 7. Unroll the puff pastry and using a 15cm/6in plate as a guide, cut out eight equal rounds. Place the pastry rounds on dampened baking sheets and, using the point of a sharp knife, score a border, 2cm/¾in inside the edge of each round.

**4** Divide the onions among the pastry rounds and top with the goat's cheese. Brush the edge of each round with beaten egg and bake for 25–30 minutes until golden. Garnish with thyme, if using, before serving with the salad leaves and tomatoes.

**VARIATION**
Ring the changes by spreading the pastry base with 45ml/3 tbsp pesto or tapenade (see recipe above) before you add the onion filling.

# diva desserts

Ensure that your guests leave the party on a high note
after sampling one (or more!) of these
superlative, mouthwatering sweet dishes.

# Summer Berries in Warm Sabayon Glaze

This luxurious combination of summer berries under a light and fluffy alcoholic sauce is lightly grilled to form a deliciously crisp, caramelized topping.

## Serves 8

*900g/2lb/8 cups mixed summer berries, or soft fruit*
*8 egg yolks*
*115g/4oz/generous ½ cup vanilla sugar or caster (superfine) sugar*
*250ml/8fl oz/1 cup liqueur, such as Cointreau, Kirsch or Grand Marnier, or white dessert wine, plus extra for drizzling (optional)*
*a little icing (confectioners') sugar, sifted, and mint leaves, to decorate (optional)*

**1** Divide the fruit among eight individual heatproof glass dishes or ramekins. Preheat the grill (broiler).

**2** Whisk the yolks in a large heatproof bowl with the sugar and liqueur or wine. Place the bowl over a pan of hot boiling water and whisk constantly until the yolks have become thick, fluffy and pale.

**3** Pour equal quantities of the sauce into each dish. Place under the grill for 1–2 minutes, or until just turning brown. Sprinkle the fruit with icing sugar and scatter with mint leaves just before serving, if you like.

### COOK'S TIP
To omit the alcohol, use a juice substitute such as grape, mango or apricot.

# Fig, Port and Clementine Sundaes

These exotic sundaes will make an ideal finale to a rich meal. The fresh flavours of figs and clementines contrast beautifully with the warm spices and port.

## Serves 6

*6 clementines*
*30ml/2 tbsp clear honey*
*1 cinnamon stick, halved*
*15ml/1 tbsp light muscovado (brown) sugar*
*60ml/4 tbsp port*
*6 fresh figs*
*about 500ml/17fl oz/2¼ cups orange sorbet (sherbet)*

**1** Finely grate the rind from two clementines and put it in a small, heavy pan. Cut the peel off the clementines, then slice the flesh thinly. Add the honey, cinnamon, sugar and port to the rind. Heat gently until the sugar has dissolved, to make a syrup.

**2** Put the clementine slices in a heatproof bowl and pour over the syrup. Cool completely, then chill.

**3** Slice the figs thinly and add to the clementines and syrup, tossing the ingredients together gently. Leave to stand for 10 minutes, then discard the cinnamon stick.

**4** Arrange half the fig and clementine slices around the sides of six serving glasses. Half fill the glasses with scoops of sorbet. Arrange the remaining fruit slices around the sides of the glasses, then pile more sorbet into the centre. Pour over the port syrup and serve.

**COOK'S TIPS**
A variety of different types of fresh figs are available. Dark purple skinned figs have a deep red flesh; yellowy-green figs have a pink flesh and green skinned figs have an amber coloured flesh. All types can be eaten, complete with the skin, simply as they are or baked and served with Greek (US strained plain) yogurt and honey for a quick dessert. When they are ripe, you can split them open with your fingers to reveal the soft, sweet flesh full of edible seeds.

# Tropical Scented Red and Orange Fruit Salad

This fresh fruit salad, with its bright colour and exotic flavour, is perfect after a rich, heavy meal or on the buffet table. It is also a refreshing dish to serve at a summer picnic or barbecue.

**Serves 4 to 6**

350–400g/12–14oz/3–3½ cups
   strawberries, hulled and halved
3 oranges, peeled and segmented
3 small blood oranges, peeled
   and segmented
1–2 passion fruit
120ml/4fl oz/½ cup dry white wine
sugar, to taste

**1** Put the strawberries and oranges into a serving bowl. Halve the passion fruit and spoon the flesh into the bowl.

**COOK'S TIP**
Omit the white wine if you wish and replace with orange or tropical juice.

**2** Pour the wine over the fruit and add sugar to taste. Toss gently and then chill until ready to serve.

**VARIATION**
Other fruit that can be added include pear, kiwi fruit and banana.

# Boston Banoffee Pie

This is a simple but impressive party dish. You can press the wonderfully biscuity pastry into the tin, rather than rolling it out. You can make the pastry case and the fudge-toffee filling in advance and then arrange the sliced banana topping and cream before serving. It will prove irresistible.

**Serves 6**

*115g/4oz/¹⁄₂ cup butter, diced*
*200g/7oz can skimmed, sweetened*
  *condensed milk*
*115g/4oz/¹⁄₂ cup soft brown sugar*
*30ml/2 tbsp golden (light corn) syrup*
*2 small bananas, sliced*
*a little lemon juice*
*whipped cream, to decorate*
*5ml/1 tsp grated plain*
  *(semisweet) chocolate*

**For the pastry**
*150g/5oz/1¹⁄₄ cups plain*
  *(all-purpose) flour*
*115g/4oz/¹⁄₂ cup butter, diced*
*50g/2oz/¹⁄₄ cup caster*
  *(superfine) sugar*

**1** Preheat the oven to 160°C/325°F/ Gas 3. In a food processor, process the flour and diced butter until crumbed. Stir in the caster sugar and mix to form a soft, pliable dough.

**2** Press the dough into a 20cm/8in loose-based flan tin (quiche pan). Bake for 30 minutes.

**3** To make the filling, place the butter in a pan with the condensed milk, brown sugar and syrup. Heat gently, stirring, until the butter has melted and the sugar has completely dissolved.

**4** Bring to a gentle boil and cook for 7–10 minutes, stirring constantly, until the mixture thickens and turns a light caramel colour.

**5** Pour the hot caramel filling into the pastry case and leave until it is completely cold. Sprinkle the banana slices with lemon juice to stop them going brown and arrange them in overlapping circles on top of the filling, leaving a gap in the centre. Pipe a generous swirl of whipped cream in the centre and sprinkle with the grated chocolate.

# Passion Fruit Crème Caramels with Dipped Physalis

The aromatic flavour of the fruit permeates these crème caramels, which are perfect for a dinner party.

**Serves 8**

*375g/13oz/generous 1³⁄₄ cups caster (superfine) sugar*
*150ml/¹⁄₄ pint/²⁄₃ cup water*
*8 passion fruit*
*8 physalis*
*6 eggs plus 2 egg yolks*
*300ml/¹⁄₂ pint/1¹⁄₄ cups double (heavy) cream*
*300ml/¹⁄₂ pint/1¹⁄₄ cups full cream (whole) milk*

**1** Place 300g/11oz/1½ cups of the caster sugar in a heavy pan. Add the water and heat the mixture gently until the sugar has dissolved. Increase the heat and boil until the syrup turns a dark golden colour.

**2** Meanwhile, cut each passion fruit in half. Scoop out the seeds from the passion fruit into a sieve set over a bowl. Press the seeds against the sieve to extract all their juice. Spoon a few of the seeds into each of eight 150ml/ ¼ pint/²⁄₃ cup ramekins. Reserve the passion fruit juice.

**3** Peel back the papery casing from each physalis and dip the orange berries into the caramel. Place on a sheet of baking parchment and set aside. Pour the remaining caramel carefully into the ramekins.

**4** Preheat the oven to 150°C/300°F/ Gas 2. Whisk the eggs, egg yolks and remaining sugar in a bowl. Whisk in the cream and milk, then the passion fruit juice. Strain through a sieve into each ramekin, then place the ramekins in a baking tin (pan). Pour in hot water to come halfway up the sides of the dishes and bake for 40–45 minutes, or until just set.

**5** Remove the custards from the tin and leave to cool, then cover and chill them for 4 hours before serving. Run a knife between the edge of each ramekin and the custard and invert each in turn on to a dessert plate. Shake the ramekins firmly to release the custards before lifting them off the desserts. Decorate each with a dipped physalis.

# Frozen Grand Marnier Soufflés

**2** Heat the milk until almost boiling and pour it on to the yolks, whisking constantly. Return to the pan and stir over a gentle heat until the custard is thick enough to coat the back of the spoon. Remove the pan from the heat. Stir the soaked gelatine into the custard. Pour the custard into a bowl and leave to cool. Whisk occasionally, until on the point of setting.

**3** Put the remaining sugar in a pan with 45ml/3 tbsp water and dissolve it over a low heat. Bring to the boil and boil rapidly until it reaches the soft ball stage or 119°C/238°F on a sugar thermometer. Remove from the heat. In a clean bowl, whisk the egg whites until stiff. Pour the hot syrup on to the whites, whisking constantly. Leave the meringue to cool.

**4** Add the Grand Marnier to the cold custard. Whisk the cream until it holds soft peaks and fold into the cooled meringue, with the custard. Pour into the prepared glasses or dishes. Freeze overnight. Remove the paper collars and leave at room temperature for 15 minutes before serving.

Light and fluffy yet almost ice cream, these delicious soufflés are perfect and wonderfully easy for a special dinner. Start preparations the day before as the desserts have to be frozen overnight.

**Serves 8**

*200g/7oz/1 cup caster (superfine) sugar*
*6 large (US extra large) eggs,*
*  separated*
*250ml/8fl oz/1 cup milk*
*15ml/1 tbsp powdered gelatine,*
*  soaked in 45ml/3 tbsp cold water*
*60ml/4 tbsp Grand Marnier*
*450ml/¾ pint/scant 2 cups double*
*  (heavy) cream*

**1** Wrap a double collar of baking parchment around eight dessert glasses or ramekin dishes and tie with string. Whisk together 75g/3oz/scant ½ cup of the caster sugar with the egg yolks, until the yolks are pale. This will take about 5 minutes by hand or about 3 minutes with an electric hand mixer.

**COOK'S TIPS**
• The soft ball stage of a syrup is when a teaspoon of the mixture dropped into a glass of cold water sets into a ball.
• If you prefer, you can make just one dessert in a large soufflé dish, rather than eight individual ones, or serve in very small glasses for a buffet.

# Classic Lemon Tart

This citrus tart can be served warm or chilled and would be suitable for a formal dinner party or a buffet. It is very lemony, so serve with cream or vanilla ice cream.

**Serves 8**

*150g/5oz/1 ¼ cups plain (all-purpose) flour, sifted*
*50g/2oz/½ cup hazelnuts, toasted and finely ground*
*175g/6oz/scant 1 cup caster (superfine) sugar*
*115g/4oz/½ cup unsalted (sweet) butter, softened*
*4 eggs*
*finely grated rind of 2 lemons and at least 175ml/6fl oz/¾ cup lemon juice*
*150ml/¼ pint/⅔ cup double (heavy) cream*
*thinly pared and shredded lemon rind, to decorate*

**1** Mix together the flour, nuts and 25g/1oz/2 tbsp sugar, then gently work in the butter and, if necessary, 15–30ml/1–2 tbsp cold water to make a soft dough. Chill for 10 minutes.

**2** Roll out the dough and use to line a 20cm/8in loose-based flan tin (tart pan). If you find it too difficult to roll out, gently press the pastry into the flan tin working it up the sides. Chill for about 20 minutes. Preheat the oven to 200°C/400°F/Gas 6.

**3** Line the pastry case with baking parchment, fill with baking beans, and bake for 15 minutes. Remove the baking parchment and baking beans, and cook for a further 5–10 minutes, or until the base is crisp.

**4** Beat the eggs, lemon rind and juice, the remaining sugar and cream until well blended. Pour into the pastry case. Bake for about 30 minutes, or until just set. Turn out of the tin, decorate with the lemon rind and serve.

# Iced Lime Cheesecake

**4** Press the cottage cheese through a sieve into a bowl. Beat in the mascarpone cheese, then the lime syrup. By hand: lightly whip the cream and then fold into the cheese mixture. Pour into a shallow container and freeze until thick. If you are using an ice cream maker, add the lightly-whipped cream and churn in an ice cream maker until thick.

**5** Meanwhile, cut a slice off either end of each of the remaining limes, stand them on a board and slice off the skins. Cut them into very thin slices.

**6** Arrange the lime slices around the sides of the tin, pressing them against the paper.

**7** Pour the cheese mixture over the biscuit base in the tin and level the surface. Cover and freeze the cheesecake overnight.

**8** About 1 hour before you are going to serve the cheesecake, carefully transfer it to a serving plate and put it in the refrigerator to soften slightly.

This frozen dessert has a deliciously tangy, sweet flavour but needs no gelatine to set the filling, unlike most unbaked cheesecakes. It is not difficult to prepare and an added advantage is that it can be made several days beforehand.

**Serves 10**

*175g/6oz almond biscuits (cookies)*
*65g/2½oz/5 tbsp unsalted*
*   (sweet) butter*
*8 limes*
*115g/4oz/generous ½ cup caster*
*   (superfine) sugar*
*90ml/6 tbsp water*
*200g/7oz/scant 1 cup cottage cheese*
*250g/9oz/generous 1 cup mascarpone*
*   cheese*
*300ml/½ pint/1¼ cups double*
*   (heavy) cream*

**1** Lightly grease the sides of a 20cm/8in springform cake tin (pan) and line with a strip of baking parchment. Break up the almond biscuits slightly, put them in a strong plastic bag and crush them with a rolling pin.

**2** Melt the butter in a small pan and stir in the biscuit crumbs until evenly combined. Spoon the mixture into the tin and pack it down with the back of a spoon. Freeze the biscuit mixture while you make the filling.

**3** Finely grate the rind and squeeze the juice from five of the limes. Heat the sugar and water in a small pan, stirring until the sugar dissolves. Bring to the boil and boil for 2 minutes without stirring, then remove the syrup from the heat, stir in the lime juice and rind and leave to cool.

# Cold Lemon Soufflé with Almonds

Terrific to look at yet easy to make, this dessert is mouthwatering, ideal for the end of any party meal.

**Serves 6**

oil, for greasing
grated rind and juice of 3 large lemons
5 large (US extra large) eggs, separated
115g/4oz/generous ½ cup caster
   (superfine) sugar
25ml/1½ tbsp powdered gelatine
450ml/¾ pint/scant 2 cups double
   (heavy) cream

### For the almond topping

75g/3oz/¾ cup flaked (sliced) almonds
75g/3oz/¾ cup icing
   (confectioner's) sugar

**1** To make the soufflé collar, cut a strip of baking parchment long enough to fit around a 900ml/1½ pint/3¾ cup soufflé dish and wide enough to extend 7.5cm/3in above the rim. Fit the strip around the dish, tape, and then tie it around the top of the dish with string. Using a pastry brush, lightly coat the inside of the paper collar with oil.

**2** Put the lemon rind and yolks in a bowl. Add 75g/3oz/6 tbsp of the caster sugar and whisk until the mixture is creamy.

### COOK'S TIP

Heat the lemon juice and gelatine in a microwave, on full power, in 30-second bursts, stirring between each burst, until it is fully dissolved.

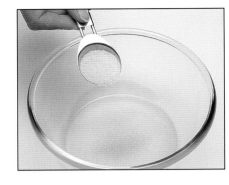

**3** Place the lemon juice in a small heatproof bowl and sprinkle over the gelatine. Set aside for 5 minutes, then place the bowl in a pan of simmering water. Heat, stirring occasionally, until the gelatine has dissolved. Cool slightly, then stir the gelatine and lemon juice into the egg yolk mixture.

**4** In a separate bowl, lightly whip the cream to soft peaks. Fold into the egg yolk mixture and set aside.

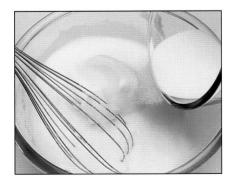

**5** Whisk the whites to stiff peaks. Gradually whisk in the remaining caster sugar until stiff and glossy. Quickly and lightly fold the whites into the yolk mix. Pour into the prepared dish, smooth the surface and chill for 4–5 hours.

**6** To make the almond topping, brush a baking tray lightly with oil. Preheat the grill (broiler). Sprinkle the flaked almonds across the baking tray and sift the icing sugar over. Grill (broil) until the nuts turn a rich golden colour and the sugar has caramelized.

**7** Allow to cool, then remove the almond mixture from the tray with a palette knife (metal spatula) and break it into pieces.

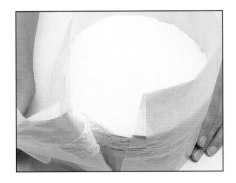

**8** When the soufflé has set, carefully peel off the paper. If the paper does not come away easily, hold the blade of a knife against the set soufflé to help it keep its shape. Sprinkle the caramelized almonds over the top before serving.

### VARIATIONS

• This soufflé is wonderfully refreshing when served semi-frozen. Place the undecorated, set soufflé in the freezer for about an hour. Just before serving, remove from the freezer and decorate with the caramelized almonds.

• You can also vary the flavour slightly by using the juice and rind of 5 limes.

# Chocolate Chestnut Roulade

This is a dream dinner party finalé to have chocoholics swooning. The combination of intense flavours produces a very rich dessert, so serve it well chilled and in thin slices. It slices better when it is cold.

**Serves 10 to 12**

oil, for greasing
175g/6oz dark (bittersweet)
    chocolate, chopped
30ml/2 tbsp cocoa powder
    (unsweetened), sifted,
    plus extra for dusting
50ml/2fl oz/¼ cup freshly brewed
    strong coffee or espresso
6 eggs, separated
75g/3oz/6 tbsp caster (superfine) sugar
pinch of cream of tartar
5ml/1 tsp vanilla essence (extract)
glacé (candied) chestnuts,
    to decorate (optional)

For the chestnut cream filling
475ml/16fl oz/2 cups double
    (heavy) cream
30ml/2 tbsp rum or coffee-
    flavoured liqueur
350g/12oz can sweetened
    chestnut purée
115g/4oz dark chocolate, grated
thick cream, to serve

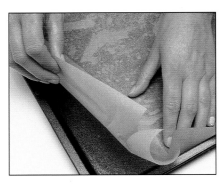

**1** Preheat the oven to 180°C/350°F/Gas 4. Oil the base and sides of a 38 × 25cm/15 × 10in Swiss roll tin (jelly roll pan). Line with baking parchment, allowing a 2.5cm/1in overhang.

**2** Melt the chocolate in the top of a double boiler, over a low heat, stirring frequently. Set aside. Dissolve the cocoa in the coffee. Stir to make a smooth paste. Set aside.

**3** In an electric mixer or in a bowl using a whisk, beat the egg yolks with half the sugar for about 3–5 minutes, or until pale and thick. Slowly beat in the melted chocolate and cocoa-coffee paste until just blended.

**4** In another bowl, beat the egg whites and cream of tartar until stiff peaks form. Sprinkle the remaining sugar over in two batches incorporating each thoroughly, and continue to beat until they are stiff and glossy. Then beat in the vanilla essence.

**5** Stir a spoonful of the whisked whites into the chocolate mixture to lighten it, then fold in the remainder.

**6** Spoon the mixture into the tin and level the top. Bake for 20–25 minutes, or until the cake is firm, set and risen, and springs back when lightly pressed with the fingertips.

**7** Meanwhile, dust a clean dishtowel with the extra cocoa powder. As soon as the cake is cooked, carefully turn it out on to the towel and gently peel off the baking parchment from the base. Starting at a narrow end, roll the cake and towel together Swiss-roll fashion. Cool completely.

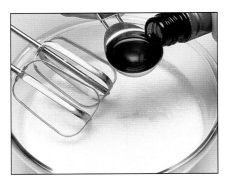

**8** To make the filling, whip the cream and rum or liqueur until soft peaks form. Beat a spoonful of cream into the chestnut purée to lighten it, then fold in the remaining cream and most of the grated chocolate. Reserve a quarter of the chestnut cream mixture.

**9** To assemble the roulade, unroll the cake and spread with the filling, to within 2.5cm/1in of the edges. Gently roll it up, using the towel for support.

**10** Place the roulade on a serving plate. Spoon the reserved chestnut cream into a small icing bag and pipe rosettes along the top of the roulade. Dust with more cocoa and decorate with glacé chestnuts and grated chocolate.

# Iced Christmas Torte

Not everyone likes traditional Christmas pudding. This makes an exciting alternative but do not feel that you have to limit it to the festive season. Packed with dried fruit and nuts, it is perfect for any special occasion.

**Serves 8 to 10**

*75g/3oz/³⁄₄ cup dried cranberries*
*75g/3oz/scant ¹⁄₂ cup pitted prunes*
*50g/2oz/¹⁄₃ cup sultanas (golden raisins)*
*175ml/6fl oz/³⁄₄ cup port*
*2 pieces preserved stem ginger,*
  *finely chopped*
*25g/1oz/2 tbsp unsalted (sweet) butter*
*45ml/3 tbsp light muscovado*
  *(brown) sugar*
*90g/3¹⁄₂oz/scant 2 cups fresh*
  *white breadcrumbs*
*600ml/1 pint/2¹⁄₂ cups double*
  *(heavy) cream*
*30ml/2 tbsp icing (confectioners') sugar*
*5ml/1 tsp mixed (pumpkin pie) spice*
*75g/3oz/³⁄₄ cup brazil nuts,*
  *finely chopped*
*sugared bay leaves (see Cook's Tip)*
  *and fresh cherries, to decorate*

**1** Put the cranberries, prunes and sultanas in a food processor and process briefly. Tip them into a bowl and add the port and ginger. Leave to absorb the port for 2 hours.

**2** Melt the butter in a frying pan. Add the sugar and heat gently until it has dissolved. Tip in the breadcrumbs, stir, then fry over a low heat for about 5 minutes, or until lightly coloured and turning crisp. Leave to cool.

**COOK'S TIP**
To make the sugared bay leaves wash and dry the leaves, then paint both sides with beaten egg white. Sprinkle with caster (superfine) sugar. Leave to dry on baking parchment for 2–3 hours.

**3** Tip the breadcrumbs into a food processor or blender and process to finer crumbs. Sprinkle a third into an 18cm/7in loose-based springform cake tin (pan) and spread them out to cover the base of the tin evenly. Freeze until firm.

**4** Whip the cream with the icing sugar and mixed spice until it is thick but not yet standing in peaks. Fold in the brazil nuts with the fruit mixture and any port that has not been absorbed.

**5** Spread a third of the mixture over the breadcrumb base in the tin, taking care not to dislodge the crumbs. Sprinkle with another layer of the breadcrumbs. Repeat the layering, finishing with a layer of the cream mixture. Freeze the torte overnight.

**6** Chill the torte for about 1 hour before serving, decorated with sugared bay leaves and fresh cherries.

# Blackforest Gâteau

Morello cherries and Kirsch lend their distinctive flavours to this ever-popular chocolate gâteau.

**Serves 8 to 10**

*6 eggs*
*200g/7oz/1 cup caster (superfine) sugar*
*5ml/1 tsp vanilla essence (extract)*
*50g/2oz/½ cup plain (all-purpose) flour*
*50g/2oz/½ cup cocoa powder*
*    (unsweetened)*
*115g/4oz/½ cup unsalted (sweet)*
*    butter, melted*

**For the filling and topping**
*60ml/4 tbsp Kirsch*
*600ml/1 pint/2½ cups double*
*    (heavy) cream*
*30ml/2 tbsp icing (confectioners') sugar*
*2.5ml/½ tsp vanilla essence (extract)*
*675g/1½ lb jar pitted morello cherries,*
*    well drained*

**To decorate**
*icing (confectioner's) sugar, for dusting*
*grated chocolate*
*chocolate curls (see Cook's Tip)*
*fresh or drained canned morello cherries*

**1** Preheat oven to 180°C/350°F/Gas 4. Grease three 19cm/7½in sandwich cake tins (pans). Line the bottom of each with baking parchment. Combine the eggs with the sugar and vanilla essence in a bowl and beat with a hand-held electric mixer until pale and thick.

**2** Sift the flour and cocoa powder over the mixture and fold in lightly and evenly with a metal spoon. Gently stir in the melted butter.

**COOK'S TIP**
To make chocolate curls, spread melted chocolate over a marble slab to a depth of about 5mm/¼in. Leave to set. Draw a knife across the chocolate at a 45° angle, using a seesaw action to make long curls.

**3** Divide the mixture among the prepared cake tins, smoothing them level. Bake for 15–18 minutes, or until the cakes have risen and are springy to the touch. Leave them to cool in the tins for about 5 minutes, then turn out on to wire racks and leave to cool completely. Remove the lining paper from each cake layer.

**4** Prick each layer all over with a skewer or fork, then sprinkle with Kirsch. Using a hand-held electric mixer, whip the cream until it starts to thicken then beat in the icing sugar and vanilla until the mixture begins to hold its shape.

**5** To assemble, spread one cake layer with a thick layer of flavoured cream and top with about half the cherries.

**6** Spread a second cake layer with cream, top with the remaining cherries, then place it on top of the first layer. Top with the final cake layer.

**7** Spread the remaining cream all over the cake. Dust a serving plate with icing sugar, and position the cake carefully in the centre. Press grated chocolate over the sides and decorate the top of the cake with the chocolate curls and fresh or drained cherries.

# Coconut and Coffee Trifle

Serve this lavish dessert in a large glass bowl for maximum impact.

**Serves 6 to 8**

**For the coffee sponge**
45ml/3 tbsp strong-flavoured
   ground coffee
45ml/3 tbsp near-boiling water
2 eggs
50g/2oz/¼ cup soft dark brown sugar
40g/1½oz/⅓ cup self-raising
   (self-rising) flour, sifted
25ml/1½ tbsp hazelnut or
   sunflower oil

**For the coconut custard**
400ml/14fl oz/1⅔ cup coconut milk
3 eggs
40g/1½oz/3 tbsp caster
   (superfine) sugar
10ml/2 tsp cornflour (cornstarch)

**For the filling and topping**
2 medium bananas
60ml/4 tbsp coffee liqueur
300ml/½ pint/1¼ cups double
   (heavy) cream
30ml/2 tbsp icing (confectioners')
   sugar, sifted
ribbons of fresh coconut, to decorate

**1** Preheat the oven to 160°C/325°F/Gas 3. Grease and line an 18cm/7in baking tin (pan) with baking parchment.

**2** Put the coffee in a jug (pitcher). Pour the hot water over and leave for 4 minutes. Strain through a fine sieve.

**3** Whisk the eggs and soft dark brown sugar in a large bowl.

**4** Gently fold in the flour, followed by 15ml/1 tbsp of the coffee and the oil. Spoon the mixture into the tin and bake for 20 minutes, until firm. Turn out on to a wire rack, remove the lining paper and leave to cool.

**5** To make the coconut custard, heat the coconut milk in a pan until it is almost boiling.

**6** Whisk the eggs, sugar and cornflour until frothy. Pour on the hot coconut milk. Add to the pan and heat gently, stirring for 1–2 minutes, until the custard thickens, but do not boil.

**7** Set the custard aside to cool for about 10 minutes, stirring occasionally.

**8** Cut the coffee sponge into 5cm/2in squares and arrange in the base of a large glass bowl. Slice the bananas and arrange on top of the sponge. Drizzle the coffee liqueur on top. Pour the custard over and leave until cold.

**9** Whip the cream with the remaining coffee and icing sugar until soft peaks form. Spoon the cream over the custard. Cover and chill for several hours. Sprinkle with ribbons of fresh coconut before serving.

**COOK'S TIP**
To make coconut ribbons, use a vegetable peeler to cut thin ribbons from the flesh of a fresh coconut, or buy desiccated (dry unsweetened shredded) coconut and toast until it is a pale golden brown colour.

**VARIATION**
Coffee liqueurs such as Tia Maria or Kahlúa can be used in the trifle or if you prefer use brandy or whisky.

# Chocolate Truffles

These irresistible, melt-in-the-mouth truffles will make a dainty addition to the buffet table as a dessert or as an after-dinner treat. Use a good quality chocolate with a high percentage of cocoa solids to give a real depth of flavour.

### Makes 20 to 30

*175ml/6fl oz/¾ cup double*
*    (heavy) cream*
*1 egg yolk, beaten*
*275g/10oz plain (semisweet)*
*    Belgian chocolate, chopped*
*25g/1oz/2 tbsp unsalted (sweet)*
*    butter, cut into pieces*
*30–45ml/2–3 tbsp brandy (optional)*

### For the coatings
*cocoa powder (unsweetened)*
*finely chopped pistachio nuts*
*    or hazelnuts*
*400g/14oz plain (semisweet), milk*
*    or white chocolate, or a mixture*

**1** Bring the cream to the boil, then remove the pan from the heat and beat in the egg yolk. Add the chocolate, then stir until melted and smooth. Stir in the butter and the brandy, if using, then pour into a bowl and leave to cool. Cover and chill in the refrigerator for 6–8 hours.

### COOK'S TIP
Chocolate truffles will delight guests at a drinks party – serve them with coffee to follow all the savoury bites.

**2** Line a large baking sheet with baking parchment. Using a very small ice-cream scoop or two teaspoons, form the chocolate mixture into 20–30 balls and place on the parchment. Chill if the mixture becomes too soft.

**3** To coat the truffles with cocoa, sift some powder into a small bowl, drop in the truffles, one at a time, and roll to coat well. To coat them with nuts, roll the truffles in finely chopped pistachio nuts or hazelnuts.

**4** To coat with chocolate, freeze the truffles for at least 1 hour. In a small bowl, melt the plain, milk or white chocolate over a pan of barely simmering water, stirring until melted and smooth, then allow to cool slightly.

**5** Using a fork, dip the frozen truffles into the cooled chocolate, one at a time, tapping the fork on the edge of the bowl to shake off the excess. Place on a baking sheet lined with baking parchment and chill. If the melted chocolate thickens, reheat until smooth. All the truffles can be stored, well wrapped, in the refrigerator for up to 10 days.

# Mint Chocolate Meringues

Omit the alcohol and these mini meringues are perfect for a child's birthday party.

**Makes about 50**

2 egg whites
115g/4oz/generous ½ cup caster (superfine) sugar
50g/2oz chocolate mint sticks, chopped
cocoa powder (unsweetened), sifted (optional)

**For the filling**
150ml/¼ pint/⅔ cup double (heavy) or whipping cream
5–10ml/1–2 tsp crème de menthe, or mint essence

**1** Preheat the oven to 110°C/225°F/ Gas ¼. Line two or three baking sheets with baking parchment. Whisk the egg whites until stiff, then gradually whisk in the sugar until it is thick and glossy.

**2** Fold in the chopped mint sticks and then place teaspoons of the mixture on the prepared baking sheets.

**3** Bake for 1 hour or until crisp. Remove from the oven and allow to cool, then dust with cocoa, if using.

**4** Lightly whip the cream until it stands in soft peaks and stir in the crème de menthe or mint essence. Use the cream to sandwich the meringues together in pairs just before serving.

# Index